giant book of TOFU cooking

giant book of TOFU cooking

K. Lee Evans & Chris Rankin

Sterling Publishing Co., Inc.

New York

Chris Rankin Editor

Theresa Gwynn Book and cover design

Evan Bracken, Richard Hasselberg Photographers

Skip Wade Photo stylist

Robert G. Wysong and David W. Rowland,
Executive Sous Chefs at Grove Park Inn Resort, Asheville, NC Food stylists

Dana Irwin Illustrator

Megan Kirby Production assistant

Catharine Sutherland Proofreader

Library of Congress Cataloging-in-Publication Data
Evans, K. Lee
    Giant book of tofu cooking / K. Lee Evans & Chris Rankin
          p. Cm
    Includes index.
    ISBN 0-8069-2957-X (paperback)
    ISBN 0-8069-5878-2 (hardcover)
    1. Cookery (Tofu) I. Rankin, Chris. II. Title.

T X 814.5.T63 E93 2000
641.6'5655--dc21

    00-030815

10 9 8 7 6 5 4 3 2 1

Published by Sterling Publishing Company, Inc.
387 Park Avenue South
New York, N.Y. 10016

© 2000 by Sterling Publishing Company, Inc

Distributed in Canada by Sterling Publishing,
c/o Canadian Manda Group, One Atlantic Ave., Suite 105
Toronto, Ontario, Canada M6K 3E7

Distributed in Great Britain and Europe by Cassell PLC
Wellington House, 125 Strand, London WC2R OBB, England

Distributed in Australia by Capricorn Link (Australia) Pty Ltd.
P.O. Box 6651, Baulkham Hills, Business Centre, NSW 2153, Australia

Manufactured in China
All rights reserved

Sterling ISBN 0-8069-2957-X (paperback)
        ISBN 0-8069-5878-2 (hardcover)

Contents

Introduction

Tofu, the super food of the East for the last 2,000 years or so, used to have an image problem here in the West. For years, tofu suffered the peaks and valleys of popularity from a culture that, largely speaking, just didn't get it. Well, tofu is no longer simply that white gelatinous mass the kids poked at on that rare trip to the specialty market. Tofu has finally made a name for itself, and is becoming a major player in the lives and diets of more and more people every year. Perhaps tofu's health benefits are too overwhelming to ignore—even if tofu does look funny. Or, it could be because people are beginning to realize the incredible, delicious potential tofu brings to almost anything to which it is added. Whatever the reason, tofu, that strange food substance you once laughed at, is now the rising ingredient in American recipes. Tofu is now being served.

But, Really...What is Tofu? And Why Should I Eat It?

Tofu, which is the Japanese word for *bean curd*, is a soft, cheeselike food that has been made in the same manner since it was first concocted 2,000 years ago by a Chinese cook whose name is lost to the ages. *Nigari*, a compound found in natural ocean water, or *calcium sulphate*, a natural mineral, is added to hot soy milk to begin a curdling process. Excess moisture is squeezed out, and the resulting curds are then strained and pressed into that solid white block you buy at the supermarket.

By itself, tofu is virtually tasteless. However, when it is added to recipes, it becomes a flavorful ingredient with endless possibilities. Tofu has a remarkable ability to act like a sponge, taking on the flavor of the foods it is prepared with or the seasoning it is marinated in. Also, tofu comes in different textures, which allows cooks to substitute tofu for a variety of recipe items, including meat, fish, cheese, milk, eggs, and more. And, to add to this already impressive résumé, tofu is healthful eating at its best. In Asia, where tofu and other soy-based foods are eaten regularly, there is less incidence of chronic disease, and the rates of breast cancer and cardiovascular disease are four times lower than in

the United States. Researchers point to tofu and other soy products as one of the main ingredients of these health statistics (see the Tofu Basics and Techniques chapter for more of tofu's amazing nutritional benefits).

This comprehensive, all-vegetarian tofu cookbook was created to celebrate tofu's versatility. Tofu can take you from appetizers, through the main course, and on to a dessert, without ever sacrificing taste. We've used tofu to create healthier versions of the classic recipes you love—giving you 350 delicious reasons to add tofu to your diet. The recipes are easy to follow, and don't rely heavily on hard-to-find ingredients.

So, we cordially invite you to expand your horizons, jump on the tofu band-wagon, and slip some tofu into your family's meal today.

Tofu Basics AND *Techniques*

If you want to cook with tofu, but are not sure how
to start, well, start here. Learn how to buy, store,
and prepare tofu. Also find out what other kinds of
soy products are on the market, why tofu should
become a healthful part of your diet, and
how to make any recipe more healthful.

• • •

Getting Started

Buying Tofu

Back in the old days (when health food meant bland and boring), tofu could only be found in large water-filled tubs in health food stores and Asian markets. Today, most supermarkets offer a wide variety of packaged tofu, which can make choosing tofu a little daunting for beginners.

Tofu is usually sold in 12- or 16-ounce blocks, and can be found either vacuum-packed or in covered tubs in the refrigerated produce or dairy section. Most brands of tofu are pasteurized at the processing plant and kept refrigerated during distribution. As with all perishable foods, check the expiration date on the package. Fresh tofu has a slightly sweet smell, with a slight vegetable odor. If the tofu smells sour, appears swollen, or has a slightly pink or green tint to it, it has begun to spoil, and should not be purchased.

Aseptically packaged tofu is also available, requiring no refrigeration until it is opened. Aseptically packaged tofu can be stored for months, but it must be consumed or frozen within three days after opening.

Before you purchase tofu, decide which style would be best suited for the recipe you are making. Tofu style is determined by density—ranging from soft to extra-firm—and the tofu's density affects how it can be used for cooking. Also, the denser the tofu, the more protein and fat it contains.

These are the varieties of tofu most often found in supermarkets today:

SOFT TOFU

Spongelike and fibrous, soft tofu is best for blending, mashing, and crumbling. Its texture makes it a wonderful alternative to cottage or ricotta cheese, heavy cream, and eggs.

FIRM TOFU

More versatile than its soft cousin, firm tofu is the perfect meat substitute. It is wonderful when crumbled, sliced, and cubed. It can be broiled, grilled, or pan-fried. You can slice it to use in sandwiches or on the barbecue grill, cube it for soups, or stir-fry with vegetables. It has a lighter consistency than the extra-firm style.

EXTRA-FIRM TOFU

Also a perfect meat substitute that can be crumbled, sliced, cubed, broiled, grilled, or pan-fried, extra-firm tofu provides more protein than any other style of tofu.

All in the family. *Clockwise from bottom of plate:* **silken, soft, and firm tofu blocks**

SILKEN TOFU

Silken tofu has a silky smooth, creamy texture similar to a custard. This tofu, when mashed, blended, or stirred, can be used in recipes calling for a creamy texture. Silken tofu is more susceptible to breaking apart when handled, so do not expect it to hold its shape. Because of its higher water count, silken tofu will not stir-fry well and will not absorb the flavors of the dish as well as firmer varieties. Instead, use it in recipes as a milk, cream, mayonnaise, or egg substitute. Enjoy mouthwatering fruit smoothies, guilt-free creamy soups, and savory dips and toppings. Firm and extra-firm silken varieties will hold their shapes better and can be used in place of regular soft or firm tofu.

The following are examples of the kinds of prepared tofu that are becoming more readily available as tofu becomes increasingly popular. These convenient blocks can usually be eaten right out of the package.

MARINATED TOFU

Though it is simple to marinate tofu at home, pre-packaged marinated tofu is a convenient and tasty alternative. If necessary, sauté the tofu in a little oil to improve the flavor. Marinated tofu comes in a wide range of flavors.

SMOKED TOFU

Smoked tofu can be used straight from the package, sliced in sandwiches, or diced in salads. Thinly sliced and grilled or fried, it becomes crispy, making it the perfect substitute for smoked meat or fish.

FREEZE-DRIED TOFU

With a rather distinct, spongy texture, this variety of tofu is best used with marinades and sauces. Available in airtight containers, it must be reconstituted with water. Its toughness makes it a good meat substitute. It is perfect for camping and backpacking.

FERMENTED TOFU

Found in jars and tins in Chinese specialty markets, this tofu is similar to Camembert cheese. Its salt content is too high to be palatable on its own, but when mixed with other ingredients, it can bring a pleasant, distinctive flavor to a dish.

Storing Tofu

Once you've purchased the tofu that's right for your cooking needs, keep it in its original packaging until you're ready to use it. Since tofu is packaged in water to prevent it from drying out, you should store opened tofu the same way. Refrigerate any unused tofu in fresh water in a closed container. This prevents the tofu from absorbing the flavors of other foods in the

Tofu varieties. *Clockwise from the bottom of plate:* **marinated tofu, freeze-dried tofu, and smoked tofu.** *In the jar:* **fermented tofu**

refrigerator. To keep the tofu fresh, change the water frequently, at least every other day. Although the taste and texture may change slightly, tofu can be kept in the refrigerator for up to one week. Keep in mind, only the freshest tofu should be used for desserts or dips, or in any recipe that does not require cooking.

Preparing Tofu for Your Recipes

There are a number of simple tofu preparatory techniques that will help you take advantage of tofu's amazing versatility as an ingredient. Each recipe in this book lists tofu first as an ingredient, along with a word or two that explains how best to prepare it for that particular recipe. The following list takes you through each step of each technique.

DRAINING AND BLOTTING

This is a necessary step for using tofu—it helps the tofu soak in the flavors of the recipe. Simply remove the tofu from its package water; set the tofu in a strainer and allow the water to run off. If you want even more moisture removed, put a few paper towels on a cutting board or countertop, cut the tofu into slabs, and place them on the towels. Then blot the surface with more paper towels.

PRESSING

Pressing is a very important step in preparation if you want the tofu to absorb the flavors of a marinade, or if you plan to deep-fry it. An extension of the draining and blotting procedure, it helps remove as much moisture from the tofu as possible, making the entire block uniformly firmer.

After you have placed paper towels over the top surface of the tofu, place a weight on top

Always drain and blot tofu before using.

Press the tofu to remove as much moisture as possible.

You can also use two small plates to press moisture from the tofu.

For those of you who live in areas where only one type of tofu is available, pressing will come in handy. Shorter, lighter pressing keeps the tofu softer; longer, heavier pressing results in a firmer tofu. Therefore, if a recipe calls for firm tofu, and you only have soft tofu available, don't worry. Decreasing the moisture content in soft tofu by pressing will change the texture enough that you may substitute it for the firmer variety.

Frozen tofu slices and cubes being thawed

(a saucepan works well), forcing more water to drain out. Let the tofu sit under the weight for approximately one hour. You can also press the tofu between two plates over a sink. Do not press silken tofu.

FREEZING AND THAWING

Freezing and then thawing tofu make it more porous, increasing its capacity to absorb flavors. If you are looking for a distinctively chewy meatlike texture, this procedure works wonders. Besides, if you'd like to have a supply of tofu always at hand, freezing is the best way to store it.

To freeze tofu, first drain and/or press it completely. Then cut it into quarters for easier handling, place the quarters in an airtight container, plastic wrap, or aluminum foil, and freeze. When you are ready to use it, simply defrost and squeeze out any remaining water. It will take six to eight hours for the tofu to defrost at room temperature, and even longer if placed in the refrigerator. You can also

defrost it in the microwave for a couple of minutes or place it in a strainer and pour boiling water over it as needed.

Now you can crumble the tofu or break it up into chickenlike chunks and incorporate it in recipes. Tofu can be frozen for up to five months. Freezing tofu will turn it a few shades darker in color. You can also resort to freezing tofu when it has started to smell slightly sour. The freezing process tends to revive the tofu, preventing it from going to waste. Do not deep-fry frozen tofu, as it absorbs too much of the oil. Freezing is also not recommended for silken tofu, as it will ruin its creamy texture.

BLENDING

Many dessert, salad dressing, and sauce recipes require that tofu be blended or puréed. The easiest way to blend tofu is with a blender or food processor. If you are using firm tofu, it might help to mash or crumble the tofu prior to blending. Most mixtures will have to be pushed back down into the blender with a rubber spatula to guarantee even mixing. If you need to blend a large amount of tofu, you may have to blend it in batches. If you use

Crumbling tofu before sautéing

Blending tofu

puréed tofu often, you can prepare a large amount and store it, refrigerated, in a sealed container. It will keep for up to one week.

CUBING AND DICING

Many recipes require you to cut the blocks of tofu into cubes or smaller, diced squares. To do this, set the tofu on a cutting board. Using a serrated knife, cut the block into horizontal slices of the desired thickness. Then cut vertical slices of the same thickness.

CRUMBLING

When you are looking for a dense texture in dishes that usually call for ground meat,

use your hands to break the tofu into small bits resembling cottage cheese. You can accentuate the meatlike texture by freezing and thawing the tofu first. Breaking tofu into smaller pieces by crumbling generally makes it easier to work with while blending or sautéing.

SHREDDING/GRATING

Tofu can also be grated like a cheese. You can use drained firm tofu or frozen and thawed tofu. The firmer the tofu, the easier the grating.

MARINATING

Marinating is one of the most common flavoring techniques used with tofu. You can use any of the marinades or sauces in this book, or utilize the wide variety of ready-made marinades. Use a firm or extra-firm tofu, and keep in mind that frozen and thawed tofu absorbs marinades much more efficiently.

Drain the tofu well to prevent diluting the marinade. Place the tofu in a shallow dish so that the marinade covers it completely. Cover and refrigerate, turning the tofu several times. You will want to marinate your tofu long enough for it to fully absorb the flavors of the marinade—30 minutes to 3 hours, or even overnight.

BOILING

If you have tofu that has just started to sour, boiling will kill any bacteria that may have developed. Boil it in enough water to cover the tofu. Usual boiling time ranges from 5 to 20 minutes. After boiling, the outside of the tofu will be cooked more than the inside. This may, however, be just the texture you are looking for in a particular recipe. Do not boil silken tofu, as it will fall apart in the hot water.

FRYING

For a wonderful meaty texture, pan-fry your tofu in a little bit of oil. Enjoyed by itself or added to recipes, it offers a nice chewiness and flavor.

DEEP-FRYING

If done correctly, deep-frying tofu can be healthy; very little oil is actually absorbed into the tofu during the cooking process. Heat your oil to 350°F before lowering the tofu into the oil. If you have a deep-fat fryer, the temperature will automatically be regulated. Dip deep-fried tofu into your favorite sauce or condiment, add it to a brothy soup, or just pop it into your mouth by itself.

Other Soy Products

Tofu is not the only soy food that can help you get your soy protein. In fact, the humble soybean is responsible for hundreds of different products.

EDAMAME

Also known as green vegetable soybeans, these beans are sold in their pods, and have been picked at the height of maturity. They have a firm texture and are sweet and pleasant tasting. Found in Asian and natural food stores, they are boiled and used as a snack or in vegetable stir fries.

MEAT ALTERNATIVES

Nearly every form of meat available now has a soy-based counterpart. Most products are made with tofu, tempeh, textured soy protein, or soy flour. These burgers, dogs, sausages, lunch meats, and crumbles are low in fat, and don't take long to cook.

MISO

Made from fermented soybeans, miso is a salty paste with a texture similar to soft peanut butter. Used widely in Japanese cooking, miso makes a great soup stock. Miso varies considerably in color and flavor, and the darker the miso the stronger the flavor. White miso is sweet and mild and well suited for sauces, soups, and salad dressings. Red (or dark) miso has a stronger flavor, and is ideal for heavier gravies. Miso is generally fermented with rice, though other grains, such as barley, are also used.

SOY CHEESE

There is a soy version of a wide range of block, sliced, spreadable, and grated cheeses. However, many varieties include *casein*, a cow's milk protein that gives the soy cheese a dairy flavor and helps it melt when heated.

Here is a small sampling of the soy meat alternatives available.

SOY FLOUR

Made from roasted soybeans that have been ground into a fine powder, soy flour is a great protein boost for recipes. It's also high in fiber.

Say cheese (soy cheese!).

Some soy products. *Clockwise from top of plate:* **soynut butter on celery, tempeh, soy sprouts, two types of textured soy protein.** *Surrounding the plate:* **Soy flour, chocolate and vanilla soy milk, and miso**

SOY ICE CREAM

Not usually found in major supermarkets, soy ice cream is a flavorful, dairy-free alternative to ice cream.

SOY MILK

Made from soybeans that have been soaked, ground fine, and strained, soy milk is a wonderful substitute for cow's milk. Sold mostly in aseptic containers (non-refrigerated), it comes in a variety of flavors, including plain, vanilla, chocolate, and carob.

SOY SAUCE

Made from fermented soybeans, soy sauce can't boast the nutritional benefits of other soy products because of its high salt content.

SOY SPROUTS

These crisp sprouts of germinated soybeans are high in protein, and can usually be found in Korean grocery stores.

SOY "YOGURT"

A dairyless "yogurt" made from soy milk, soy yogurt comes in a variety of flavors, and tastes a lot like the original.

SOYNUT BUTTER

A peanut-butter substitute made from roasted whole soynuts, this soy product has less fat than traditional peanut butter.

SOYNUTS

Whole soybeans soaked in water, soynuts are baked until browned. They taste somewhat like peanuts.

TEMPEH

A chunky, tender soybean cake traditionally used in Indonesian food, tempeh has a distinctive nutlike taste. It's sold fermented with a variety of grains, such as quinoa and barley. Tempeh comes in several marinated flavors too.

TEXTURED SOY PROTEIN

Used as a meat substitute, textured soy protein is made from soy flour, and has all the protein, fiber, and isoflavones of other soy products.

WHOLE DRY SOYBEANS

This is the original soy food. When ripened, these beans turn yellow, although you can also find black soybeans. They can be soaked or cooked, then used in soups and sauces.

and other soy products help you reduce the risk of heart disease, but with the help of a naturally occurring "plant estrogen" called *isoflavones*, tofu may also reduce the risk of many types of cancer, decrease menopausal symptoms, and help with the prevention of bone loss due to osteoporosis. Soy foods have so many health benefits that they actually blur the line between food and medicine. Finally, soy products are also healthy for our planet, improving the soil in which they grow.

Here are the basic facts regarding soybeans and the health claims that have caught the attention of health-conscious eaters worldwide.

Tofu and a Healthier You

It says so right on the label: "Diets low in saturated fat and cholesterol that include 25 grams of soy protein per day may reduce the risk of heart disease." And this isn't advertising hype. The U.S. Food and Drug Administration has authorized this claim, and in effect, opened up a whole new world of healthful eating for people who had never even heard of tofu. If this health claim was the only thing tofu and soy foods had going for them, it would be enough—but it is only the tip of the iceberg.

In addition to being loaded with iron, phosphorus, and B-complex vitamins, tofu has absolutely no cholesterol and very little sodium. It's easy to digest and especially good for people who are allergic to dairy products. When tofu is made using calcium salt as a curdling agent, it becomes an excellent source of absorbable calcium. And, not only can tofu

Protein

Soybeans are now considered to be the most promising source of low-cost, high-quality protein available. But this isn't news to the roughly one-quarter of the world's population that relies on soy foods as its primary source of protein. Four ounces of cooked soybeans has the same amount of protein as four ounces of beef, but without the saturated fat and cholesterol. Four ounces of tofu yields up to 13 grams of protein. With all nine of the essential amino acids that our bodies require, tofu and other soy foods can safely and effectively replace animal products as the major source of protein in your diet.

Heart Disease

Soy foods are high in protein but low in saturated fat and free of cholesterol. In fact, clinical studies have shown that substituting soy protein for animal protein or simply adding soy protein to the diet significantly reduces the risk of heart disease. Soy protein has the ability to dramatically lower the undesirable low-density lipoprotein blood cholesterol

(LDL) levels that have already accumulated within the body while raising the desirable high-density lipoprotein levels. It takes at least 25 grams of soy protein per day in a low-fat, low-cholesterol diet to achieve a 10 percent reduction in cholesterol. That 10 percent decrease in cholesterol reduces the chance of having a heart attack by an astonishing 20 to 30 percent.

Cancer

Recent studies into the soy component known as isoflavones have offered promising hope for the prevention and treatment of many different types of cancers. Scientific studies have found a strong connection between isoflavones, which are found almost exclusively in soybeans, and a reduced risk of many types of cancer including breast, colon, lung, prostate, skin, and leukemia. More research needs to be done to determine exactly how isoflavones work to fight cancer, but it appears that as little as one serving of soy foods a day may be enough to obtain the benefits of isoflavones.

Menopause

Isoflavones have also been linked to a decrease in symptoms related to menopause. Often, menopausal women are forced to endure symptoms such as difficulty in the regulation of body temperature, resulting in "hot flashes" and "night sweats." A recent study showed that menopausal women who ate soy had almost a 50 percent reduction in such symptoms.

Osteoporosis

Characterized by thin, weak, and brittle bones, this disease plagues an alarming number of post-menopausal women. There are many preventative factors that can slow down the loss of bone matter and even increase overall bone density. Calcium is an essential part of this process, and the isoflavones found in tofu are known to assist in better utilization of calcium within the body, making it easily absorbed. There are some brands of tofu that are made with calcium sulfate, a naturally mined mineral, which brings a significant boost to the tofu's overall calcium content. And, when calcium chloride is used as the coagulant in the tofu-making process, the tofu boasts 23 percent more calcium than the same amount of dairy milk.

Our Planet

Soybeans are one of the only crops that actually improve the soil in which they are grown, adding valuable nitrogen to the soil. Plus, while one acre of land yields about six pounds of beef, that same acre of land will produce more than 300 pounds of soybeans a year!

Simple Ingredient Substitutions

Although tofu is an essential ingredient in all of the recipes presented in this book, we will leave it up to you to adjust each recipe to fit your dietary and nutritional needs. Some of you may have a need for strict vegan (no animal products whatsoever), no sugar, or low-sodium diets. Here are some simple substitutions you can make for some key ingredients.

Eggs

Whether you wish to cut down on eggs because you're trying to lower your cholesterol levels, or wish to eliminate them from your diet altogether as part of a nonanimal-foods diet, you do have options. There are a variety of commercial egg replacers available in the dairy case of most supermarkets. A combination of starches and leavening agents, egg replacers bind cooked and baked foods in the same way as real eggs. If a recipe requires eggs for leavening purposes, as with baked goods, you can add 1 teaspoon of baking powder for every egg. This leavening is a bit unpredictable, so results may vary. If a recipe requires eggs for binding, as in pancakes or a casserole, you can substitute 2 ounces of mashed tofu or 1 teaspoon of arrowroot per egg.

Milk

Whether you're lactose-intolerant, vegetarian, vegan, or just looking for a tasty alternative to milk, there are a wide variety of nondairy beverages currently available in natural food stores and supermarkets. Most can be used in recipes in the same manner as cow's milk. Soy milk is the most versatile, with its creamy, nutty flavor. Rice milk is great for making desserts, but it can be too sweet for savory dishes. Almond milk is the sweetest of them all, so use it in desserts only. Most often sold in aseptic (non-refrigerated) packages, nondairy beverages can be stored at room temperature for several months. Once opened, however, they must be refrigerated and will stay fresh for about five days.

Cheese

There are many cheese substitutes on the market today. Most are made from a combination of soy milk and a variety of spices and seasonings. Although these cheeses are cholesterol-free, they may contain a certain amount of oil. Vegans must be on the lookout for those soy cheeses containing casein, a cow's milk derivative, which is added to help the cheeses melt. Because of their cheeselike flavor, nutritional yeast flakes make a delicious alternative to traditional Parmesan when a recipe calls for cheese to be sprinkled on top of a dish. You can buy nutritional yeast flakes in jars at natural food stores.

Butter

All-vegetable margarines are a simple non-dairy substitute for butter, but avoid those containing hydrogenated oils. Vegetable broth may also be used for sautéing in place of butter. Just be sure to use twice the amount as required for the butter.

Salt

Salt has an amazing ability to bring out the flavors of almost any dish. But conventional table salt is mixed with chemical additives, making it less appealing to the health-conscious cook. Sea salt and Kosher salt, on the other hand, are all natural, though you may need to grind them in a pepper mill since they are coarser than table salt. Miso can also be used in place of salt in some recipes.

Sugar

Because conventional refined white sugar provides no nutritional content, some cooks opt for alternative methods of sweetening their recipes. Although there are many chemical sweeteners available on the market, many diabetics and calorie-counters look for more natural sugar substitutes. Fortunately, there are plenty of options to choose from. Grain-based sweeteners are complex sugars, releasing into the blood slowly, providing fuel for the body instead of the rush and eventual crash associated with simple sugar. Because natural sweeteners are generally less sweet than sugar, you may need to increase the amount used to suit your taste. Also keep in mind that, if you choose to use a liquid sweetener, you may need to decrease the amount of liquid called for in the recipe.

HONEY

Produced by bees from the nectar of flowers, honey is one of the most preferred alternatives to sugar. There are hundreds of varieties of honey, most of them named after the principal nectar source (clover, wildflower). Honey ranges in color from almost white to amber to dark brown. As a rule of thumb, the lighter the color of the honey, the milder the flavor.

MOLASSES

Made from 100 percent pure, natural sugar cane juices, molasses is clarified, reduced, and blended to get just the right color and consistency. Light molasses is usually preferred to the darker, heavy-tasting, blackstrap variety.

MAPLE SYRUP

Maple syrup has about the same amount of calories as white cane sugar, but also contains significant amounts of potassium, calcium, small amounts of iron and phosphorus, and trace amounts of B-vitamins. Use only pure maple syrup in recipes. You will find it with other syrups in the supermarket.

RICE SYRUP

Made from soft cooked rice, this sweetener offers a delicate sweetness with no aftertaste. It makes a perfect sweetener for cakes, cookies, and puddings. Since it is about 40 percent as sweet as white sugar, you will need to add more than the amount of sugar the recipe calls for. You can find it in most natural food stores.

BARLEY MALT SYRUP

Stronger in flavor than rice syrup, this dark, sticky sweetener is not as overpowering as molasses and not as sweet as honey. It is best used with desserts that complement its intense flavor, such as spice cakes or custards. It is available at natural food stores.

Ingredient
Glossary

Puzzled by polenta? Flustered by fennel? Though
most of our recipes are made with easy-to-find
ingredients, you may feel baffled when your
recipe calls for bulgur. Turn here for
the answers to those pesky
ingredient questions.

• • •

Ingredients

This glossary includes only the less familiar ingredients used in our recipes. Most of these ingredients are not difficult to find; they can be purchased at supermarkets or natural food stores. If you can't find a particular ingredient, try buying it through gourmet food catalogs or magazines. Of course, you can also search the Internet. Wherever possible, we offer substitutions.

ARROWROOT

A thickening agent for sauces, puddings and other foods, arrowroot is made of the ground roots of a tropical tuber. It is tasteless and becomes clear when cooked. Its thickening power is twice that of wheat flour, so be sure not to use too much. Like cornstarch, you should mix it with a cold liquid before heating or adding to hot mixtures. Find it in supermarkets, Asian markets, and natural food stores.

BALSAMIC VINEGAR

This is an intensely flavored, slightly sweet red wine vinegar. Because of its strength, use less balsamic vinegar than other varieties in cooking. Much like olive oil, it comes in a wide range of qualities and price ranges. A moderately priced vinegar is fine for everyday use. Beware of imitations that are flavored with sugar, vanilla, and caramel. Available in all supermarkets.

BAMBOO SHOOTS

Bamboo shoots are the young, edible, opaque slices from the tender stem and shoots of the bamboo plant. A common ingredient in Asian cooking, they are usually used with other Oriental vegetables or served raw. In most supermarkets, you can find canned bamboo shoots that are ready to be used in recipes. Sometimes you can find fresh ones in Asian markets.

BARLEY MALT SYRUP

Dark, sticky, and boldly flavored, barely malt sugar is not as overpowering as molasses and not as sweet as honey. High in complex carbohydrates, it serves as a natural sweetener in breads, muffins, and malted beverages.

If you cannot find it, you can substitute ⅔ cup of molasses or ¾ cup maple syrup for every cup of barley malt syrup. Available in natural food stores.

BASMATI RICE

Traditionally used in Indian and Middle Eastern cuisines, this rice is favored by many for its fragrant long grains and subtle floral or nutty flavor. Some consider white basmati to be the most easily digestible grain. Available in most supermarkets and Asian markets in white or brown form.

BEAN SPROUTS

Usually used in Asian dishes, the crisp sprouts of the mung bean have a very pleasant taste and a light, crunchy texture. They

give a crisp freshness to salads and sandwiches and can be enjoyed by themselves. They are rich in almost every important vitamin and mineral, and are considered one of the few "complete foods" available today. They are usually sold near Chinese vegetables in the produce section of the supermarket. Good-quality bean sprouts will be crisp-looking, almost dry, and bright-white.

BOK CHOY

Also known as Chinese cabbage, bok choy is actually not a cabbage at all, but a versatile crunchy vegetable with white stalks and bright green leaves. It is commonly used in stir-fries and other Asian dishes. It will keep for about a week in the produce drawer of your refrigerator.

BUCKWHEAT

Buckwheat, with its light, bland flavor, can be used in a variety of ways. Because of its size, processing, and application characteristics, buckwheat is often considered similar to cereal grains such as wheat, barley, and oats. It is, however, a leafy plant. It may come in the form of sprouts that have a mild, lettuce-like flavor. Flour, made from the triangular seeds, can be used in baked goods, such as pancakes and muffins. Dehulled buckwheat seeds are also used to add texture to breads, salads, and other dishes.

BULGUR WHEAT

If you've ever eaten tabouli, you've eaten bulgur! This cracked, parboiled wheat is often called the "rice" of the Middle East. Sold in supermarkets and natural food stores, it has a unique nutty flavor.

CAPERS

Sharp and vinegary in flavor, capers are the pickled buds of a Mediterranean flowering plant. Their strong, olive-like taste is wonderful used in a wide variety of dishes. Capers should be drained and rinsed before using. You will find them in most supermarkets.

CELERY SALT

A pungent mixture of fine-grained salt and ground celery seed, this seasoning is usually used to sprinkle on vegetables, salads, and in tomato or other vegetable juices.

CHILI PASTE

Made from a variety of ingredients, including garlic and hot chili peppers, this very hot paste adds kick to any recipe. Look for it in Asian food shops or well-stocked supermarkets.

CHIVES

A sweet, delicate member of the onion family, chives come either fresh (in long, thin green strands) or dried (in tiny pieces). When cooking, add chives near the end of the cooking time to retain their flavor. Fresh chives are preferred, as dried chives are much weaker in flavor and aroma. If fresh ones are unavailable, substitute scallion greens cut into fine strips.

CHUTNEY

This sweet and sour condiment is usually made with a combination of fruit and/or vegetables, vinegar, sugar, and spices. A variety of chutneys can be found in most supermarkets and gourmet shops, but it is easy to make your own at home.

CIDER VINEGAR

Cider vinegar adds a lively, fruity flavor to recipes. It is milder and sweeter than most wine vinegars. You can find it in almost any supermarket.

CILANTRO

Often sold as "fresh coriander" or "Chinese parsley," cilantro is an essential part of Thai, Indian, Vietnamese, and Mexican cooking. Its pungent flavor and fragrance enhance highly spiced foods. Used uncooked, the leaves make an attractive garnish. Add cilantro near the end of cooking time to retain its full flavor. If you cannot find fresh cilantro leaves, fresh flat-leaf parsley sprigs are an adequate substitute.

CLOVES

The unopened buds of myrtle flowers, cloves are available either whole or ground, and are a common spice in Middle Eastern cuisines, as well as in many desserts. Ground, they are used in cakes and soups; whole, they add great flavor to mulled wines and ciders. Available in your supermarket's spice aisle.

COCONUT MILK OR CREAM

Its fragrant, naturally sweet flavor is essential in many Thai and Southeast Asian dishes, especially soups, sauces, and curries. There are a wide variety of canned coconut milks available. The fat will naturally separate from the milk, so shake well before using. Lighter versions containing half the calories and fat of regular coconut milk are available in natural food stores, Asian markets, and select supermarkets. Avoid coconut milk that is labelled "sweetened" or "cream of coconut;" this is a syrup primarily used in desserts and mixed drinks.

CORIANDER

An ingredient in many Indian, Thai, and Malaysian dishes, this spice is made from the ground seeds of the cilantro plant. Not nearly as potent as its parent plant, it has a distinctive flavor which is slightly sweet and aromatic. Also known as a pickling spice, you can find coriander in any supermarket.

CUMIN

Popular in Middle Eastern, Indian, Asian, and South American cooking, cumin is the dried fruit of a plant in the parsley family. Its aromatic, nutty, peppery flavor is often an essential ingredient in chili and curry. You can find dried curry powder in your supermarket's spice aisle.

CURRY PASTE, THAI

Don't get this curry paste confused with chili paste. Essential in many Thai curries and sauces, it comes in red, yellow, or green, and varies in flavor and heat level. It makes a flavorful addition to any marinade. There really is no adequate substitute. Available in Asian markets and natural food stores.

CURRY POWDER

What we call "curry powder" is actually a pre-mixed blend of spices typically consisting of cayenne pepper, coriander, cumin, cloves, cinnamon, fenugreek, ginger, mace, and turmeric. In India there is no such thing as curry powder; they make fresh spice blends on a daily basis. To most cooks, the convenience of curry powder makes it an essential kitchen ingredient. It may be added to traditional Southeast Asian dishes, deviled eggs, chicken salads, soups, sauces, rice dishes, and vegetables. Be careful not to add too much—curry powder's intense flavor goes a long way and can easily overpower a dish.

EXTRACTS

These are liquid flavor essences of nuts, herbs, and fruits that can be added to recipes. You can get pure bottled extracts or artificial ones in the spice or baking aisle of the supermarket. Artificial extracts have artificial flavors which can really throw off the taste of a recipe, so, while pure extracts are considerably more expensive, they are worth it. Although extracts last a long time (store them in a cool, dark place), they will eventually lose their potency. Smell the extract—the more potent the fragrance, the fresher the extract. If the smell is weak, the flavor will be, too.

FENNEL

A fragrant vegetable with a mild licorice flavor, the edible bulb and stalks can be used like celery. Fennel seeds are used for seasoning in both sweet and savory dishes. The fresh herb is available in well-stocked produce sections, and the seeds, whole and ground, are available in the spice aisle of any supermarket.

FERMENTED CHINESE BLACK BEANS

These fermented and seasoned black soybeans have a sweet, salty, and spicy flavor that is

truly unique. Found in gourmet or specialty Asian shops, the beans add a distinct flavor to tofu stir-fry dishes. If you are concerned about salt content, rinse the beans in water before use. There is no substitute.

FILÉ POWDER

An integral part of traditional Creole cooking, filé powder is made from dried and ground sassafras leaves. It is used as a seasoning and primary thickening agent in gumbo, and has a wonderfully pungent and aromatic flavor reminiscent of root beer. It must be stirred into a recipe after the dish has been removed from the heat, because undue cooking makes filé tough and stringy. Available in the spice or gourmet section of most large supermarkets.

GALANGAL

A member of the ginger family, this knobby root hails from Indonesia and has a delicate flavor comparable to pepper and ginger. Sold in dry, hard circles resembling wood chips, it is most often used as a warm, aromatic seasoning in curries, stews, stir-fries and marinades. Find it in Asian markets or the spice aisle of a well-stocked supermarket.

GARAM MASALA

This popular Indian spice blend is a combination of many different spices, including coriander, cumin, black pepper, and cloves. Although it is more difficult to find than traditional curry powder, you can buy garam masala at your local natural food store or Indian market.

GARBANZO BEANS

Also known as chickpeas, these round, irregular shaped beans are very popular in Mediterranean cuisine. They have a mild, nutty flavor and firm texture. Canned chickpeas can be found in the bean aisle of most grocery stores.

GRATED CITRUS RIND

The outermost part of an orange, lemon, or lime, grated citrus rind adds an intense citrus flavor to dishes. When grating a fruit rind, be very careful to get only a thin layer of skin and none of the white pithy parts, as they are very bitter. A grater or citrus zester can be used to obtain grated rind. For larger pieces of grated rind, simply use a potato or vegetable peeler.

HOISON SAUCE

Mostly used in Asian stir-fry dishes, this thick, sweet, reddish-brown sauce is made from soybeans, sugar, chilies, spices, and garlic. Widely available in supermarkets and natural food stores, it can be added to marinades for a wonderful flavor.

JERK SEASONING

This Jamaican hot and spicy seasoning includes a blend of chilies, cinnamon, allspice, thyme, and lime juice or rum. The blending of the hot and sweet flavors results in a pungent flavor and an absolutely irresistible aroma.

This seasoning is excellent to have on hand to sprinkle on vegetables and snacks, or to use in a traditional marinade for grilling.

LADY FINGERS

These sweet, fairly dry, finger-shaped sponge cakes are an essential ingredient in the Italian dessert tiramisu. Ladyfingers can be made at home or purchased in bakeries, supermarkets, or gourmet shops.

LEEKS

A member of the garlic and onion family, leeks are a versatile cooking ingredient. They look like giant scallions, but have a mild flavor reminiscent of garlic and onions. When buying fresh leeks, look for firm white stalks and stiff, bright green leaves. When you pick up a leek, it should be firm, not limp. Usually, you will only use the white and/or the very pale green part of a leek.

LEMONGRASS

This tall, hard, gray-green, stalklike grass is most commonly used in Thai cooking. Used whole, smashed, or diced, it adds a wonderful citrus flavor to food. Its flavor is unique and cannot be substituted. Find it in Asian markets or the gourmet section of supermarkets.

LIQUID SMOKE

This liquid seasoning made from hickory smoke concentrate imparts a distinct smokey flavor to foods. Use it sparingly, as liquid smoke is very concentrated and a few drops will go a long way. You can buy it in the barbecue and steak sauce section of most supermarkets.

MARJORAM

Closely related to oregano, this mint-flavored herb imparts a nice flavor to salad dressings, Italian and Greek dishes, beans, and tomato-based sauces. It is available fresh, in well-stocked produce sections, or dried, in your supermarket's spice aisle.

MARSALA WINE

This wine, imported from Sicily, is Italy's most famous fortified wine. It has a rich, smoky flavor that can range from dry to sweet. Sweet Marsala is used as a dessert wine and also to add flavor to recipes.

MASCARPONE

An Italian cream cheese, mascarpone comes from a low-fat, fresh cream. Made from the milk of cows that have been fed special grasses containing fresh herbs and flowers, mascarpone is a milky-white, thick cream that is easily spread. When fresh, it smells like milk and cream, and is often used in place of butter. It is much like fresh ricotta in consistency and has a mildly acidic and buttery flavor. Because of its low sodium content, mascarpone is highly perishable. Find it in the dairy section of your supermarket.

MATZO MEAL

This coarse, flour-like ingredient is made from matzo, an unleavened bread. Available in the Kosher section of a well-stocked supermarket.

MIRIN

This low-alcohol, Japanese sweet rice wine, only used for cooking, adds flavor to a variety of sauces and main dishes. If you cannot find it, you may substitute ½ teaspoon honey or 2 tablespoons dry sherry for each tablespoon of mirin called for in the recipe. It is available in Asian markets and gourmet shops.

MISO

Known as soybean paste to Westerners, miso is a fermented paste of grain and soybeans with the consistency of peanut butter. It comes in a variety of strengths and colors,

with white (which is actually pale yellow) being the mildest, going up to red or brown. Miso can enhance the flavor of sauces, soups, and marinades. Since it's high in sodium, don't add salt or soy sauce to a recipe until you test it for taste first. You can find it in Asian grocery stores, natural food stores, and select supermarkets.

NAPA CABBAGE

This tender and delicious green is the most popular family of Chinese cabbages sold in supermarkets. It is similar in shape to romaine lettuce, and pale green to greenish-white in color. It can be eaten raw, cooked, or used in salads, soups, stews, and stir-fries.

NUTRITIONAL YEAST

This nutritional supplement is an excellent source of protein and B-vitamins, and it helps in the regulation of blood sugar. Because of its cheeselike flavor, these pale yellow flakes make a delicious topping and ingredient for main dishes and snacks. Never use a live yeast (i.e., baking yeast) as a food supplement, because it will continue to grow in the intestine and deplete the B-vitamins in the body, instead of replenishing the supply. Brewer's yeast is nutritionally the same, but as a by-product of the beer-brewing industry, it has a characteristically bitter hops flavor. Nutritional yeast is widely available in natural food stores.

PHYLO OR FILO

Pronounced "FEE-low," this pastry dough is characterized by its wafer-thin layers. It is commonly used in appetizers and dessert pastries. The layers are stacked with butter between them for a flaky consistency. The dough can be tricky to work with as it dries out quickly, so be sure to keep the portions you are not immediately working with covered with a damp cloth. You will find phylo in the freezer section of most supermarkets.

PICKLED GINGER

Traditionally served with sushi, this preserved ginger root has a cool, sharp flavor. It is pickled in sugar, vinegar, and spices. You can find it in Asian markets and well-stocked supermarkets.

PIMENTO

A variety of red bell pepper, pimentos are usually peeled and packed in brine. In cooking, pimentos are interchangeable with roasted red peppers.

PINE NUTS

An important ingredient in pesto and a tasty addition to salads, these expensive little delicacies are not actually nuts at all, but seeds from the cone of certain pine trees. There are two main varieties: Mediterranean and Chinese. The Mediterranean pine nut is more delicately flavored, and the Chinese pine nut has a stronger pine flavor. Toasting brings out

their buttery flavor. You will find them in natural food stores, gourmet shops, and well-stocked supermarkets.

POLENTA

This grainy yellow flour is a type of cornmeal made from ground maize, which is cooked into a kind of porridge. Polenta is versatile and has a wide variety of uses. It can be served by itself with various hot toppings, or molded and cut into squares to be fried or grilled.

QUINOA

Pronounced "KEEN-wah," quinoa is a newly re-discovered grain that many nutritionists, doctors, and chefs are recommending because of its great nutritional profile and its nutty, distinctive flavor. Quinoa contains high quality, easy-to-digest protein, calcium, iron, and B vitamins. Always give it a thorough rinsing under water before using. Available in natural food stores.

RASPBERRY VINEGAR

Now readily available in most supermarkets, this slightly sweet vinegar is wonderful when used in a simple vinaigrette dressing on salads, or added to other dishes for a surprising flavor.

RED PEPPER FLAKES

These dried, crushed red chili peppers and seeds add just enough spice to recipes without going over the edge. Used as a substitute for cayenne pepper, a little goes a long way. Add a few pinches to warming oil to release their full flavor. Pepper flakes are available in any supermarket.

RICE NOODLES

These very long, transparent noodles are made from rice flour and make a delightful alternative to wheat-based pastas. They are not cooked, but rather soaked in warm water for 10 to 15 minutes until soft. They are versatile enough for salads, clear soups, Asian specialties, and fried noodle dishes. Rice noodles can also be deep-fried, which causes them to expand into a tangle of light, crunchy strands. Find them in well-stocked supermarkets and Asian markets.

RICE PAPERS

These thin, translucent wrappers are most often used to make Asian spring rolls. Available in different sizes, you can find them in Asian markets and natural food stores.

RICE SYRUP

This honey-like natural sweetener is made from soft cooked rice. For diabetics, it is a great alternative to refined white sugar. It offers the added benefit of containing about 50 percent complex carbohydrates, which do not break down during digestion as quickly as refined sugars. It is about 40 percent as sweet as white sugar. Available in natural food stores.

RICE VINEGAR

Made from fermented rice, this vinegar has a low acid content and is milder and sweeter than ordinary white vinegar. To avoid those that are seasoned or sweetened, look for "pure" rice vinegar in Asian markets and most supermarkets.

ROLLED OATS

Old-fashioned rolled oats are whole grain oat flakes that make a hearty, old-fashioned porridge, or add texture to granola, cookies, muffins, and other baked goods. They are a good source of fiber and a sodium-free, low-fat, and cholesterol-free food. You may be more familiar with quick-cooking oats, which are actually oat groats that have been cut into several pieces before being steamed and rolled into thinner flakes. The two can be used interchangeably in most recipes; however, the old-fashioned, rolled variety is preferred for its richer flavor and texture. You will find them in the cereal aisle.

ROSE WATER

Rose water is an aromatic distillation of rose petals. Popular in Middle Eastern, Indian, and Chinese cooking, it is used to give flavor to jellies, creams, drinks, and baked goods. Look for it in Asian markets.

RYE FLOUR

Available in medium, light, and dark rye, this flour can be used alone or in conjunction with other flours. It adds a unique sour taste to recipes, and has a heartier flavor than wheat flour. It has a very low gluten content, resulting in a denser bread.

SAFFRON

Best known as the world's most expensive spice, this vibrantly colored spice is used throughout the world in many cuisines. Its exquisite flavor is pungent, aromatic, and truly unique. It can be purchased in threads or in powdered form. Threads should be crushed just before using. Available in gourmet shops and natural food stores.

SAKE

Pronounced "sah-kay," this Japanese fermented rice wine is used widely in cooking. Its flavor and aroma can range from fruity and flowery to spicy and nutty. Sake enhances the taste of ingredients, and is therefore widely used for preparing and seasoning both Japanese and Western-style dishes. You can find it in many liquor stores and Asian markets. For cooking purposes, inexpensive brands of sake will do just as well as the more expensive ones.

SCALLIONS OR GREEN ONIONS

These delicately flavored members of the onion family are, simply put, a young onion before the enlargement of the bulb. The leaves should be bright green and firm; the white bulbs should be firm and unblemished. As a general rule, the more slender the bottoms, the sweeter the flavor. Both the green and white parts can be used in recipes that call for scallions. Buy fresh scallions in the produce section of the supermarket.

SHALLOTS

Members of the onion family, shallots, like garlic, grow in a cluster of bulbs—usually covered by a reddish paper membrane. Known for their distinctive and slightly garlicky taste, they are often used in French and Southeast Asian cooking. Choose shallots that are plump and fresh-looking, with no signs of wrinkling or sprouting. Available in most supermarkets.

SHERRY

This wine, fortified with brandy, comes either in a dark, sweet, cream or a dry, delicate version with a hint of saltiness. As well as being a wonderful after-dinner drink, sherry is frequently used in cooking.

SHOYU

An all-purpose seasoning used in many Asian cuisines, shoyu is a high-quality Japanese soy sauce made with cultured wheat and soybeans, water, and sea salt. In most cases, 1 teaspoon of shoyu can be substituted for $\frac{1}{4}$ teaspoon salt. You can find it in cans and bottles in well-stocked supermarkets. If you can't find it, substitute soy sauce.

SOBA NOODLES

These long, flat Japanese noodles are made from buckwheat and wheat flours, giving them a brownish color and nutty flavor. Served cold or hot, they add a distinctive, earthy flavor to recipes.

STRAW MUSHROOMS

These mushrooms possess a delicate, slightly musky flavor that enhances many Asian dishes, from soups to stir-fries. Their name comes not from their shape, but rather the way in which they are grown on straw. Because of their mild flavor and plump texture, they are easily substituted for standard button mushrooms. You can find them fresh in Asian markets or dried in many supermarkets. If you are using the dried kind, simply soak them in water for about 20 minutes before using.

SUN-DRIED TOMATOES

Sun-dried tomatoes have a tart-sweet taste that can add lovely, intense bursts of flavor to your cooking. They are available in most supermarkets, either packed in oil or dried. If you buy them dried, you will need to re-hydrate them by covering them with boiling water and letting them soak for 10 to 15 minutes. The oil-packed variety are ready to use, but are higher in fat content and price.

SWEET PICKLE RELISH

Made from sweet pickled cucumbers, bell peppers, and onions, this vinegary relish adds a pleasing, zesty touch to a variety of foods. It's a common ingredient in tartar sauce and some salads.

TAHINI

An essential ingredient in many Middle Eastern recipes, tahini is a smooth, creamy paste made from ground sesame seeds. It must be refrigerated, and stirred when it separates. It is used as a base for many sauces and dips, and is delicious eaten by itself. Find it in natural food stores and select supermarkets.

TAMARIND FRUIT PASTE AND JUICE

The tamarind is a fruit with a sour but slightly sweet flavor and a pleasant aroma. It is ideal wherever a gentle sourness is required, such as with Indian curries and certain Southeast Asian dishes. The fruit and juice can be found in Asian, Indian, and Mexican specialty shops. There is no substitute.

TARRAGON

This tangy herb adds a very distinct licorice flavor to foods. Use sparingly, as it has a strong flavor. It is available fresh in well-stocked produce sections, or dried in your supermarket's spice aisle.

TOASTED SESAME OIL

This dark, amber-colored oil is made from toasted sesame seeds. Because of its strong taste, it is most commonly used as a flavoring oil. Add it toward the end of the cooking process. Add a dash to a stir-fry or a bowl of miso soup.

VEGETARIAN GELATIN

This is a plant-derived gelling powder that mimics traditional gelatin. Available in some natural food stores and supermarkets.

VEGETARIAN WORCESTERSHIRE SAUCE

If you want the flavor of this commonly used condiment, but need a vegetarian version, you can find it in a natural food store. Just like the original, it is made of soy, vinegar, and spices, but without the anchovies.

WAKAME

A delicate, leafy sea vegetable used in Japanese cooking, wakame is a nice addition to miso soup. Dulse, a red seaweed, can be used with or in place of wakame. You can find wakame in Japanese markets and natural food stores.

WATER CHESTNUTS

These walnut-sized bulbs are covered by a tough, russet-colored skin. They can be boiled plain in their jackets, peeled and simmered, or candied. Water chestnuts are usually available in cans, either whole or sliced. Find them in Asian markets or the ethnic section of the supermarket.

WHEAT GERM

This inner part of the wheat kernel adds a nutty flavor to baked goods, and can be sprinkled over breakfast cereals, yogurt, or fruit. It is a concentrated source of vitamins, minerals, and protein. Toasted wheat germ, located in the cereal aisle of most supermarkets, is preferable to raw wheat germ because of its slightly crunchy texture. Keep it refrigerated, in a closed container.

Breakfast

Start your day with a revitalized breakfast favorite.
From smoothies to scrambles, we've got a
breakfast for you that will taste great and
get you going. Tofu isn't just
for dinner anymore.

• • •

Tofu-Pumpkin Pancakes

• • •

This interesting combination is a veritable taste explosion. You won't be able to get enough of these savory cakes.

• • •

Serves 4 to 6

INGREDIENTS

8 ounces soft tofu, blended
1½ cups pumpkin, puréed
1 cup unbleached, all-purpose flour
1 teaspoon ground allspice
1 teaspoon baking powder
2 eggs
Butter, for griddle

PREPARATION

1 In a large mixing bowl, mix the pumpkin purée and tofu.

2 In another bowl, sift the flour, allspice, and baking powder together. Stir into the pumpkin-tofu mixture, mixing well.

3 Beat in the eggs, and let the batter stand for 30 minutes.

4 In a griddle, melt the butter over medium-high heat. Drop the batter onto the griddle by tablespoonfuls.

5 Brown the cakes on both sides, and serve immediately with syrup or jam.

'Tater Cakes

• • •

Make extra mashed potatoes for dinner, and use the leftovers the next morning in these quick and easy potato cakes. Don't laugh, but we dip ours in ketchup.

• • •

Yields 12 cakes

INGREDIENTS

6 ounces firm tofu, mashed
3 tablespoons vegetable oil
1 medium onion, chopped
3 cups mashed potatoes
¼ cup fresh parsley springs, minced
½ teaspoon salt
¼ teaspoon pepper

PREPARATION

1 In a frying pan, sauté the onion in 1 tablespoon of oil until golden.

2 In a large mixing bowl, mix the onions, potatoes, tofu, parsley, salt, and pepper.

3 Mold the mixture into ½-inch patties, and fry in the rest of the oil until browned on each side.

French Toast Sans Eggs

• • •

Savor this updated breakfast staple with your favorite fruit spread or syrup.

• • •

Serves 4

INGREDIENTS

12 ounces silken tofu
½ cup milk or soy milk
2 tablespoons honey or maple syrup
1 teaspoon cinnamon
½ teaspoon salt
2 tablespoons vegetable oil
4 to 6 slices bread

➡

Tofu-Pumpkin Pancakes (see opposite page)

PREPARATION

1 In a blender, combine all the ingredients and mix until smooth. Pour the mixture into a bowl.

2 Dip each slice of bread into the mixture until coated.

3 On a lightly oiled griddle, brown the battered bread on each side. Serve hot.

Tofu Pancakes

• • •

To create color and texture, add a cup of your favorite fruit (frozen or fresh) to the pancake batter just before cooking.

• • •

Serves 4

INGREDIENTS

6 ounces soft tofu, mashed
2 cups flour
½ cup cornmeal
4½ teaspoons baking powder
3 cups milk (or soy milk)
2 tablespoons vegetable oil
1 teaspoon salt
¼ cup sugar
1 teaspoon vanilla

PREPARATION

1 In a large mixing bowl, thoroughly mix the flour, cornmeal, and baking powder.

2 Stir in the milk, oil, salt, sugar, vanilla, and tofu.

3 Heat a lightly oiled griddle over medium-high heat. Pour about ¼ cup of batter for each pancake. When the tops of the pancakes bubble, flip them, and brown the other side. Serve hot with maple syrup or your favorite jam.

Tofruity Smoothie

• • •

You can dream up a different concoction every morning with this creamy, fruity drink.

• • •

Yields 3 cups

INGREDIENTS

12 ounces soft tofu, drained
1 ripe banana, peeled
1 cup frozen strawberries, thawed
1 cup apple juice
2 tablespoons wheat germ (optional)

PREPARATION

1 In a blender, combine all the ingredients and blend until smooth. Serve chilled.

Tofruity Smoothie (see above)

Hash Browns with Tofu, Green Chili, and Cheese

• • •

Serve alongside the Breakfast Tofu Scramble (see recipe on page 39), or heat up some tortillas, and make a breakfast burrito.

• • •

Serves 4

INGREDIENTS

8 ounces soft tofu, crumbled
water for boiling
2 pounds russet potatoes
¼ cup onion, finely diced
3 tablespoons oil
1 teaspoon salt
¼ teaspoon black pepper
3 tablespoons green chili
2 tablespoons fresh cilantro leaves, chopped
¼ cup Monterey Jack or Cheddar cheese, grated

PREPARATION

1 In a large pot, boil the potatoes until tender, then drain. Let the potatoes cool, and remove the skins.

2 In a mixing bowl, grate the potatoes coarsely, and mix with the onions and tofu.

3 In a large frying pan, heat the oil and add the potato mixture. Season with salt and pepper.

4 Fry on medium heat. Add the green chilies, and fry for 5 minutes, or until golden on the bottom.

5 Flip the hash browns and fry for five minutes on the other side, or just stir them around in the frying pan every few minutes.

6 Once lightly browned, stir in the cilantro and cheese. Serve hot.

Recipe Tip

To save time in the morning, boil, peel, and grate the potatoes for the hash browns the night before.

Tofu Benedict

• • •

Here's another great recipe to try if you are looking to get rid of the cholesterol in your diet without sacrificing taste.

• • •

Serves 4

INGREDIENTS

12 ounces smoked tofu, cut lengthwise into 4 slices
¼ cup fresh orange juice
2 garlic cloves, minced
1 teaspoon salt
1 large red onion, cut into ⅓-inch slices
2 tomatoes, halved
4 teaspoons olive oil
4 cups packed spinach leaves
1 teaspoon canola oil
4 English muffin halves, toasted
1 cup Mock Béarnaise Sauce (see recipe on page 208)
Fresh parsley springs, chopped

PREPARATION

1 In a shallow bowl, combine the orange juice, minced garlic clove, ½ teaspoon of the salt, onion, tomatoes, and 2 teaspoons of the olive oil. Let sit for 10 minutes.

2 On an oiled baking sheet, broil the onions and tomato halves for 10 minutes, or until the onions are soft. Set aside.

➡

Tofu Benedict (see page 37) with
Mock Béarnaise Sauce (see page 208)

3 In a medium frying pan, sauté the other minced garlic clove in the rest of the olive oil over medium heat until browned. Remove from the heat.

4 Add the spinach, and toss until wilted. Add salt to taste, and set aside.

5 Brush the tofu slices with the canola oil. Broil for 2 minutes, or until the tops are browned and blistered.

6 For each serving, place an English muffin slice in the center of a plate. Top with a slice of tofu, a portion of spinach, slices of onion, and a grilled tomato half. Ladle ⅓ cup of the Mock Béarnaise Sauce over each muffin, and garnish with the parsley. Serve immediately.

Breakfast Tofu Scramble

• • •

Scrambled tofu looks and tastes like scrambled eggs. Anything you add to your scrambled eggs, you can add to this recipe.

• • •

Serves 4

INGREDIENTS

16 ounces firm tofu, crumbled
2 chopped scallions or ½ cup chopped onions
1 garlic clove, minced
½ teaspoon turmeric
Salt to taste
Pepper to taste
1 teaspoon dried parsley
1 tablespoon butter

PREPARATION

1 In a small bowl, combine the scallions or onions, garlic, turmeric, pepper, salt and parsley.

2 Melt the butter in a frying pan, and add the tofu. Sprinkle the combined seasonings over the tofu and cook, stirring frequently.

3 Cover and cook on medium heat until heated through. Serve hot.

Recipe Tip

Don't overdo it with the turmeric. It is used here for coloring, and too much will make the scrambles bitter.

VARIATION: Sauté ½ cup each of sliced peppers, mushrooms, and tomatoes before adding the tofu to the frying pan.

VARIATION: Sauté 1 cup of serrano chilies, and add a salsa of your choice, before adding the tofu to the frying pan.

Savory Potato Frittata

• • •

Impress brunch guests with this gourmet-style meal. You don't have to tell them how easy it is to make.

• • •

Serves 4

INGREDIENTS

8 ounces soft tofu, crumbled
1 egg, plus 2 egg whites
¼ teaspoon salt
Black pepper to taste
3½ tablespoons canola oil
2 medium potatoes, peeled
1 cup sliced mushrooms
2 garlic cloves, minced
½ teaspoon dried thyme
3 scallions, chopped
2 jalapeño chilies, seeds and stems removed, minced

1 small red bell pepper, diced
½ cup frozen corn kernels, thawed and rinsed
1 teaspoon fresh lemon juice
2 tablespoons grated Parmesan cheese
1 cup grated Monterey Jack cheese
2 to 3 tablespoons cilantro leaves, chopped

PREPARATION

1 Whisk the egg, egg whites, half the salt, a dash of pepper, and ½ tablespoon of the oil together in a bowl. Set aside.

2 Grate the potatoes, and rinse them three times. Squeeze them dry.

3 In a large frying pan, heat 2 tablespoons of canola oil over medium-high heat. Add the potatoes and tofu to the hot oil, and cook until they are crisp and browned. Stir as needed.

4 In another frying pan, heat the remaining tablespoon of oil. Add the mushrooms,

Savory Potato Frittata (see above)

garlic, thyme, scallions, jalapeño chili, and red pepper.

5 Sauté for 2 to 3 minutes, and then add the corn, remaining salt, and lemon juice.

6 Sauté the mixture until the vegetables are tender and all of the liquid has evaporated. Stir in the Parmesan cheese.

7 Reduce the heat under the potatoes and tofu to low, and pour in the egg mixture. Cook about 1 minute.

8 Spread the vegetables over the mixture. Sprinkle the cheese over the top and cover.

9 Cook until the cheese melts. Slide the cooked frittata onto a warm serving plate, garnish with the cilantro, and cut it into wedges.

Fakin' Bacon

• • •

A great meat substitute, these tofu "bacon" strips taste great served with eggs or in a sandwich.

• • •

Yields 6 slices

INGREDIENTS

12 ounces firm tofu
Vegetable oil for frying
1 tablespoon liquid smoke
Salt to taste
Soy sauce to taste

PREPARATION

1 Slice the tofu into ⅛ to ¼-inch slices.

2 Cover the bottom of a frying pan with a thin layer of oil, and place the tofu slices on top.

3 Sprinkle the tofu slices with liquid smoke and salt, and sauté over medium heat until golden brown.

4 Flip the slices and brown on the other side for an additional 15 minutes.

5 After the slices are browned, sprinkle soy sauce over them, and sauté for 5 minutes longer. Serve hot.

Southwestern Breakfast Burritos

• • •

This Tex-Mex classic is served here without the fried eggs.

• • •

Serves 6

INGREDIENTS

16 ounces firm tofu, drained and cubed
Vegetable oil for frying
1 medium onion, chopped
1 garlic clove, minced
1 small green bell pepper, finely diced
16-ounce can crushed tomatoes
4-ounce can chopped green chilies
½ teaspoon dried oregano
½ teaspoon cumin
Salt to taste
¼ cup cornmeal
6 corn tortillas
1¼ cup grated Monterey Jack or Cheddar cheese
1 medium avocado, sliced

PREPARATION

1 In a 5-quart saucepan, sauté the onion and garlic in oil for 3 to 5 minutes.

2 Add the pepper, and continue to sauté until the onion is golden.

3 Add the tomatoes, chilies, oregano, cumin, and salt, and simmer, covered, for 10 to 15 minutes.

Southwestern Breakfast Burritos (see page 41)

4 Place the tofu cubes in a plastic bag with the cornmeal. Shake gently to coat the cubes.

5 In a medium-sized frying pan, sauté the tofu in oil. Stir frequently until golden. Remove from heat.

6 Quickly dunk each tortilla in the sauce, and place it on an individual serving plate.

7 Divide the tofu among the tortillas, then top with more sauce and grated cheese.

8 Fold the tortillas over the tofu and sauce, and garnish with avocado slices.

Toffles

• • •

Tofu stands in for the eggs in this delicious version of homemade waffles.

• • •

Yields 8 waffles

INGREDIENTS

32 ounces soft tofu
2½ cups vanilla soy milk
4 tablespoons honey
½ teaspoon salt
2 teaspoons baking powder
2 teaspoons vanilla
2 cups whole wheat flour

PREPARATION

1 Pour all the ingredients, except for the flour, into a blender or food processor, and mix until smooth.

2 Add the flour to the mixture, and blend again.

3 Bake in a preheated waffle iron according to manufacturer's instructions.

Recipe Tip

Add blueberries, strawberries, peaches, or whatever fruit you desire to the batter to create your very own fruit toffles.

Huevos Rancheros with Tofu

• • •

Travel south of the border with this mild, yet wild, egg and tofu breakfast bonanza.

• • •

Serves 4

INGREDIENTS

16 ounces firm tofu, frozen, thawed, and crumbled
1 medium onion, chopped
1 bell pepper, chopped
2 tablespoons vegetable oil
3 garlic cloves, minced
15-ounce can tomato sauce
½ cup water
½ teaspoon dried oregano
1½ teaspoon chili powder
½ teaspoon cumin
2 teaspoons vegetable-flavored bouillon
¼ teaspoon black pepper
4 eggs

PREPARATION

1 In a 5-quart saucepan, sauté the onion and pepper in oil for 5 minutes.

2 Add the garlic, tomato sauce, water, tofu, oregano, chili powder, cumin, bouillon, and pepper. Bring to a boil, reduce heat, and simmer, covered, for 10 minutes.

3 Make four indentations in the thick sauce, and break an egg into each one.

4 Simmer, covered, for 5 to 10 minutes more, or until the eggs are poached as desired.

5 Scoop out each egg with sauce to serve.

Baked Spinach Omelet

• • •

This omelet bakes up plump and cheesy.

• • •

Serves 6

INGREDIENTS

8 ounces firm tofu, crumbled

2 10-ounce packages frozen, chopped spinach, thawed

½ cup matzo meal or bread crumbs

1 cup grated sharp Cheddar cheese

6 eggs, thoroughly beaten

1 pound cottage or feta cheese (or a mixture of both)

½ cup grated Romano or Parmesan cheese

2 tablespoons olive oil

Salt to taste

Pepper to taste

¼ teaspoon nutmeg

PREPARATION

1 Squeeze the excess liquid from the thawed spinach, and mix in a large bowl with ¼ cup of matzo meal or bread crumbs, tofu, ¼ cup of Cheddar cheese, eggs, cottage or feta cheese, Romano or Parmesan cheese, oil, salt, pepper, and nutmeg.

2 Dust an oiled baking pan with the rest of the matzo meal or bread crumbs.

3 Spread the spinach mixture evenly in the pan. Sprinkle the top with the rest of the Cheddar.

4 Bake at 350°F for 45 to 60 minutes, or until the top is firm to the touch.

5 Cut into squares and serve.

Recipe Tip

For a summer brunch, garnish the omelet with slices of cantaloupe or honeydew melon.

Blueberry "Yogurt"

• • •

Serve as is over cereal, or on its own. You can also freeze the "yogurt" in an ice cream machine or in ice cube trays.

• • •

Serves 4

INGREDIENTS

20 ounces firm tofu

½ cup water

⅔ cup brown rice syrup

2 cups frozen blueberries

1 teaspoon blueberry extract

1 teaspoon raspberry extract

½ teaspoon lemon juice

1 teaspoon orange juice concentrate

PREPARATION

1 In blender, combine all the ingredients and blend until smooth.

Spanish "Omelet"

• • •

There's no cholesterol in this eggless
version of a traditional Spanish omelet—
but you'll never notice the difference.

• • •

Yields 4 patties

INGREDIENTS

24 ounces firm tofu
¾ pound potatoes
2 small onions, chopped
3 tablespoons olive oil
2 canned pimentos, chopped
2 tomatoes, peeled and chopped
4 tablespoons cooked peas
½ cup whole wheat flour
1½ teaspoons baking powder
Salt to taste
Pepper to taste

PREPARATION

1 Boil the potatoes until tender. Drain, peel,
and dice.

2 Sauté the onions in oil for 3 minutes, then
add the potatoes, pimentos, tomatoes, and
peas. Sauté for 2 to 3 minutes, stirring frequently.

3 In a blender, blend 6 ounces of the tofu
until smooth and creamy.

4 In a large mixing bowl, mash the rest of
the tofu. Add the blended tofu, flour, and
baking powder. Mix well.

5 Add the sautéed vegetables to the tofu
mixture, and mix well. Add the salt and
pepper.

6 Mold the mixture into four patties, and
place on a slightly oiled baking sheet. Bake
at 325°F for 30 minutes.

7 Flip the patties, and bake for 15 minutes
more.

Polenta, Tofu, and Vegetable Torte

• • •

Polenta, a cornmeal mush, makes a great
base for this layered brunch.

• • •

Serves 6

INGREDIENTS

24 ounces firm tofu, finely crumbled
4 cups water
1½ teaspoons salt
1 cup polenta
½ teaspoon dried oregano
¼ teaspoon rosemary sprigs, minced
2 garlic cloves, minced
1 bunch fresh basil, stemmed
2 tablespoons light miso
2 teaspoons rice vinegar
2 teaspoons nutritional yeast
⅓ teaspoon ground nutmeg
2 leeks, white part only, washed well and cut
into ½-inch-thick slices
2 teaspoons olive oil
8 ounces button mushrooms, thinly sliced
1 zucchini, thinly sliced
¼ teaspoon ground black pepper
1 tomato, thinly sliced
Dried oregano, parsley, basil, tarragon, and
rosemary to taste
½ cup bread crumbs
Mock Béarnaise Sauce (see recipe on page 208)

PREPARATION

1 In a medium saucepan, bring the water to
a boil, and add the salt. Gradually add the
polenta.

2 Reduce heat to low, add the oregano and
rosemary, and whisk for 5 minutes.

3 Cook for another 10 minutes, or until the
polenta pulls away from the sides of the
pot.

4 Pour the polenta into an 8-inch square
baking dish. Let it cool for 1 hour.

5 Meanwhile, in a large bowl, combine the garlic, basil, miso, tofu, vinegar, yeast, and nutmeg.

6 Transfer half the mixture to a blender and blend until smooth. Return the blended portion to the bowl, and set aside.

7 In a large frying pan, sauté the leeks and garlic in the oil for about 5 minutes, or until the leeks are wilted. Add the mushrooms and zucchini, and sauté until the vegetables are soft.

8 Add the salt and pepper, and remove from the heat.

9 Add the tofu mixture, and stir well. Spread this mixture on the polenta in the baking dish.

10 Cover the dish with aluminum foil, and bake at 400°F for 20 minutes.

11 Remove the foil, and top with the tomatoes, herbs, and bread crumbs.

12 Bake, uncovered, for 20 minutes more, or until the top is lightly browned.

13 Let cool for 10 minutes, and serve with the Mock Béarnaise Sauce.

Marinated Tofu with Olives and Tomatoes

• • •

For something a little different, try this updated Israeli breakfast fare.

• • •

Serves 6

INGREDIENTS

24 ounces extra-firm tofu, pressed, and cubed
3 tablespoons rice wine vinegar
2 garlic cloves, minced
1 teaspoon Dijon mustard
Fresh parsley, to taste
¼ teaspoon dried tarragon
¼ teaspoon dried marjoram
Salt to taste
Pepper to taste
⅓ cup olive oil
Lettuce leaves
1 can olives
6 medium tomatoes, sliced
Fresh cilantro leaves

PREPARATION

1 Place the tofu cubes in a medium mixing bowl.

2 In a small mixing bowl, combine the vinegar, garlic, mustard, parsley, tarragon, marjoram, salt, and pepper.

3 Mix in the olive oil, pour the mixture over the tofu, and toss.

4 Place the lettuce leaves on plates, and pour the tofu mixture over the lettuce.

5 Garnish each plate with olives, tomatoes, and cilantro.

Tomato, Spinach, and Tofu Quiche

• • •

Tofu is perfect for quiches—adding protein and subtracting cholesterol, while taking on the flavor of whatever you add to your recipe. Experiment and enjoy.

• • •

Serves 6

INGREDIENTS

12 ounces firm tofu
1 tablespoon vegetable oil
½ small onion, chopped
2 garlic cloves, minced
10-ounce package frozen chopped spinach, thawed and drained
3 medium tomatoes, coarsely chopped
1 teaspoon salt
9-inch pie crust
¼ cup mozzarella cheese, grated

PREPARATION

1 In a blender, purée the tofu until smooth.

2 In a large saucepan, sauté the onion and garlic over medium-high heat for 5 minutes.

3 Stir in the spinach and tomatoes, and simmer for 2 to 3 minutes. Remove from the heat.

4 Add the tofu and salt to the mixture. Pour the mixture into the pie crust. Sprinkle the cheese on top, and bake at 350°F for 35 minutes or more, until browned. Serve hot.

Sweet Noodle Casserole

• • •

For those watching fat and cholesterol intake, this modified version of a traditional kugel avoids the eggs and cheese without sacrificing taste.

• • •

Serves 6

INGREDIENTS

8 ounces soft tofu
½ cup plain, low-fat yogurt
¼ cup mild honey
1 tablespoon sesame tahini
3 tablespoons lemon juice
1 teaspoon cinnamon
½ teaspoon nutmeg
1 teaspoon vanilla
¼ pound flat noodles or 1 cup macaroni
¼ cup raisins or currants
1 apple, pear, or peach, cored or pitted, and chopped

PREPARATION

1 In a blender, blend the tofu, yogurt, honey, tahini, lemon juice, cinnamon, nutmeg, and vanilla until smooth.

2 Cook the noodles al dente, drain, and rinse with cold water. Drain again, place in a large mixing bowl, and mix with the tofu mixture, currants or raisins, and fruit.

3 Pour into an oiled casserole dish, and bake at 325°F for 40 minutes.

4 Remove when a crust has formed around the outside. Let stand for 10 minutes before serving.

Zesty Curried Tofu Sauté

• • •

This healthy breakfast looks a lot like scrambled eggs, but the curry powder adds a kick you will savor. Use to top your morning bagel or toast.

• • •

Serves 6 to 8

INGREDIENTS

48 ounces silken tofu, cubed
1 tablespoon vegetable oil
½ small onion, chopped
½ red bell pepper, chopped
1 tablespoon curry powder

PREPARATION

1 In a large saucepan, sauté the onions and peppers in oil for 5 minutes. Stir in the curry powder.

2 Add the tofu cubes. Cook, stirring gently, until heated through. Serve hot.

Blueberry Bars

• • •

Wrap 'em, refrigerate 'em, and grab 'em for those mornings when you're running out the door.

• • •

Yields 15 pieces

INGREDIENTS

10 ounces silken tofu
2 cups unbleached white flour
2½ teaspoons baking powder
⅓ cup vegetable oil
½ cup honey
½ cup water
1 teaspoon vanilla
1 cup fresh or frozen blueberries

PREPARATION

1 In a large mixing bowl, combine the flour and baking powder.

2 In a blender, blend the oil, honey, tofu, water, and vanilla until smooth.

3 Add the dry ingredients to the blender, and blend until mixed. Then add the blueberries.

4 Pour the mixture into a 9 by 13-inch pan, and bake at 350°F for 25 minutes.

Tofu Toast Topper I

• • •

Great for toast, bagels, or anyplace you'd spread cream cheese. This breakfast spread has a great taste, but it's surprisingly low in fat.

• • •

Yields 2 cups

INGREDIENTS

8 ounces soft tofu
2 medium tart apples, unpeeled
¼ cup plain, low-fat yogurt
1 to 2 tablespoons honey or maple syrup
1 to 2 tablespoons lemon juice to taste
½ teaspoon ground cinnamon
¼ to ½ teaspoon grated nutmeg, to taste
1 tablespoon sesame tahini
1 teaspoon vanilla
2 teaspoons whole wheat pastry flour
1 teaspoon butter

PREPARATION

1 Place the apples in a baking dish, and bake at 350°F for 30 to 45 minutes, or until thoroughly soft. Remove from the oven, let cool, and core.

2 In a blender or food processor, blend the apples along with the remaining ingredients, except for the butter, until very smooth.

3 Pour the mixture into a buttered baking dish, and bake at 350°F for 30 to 40 minutes, or until firm and browned.

4 Cover, refrigerate, and use for up to two weeks.

> ## Recipe Tip
>
> Try serving Tofu Topper I in a pudding dish as a dessert for the kids.

Tofu Toast Topper II

• • •

This spread utilizes the combination of walnuts and dates to create a palate-pleasing topping for toast, muffins, and pastries.

• • •

Yields 4 to 5 cups

INGREDIENTS

10 ounces silken tofu
1 cup walnuts
3 cups warm water
1 cup pitted dates
1 tablespoon light miso
1 tablespoon maple syrup
½ teaspoon ground nutmeg
½ teaspoon salt

PREPARATION

1 Soak the walnuts in 2 cups of warm water for 30 minutes. Drain.

2 Place nuts on a baking sheet, and bake at 350°F for 30 minutes. Turn every 10 minutes. Set aside.

3 Soak the dates in 1 cup of warm water for 15 minutes, or until soft. Drain.

4 In a blender or food processor, combine the dates, walnuts, miso, tofu, syrup, nutmeg, and salt, and blend until smooth.

5 Refrigerate in an airtight container. Use the spread within four days.

Tofu Toast Topper III

• • •

Great for breakfasts, this topper features onions, garlic, and herbs. It can also be served as a dip or pâté at your next party.

• • •

Yields 2 cups

INGREDIENTS

12 ounces firm tofu, drained
1 yellow onion, cut lengthwise into thin crescents
3 garlic cloves, peeled
1 teaspoon salt
¾ cup vegetable broth or stock (see recipe on page 81)
½ teaspoon dried thyme
½ teaspoon dried sage
½ teaspoon fresh rosemary sprigs, minced
½ teaspoon dried basil
½ teaspoon dried oregano
¾ teaspoon ground pepper
¼ teaspoon ground nutmeg
¼ cup light miso

PREPARATION

1 In a large frying pan, cook the onions, garlic, salt, and ¼ cup of the broth or stock, over medium heat for 5 minutes, or until the onions start to soften.

2 Add the thyme, sage, rosemary, basil, oregano, pepper, nutmeg, and the rest of the stock or broth.

3 Cover and cook for 20 minutes, or until the liquid evaporates. Remove from the heat and let cool.

4 In a medium-sized mixing bowl, crumble the tofu, add the miso and the onion mixture, and mix well.

5 In a blender, blend the mixture until smooth. Serve chilled or at room temperature.

Crunchy Cream Scones

...

English scones are a kind of sweet biscuit. These tofu treats will surprise the palates of family and friends, bored with the same old muffins. Serve with fruit spread, honey, or syrup.

• • •

Yields 8 scones

INGREDIENTS

6 ounces soft tofu
2 cups all-purpose flour
1/2 cup sugar
1 tablespoon baking powder
1 teaspoon salt
2 tablespoons poppy seeds
1/2 cup margarine or butter, chilled
1/3 cup milk
2 teaspoons vanilla extract
Grated rind of 1 large lemon

PREPARATION

1 In a large mixing bowl, combine the flour, sugar, baking powder, salt, and poppy seeds.

2 Cut the margarine or butter into small cubes, and mix into the dry ingredients until the margarine or butter looks like crumbs.

3 In a blender, combine the tofu, milk, and vanilla, and mix until smooth.

4 Pour into the flour mixture, stirring to combine thoroughly. Add the grated lemon rind.

5 On a lightly floured surface, roll the dough out to a 1/2-inch thickness. Cut into 3-inch circles, and place on a greased baking sheet.

6 Bake at 400°F for 15 minutes, or until slightly browned. Remove from the oven, and let cool before serving.

Banana-Walnut Breakfast Muffins

...

Next to the smell of coffee brewing, nothing livens up breakfast better than the delectable odor of these tasty breakfast treats.

• • •

Yields 12 muffins

INGREDIENTS

6 ounces soft tofu
1/4 cup vegetable oil
1/4 cup honey
1 cup rolled oats
1 1/4 cups apple juice
1 cup banana, chopped
1/2 cup walnuts, chopped
1 cup whole wheat flour
1 cup rice flour
4 teaspoons baking powder
1/8 teaspoon salt

PREPARATION

1 In a blender, crumble the tofu, and add the oil and honey. Whip until creamy.

2 In a large mixing bowl, combine the tofu mixture with the rolled oats, apple juice, bananas, and walnuts. Stir well.

Banana-Walnut Breakfast Muffins (see opposite page)
with Tofu Toast Topper II (see page 49)

3 In a separate bowl, mix the whole wheat flour, rice flour, baking powder, and salt. Pour the dry ingredients into the tofu mixture, and stir well.

4 Spoon the batter into an oiled muffin tin. Bake at 400°F for 10 minutes.

5 Reduce heat to 350°F, and bake for 25 minutes more.

6 Remove, let cool for 5 minutes, and enjoy.

Recipe Tip

For a tasty muffin variation, substitute cranberries or blueberries for the bananas. You may also omit the walnuts.

Banana Bread

• • •

In this updated family favorite, nobody ever notices the tofu.

• • •

Yields 9 slices

INGREDIENTS

12 ounces silken tofu
2 cups flour
½ teaspoon baking soda
½ teaspoon baking powder
¼ teaspoon salt
1 cup sugar
¼ cup vegetable oil
1 teaspoon vanilla
1 cup ripe bananas, mashed
¾ cup walnut pieces

PREPARATION

1 In a large mixing bowl, combine the flour, baking soda, baking powder, and salt.

2 In a separate bowl, beat the sugar, oil, vanilla, and bananas.

3 In a blender, blend the tofu until it's creamy.

4 Beat everything except the walnuts together in one bowl. Fold the walnuts into the mixture.

5 Pour the mixture into an oiled loaf pan, and bake at 350°F for 1 hour. Serve warm.

Raisin-Rum Rolls

• • •

Enjoy these tasty rolls straight from the oven, or freeze them to await an impromptu brunch.

• • •

Yields 24 rolls

INGREDIENTS

DOUGH

1 tablespoon active dry yeast
¼ cup sugar
½ cup warm water
5 cups unbleached white flour
¼ cup vegetable oil
1 teaspoon salt

FILLING

8 ounces soft tofu, crumbled
¾ cup brown sugar
2 tablespoons vegetable oil
2 teaspoons rum flavoring
½ teaspoon salt
1 cup raisins, soaked in hot water and drained

FROSTING

1 cup powdered sugar
2 to 3 tablespoons hot water
1 teaspoon rum flavoring

PREPARATION

1 In a large mixing bowl, mix the yeast, sugar, and warm water, and let sit in a warm place until the mixture begins to foam.

2 Mix in 1 cup of the flour, and let sit for 10 more minutes.

3 Mix in the oil, the rest of the flour, and salt, and stir until blended.

4 Cover and let rise in a warm place.

5 While the dough is rising, prepare the filling. In a large mixing bowl, combine the brown sugar, tofu, oil, rum flavoring, and salt. Beat well, then stir in the raisins.

6 Punch the risen dough down and divide it in half. Roll each half into a ⅜-inch thick rectangle.

7 Spread each rectangle with filling and roll it up. Cut the rectangles into 1-inch thick slices.

8 Place each slice into a muffin cup. Cover and let rise until almost double in size.

9 Bake at 350°F for 15 to 20 minutes.

10 In a small mixing bowl, combine the powdered sugar, hot water and rum flavoring. Brush the frosting over the finished rolls.

4 Knead the dough on a floured surface for approximately 5 minutes.

5 In a large mixing bowl, let the dough rise until it is almost double in size. Punch it down and roll it out on a thin bed of cornmeal. The dough should be ½-inch thick.

6 Cut the dough in circles (3 to 4 inches in diameter), and let rise for 10 minutes.

7 Cook each dough circle in a frying pan over low heat for about 5 minutes on each side, or until golden brown.

8 Split each muffin with a fork, and toast.

English Muffins

• • •

You won't know what a fresh (really fresh!) English muffin tastes like until you try these.

• • •

Yields 18 muffins

INGREDIENTS

8 ounces silken tofu
1 tablespoon active dry yeast
1½ cups warm water
2 tablespoons sugar
1 teaspoon salt
3 tablespoons vegetable oil
5 cups unbleached white flour
½ cup cornmeal

PREPARATION

1 In a large mixing bowl, mix the yeast, 1 cup of the warm water, and sugar and let sit in a warm place for 10 minutes, or until it begins to foam.

2 In a blender, add the tofu, the rest of the warm water, and the salt. Blend until creamy, and pour into the foaming yeast mixture along with the oil.

3 Gradually stir in the flour until the dough is smooth and soft.

Classic Country Cornbread

• • •

Serve these golden morsels right out of the pan, slathered with molasses or honey. Yum.

• • •

Yields 9 squares

INGREDIENTS

16 ounces soft tofu
2 eggs
3 tablespoons vegetable oil
¼ cup honey
1 cup instant nonfat milk powder
¼ cup whole wheat flour
1 teaspoon salt
1½ teaspoons baking powder
½ teaspoon baking soda
1½ cups cornmeal

PREPARATION

1 In a blender, combine the tofu, eggs, oil, honey, milk powder, flour, salt, baking powder, and baking soda, and blend until smooth.

2 Stir in the cornmeal.

3 Pour the mixture into an oiled 9 by 9-inch pan, and bake at 425°F for 25 to 30 minutes.

Low-Fat Peach Coffee Cake

• • •

This coffee cake has "guilt-free" written all over it. So, don't be afraid to go for seconds.

• • •

Yields 8 slices

INGREDIENTS

12 ounces soft tofu, puréed
3 tablespoons water
3 tablespoons vegetable oil
3 tablespoons maple syrup
1 egg
6 tablespoons fresh orange juice
1 cup sugar
1 tablespoon vanilla extract
1½ teaspoons orange extract
Grated rind of 1 orange
2 cups cake flour
½ cup whole wheat pastry flour
1½ teaspoons baking powder
½ teaspoon baking soda
½ teaspoon salt
1½ cups frozen or fresh peaches

TOPPING RECIPE

2 tablespoons sugar
2 tablespoons wheat germ
¼ teaspoon cinnamon
2 tablespoons granola
1 teaspoon maple syrup
1 teaspoon vegetable oil
2 teaspoons orange juice

PREPARATION

1 In a large mixing bowl, combine the water, oil, syrup, egg, orange juice, sugar, vanilla, orange extract, grated orange rind, and tofu. Mix well.

2 In another bowl, sift the flours, baking powder, baking soda, and salt. Add to the liquid mixture, and blend lightly. Pour in the peaches.

3 Pour the batter into a floured, 10-inch, round baking pan.

4 Sprinkle the topping (see Topping Preparation below) over the batter. Bake at 350°F for 40 minutes. Serve warm.

TOPPING PREPARATION

1 In a medium-sized mixing bowl, mix the sugar, wheat germ, cinnamon, and granola.

2 Add the syrup, oil, and orange juice, and whisk together.

Cinnamon Muffins

• • •

The tofu adds a protein punch to these delightfully mouth-watering muffins.

• • •

Yields 12 muffins

INGREDIENTS

8 ounces soft tofu
1 cup whole wheat flour
1 cup rolled oats
¼ cup raisins
2 eggs
¼ cup oil
½ cup honey
1½ teaspoons cinnamon
½ teaspoon salt
2 teaspoons baking powder
¼ teaspoon baking soda

PREPARATION

1 In a large mixing bowl, combine the flour, oats, and raisins.

2 In a blender, mix the tofu, eggs, oil, honey, cinnamon, salt, baking powder, and baking soda until smooth.

3 Pour the blended ingredients into the flour mixture. Stir well.

4 Fill the muffin tins two-thirds full. Bake at 425°F for 12 to 15 minutes.

Upside-Down Carrot-Onion Cornbread

• • •

Lots of onions, peppers, corn, and carrots start off on the bottom of this scrumptious bread, but end up as a savory topping to wake up your taste buds.

• • •

Serves 6 to 8

INGREDIENTS

5 ounces soft tofu, mashed

6 tablespoons canola oil

2 large onions, peeled and thinly sliced

¼ teaspoon dried thyme

1 small red bell pepper, cut into thin strips

1 cup uncooked corn kernels

1 cup carrots, grated

1½ cups yellow cornmeal

1½ cups whole wheat pastry flour

1 tablespoon baking powder

1 teaspoon baking soda

½ teaspoon salt

¾ teaspoon pepper

Dash cayenne pepper

1¼ cups vegetable stock (see recipe on page 81) or water

2 tablespoons barley malt syrup

1 tablespoon apple cider vinegar

PREPARATION

1 In a large frying pan, sauté the onions in 1 tablespoon of oil for 8 to 10 minutes, or until they are browned. Stir in the thyme, red pepper, corn, and carrots. Sauté for 2 minutes more. Set aside.

2 In a large mixing bowl, combine the cornmeal, flour, baking powder, baking soda, salt, cracked pepper, and cayenne pepper.

3 In a blender, combine the stock, tofu, the rest of the oil, barley syrup, and vinegar, and mix until the liquid is frothy.

4 Stir the blended ingredients into the dry ingredients, and mix until the flour is absorbed.

5 Pour the onion mixture into a 9-inch pie pan, then pour the batter over the onions. Bake at 375°F for 20 to 25 minutes, or until a skewer inserted into the center comes out clean.

6 To serve, cut the cornbread into slices, and, using a spatula, lift each slice and turn it over onto a plate.

Upside-Down Carrot-Onion Cornbread (see above)

Appetizers

Like the name suggests, these tofu side dishes are
appetizing, as well as good for you. From finger
foods to dips, these recipes all rely on tofu
for enhancing taste and providing
healthful pre-dinner treats.

• • •

Nachos with Tofu and Black Beans

• • •

You can whip these up before a big party and watch them quickly disappear. They're great with a bowl of fresh salsa and a big dollop of cold sour cream or guacamole.

• • •

Yields 3 dozen nachos

INGREDIENTS

8 ounces extra-firm tofu, crumbled
1 medium onion, chopped
3 garlic cloves, minced
2 tablespoons olive oil
1 15-ounce can black beans, rinsed and drained
2 cups water
2 tablespoons fresh cilantro leaves, chopped
1 teaspoon ground cumin
1 teaspoon chili powder
1 bag of tortilla chips
1 4-ounce can jalapeños, sliced
1 cup Cheddar or Monterey Jack cheese, grated

PREPARATION

1 In a large saucepan, sauté the onion and garlic in oil until the onion becomes translucent.

2 Add the beans and water, and bring to a boil. Add the cilantro, cumin, and chili powder.

3 Reduce the heat and simmer, covered, until the liquid is thick.

4 Remove from the heat.

5 Arrange a layer of tortilla chips on a baking sheet. Spoon half of the black bean mixture over the chips, making sure each chip is covered.

6 Sprinkle half of the crumbled tofu over the top.

7 Top with jalapeños and cheese.

8 Repeat this procedure on another baking sheet until the bean mixture and tofu are used up.

9 Bake at 350°F for 15 minutes, or until the cheese melts.

10 Serve immediately.

Tofu "Fries"

• • •

This is a favorite with the kids. Similar to crispy french fries, these cracker-crumb encrusted sticks are great dipped in ketchup or barbecue sauce.

• • •

Serves 6

INGREDIENTS

24 ounces firm tofu, drained and pressed
⅓ cup fine cracker crumbs
2 tablespoons cornmeal
¼ teaspoon garlic powder
½ teaspoon ground chili powder
¼ teaspoon salt
Olive oil

PREPARATION

1 In a medium-sized bowl, combine the cracker crumbs, cornmeal, garlic powder, chili powder, and salt. Set aside.

2 Cut each block of tofu into 12 sticks about 3 inches long and ¾ inch thick.

3 Coat each stick with the crumb mixture, covering it completely.

4 Place the sticks on a lightly oiled wire cooling rack, and bake at 375°F for 35 to 45 minutes, or until crisp and brown.

5 Serve warm with your favorite dipping sauce.

Tofu-Stuffed Mushrooms

• • •

For those of us who love mushrooms, these are as good as it gets. Packed with flavorful spices, bread crumbs, and cheese, you may need to double this recipe to make sure there are plenty to share.

• • •

Yields 15 mushrooms

INGREDIENTS

12 ounces extra-firm tofu, frozen, thawed, and mashed

16 large fresh mushrooms, washed, drained, stems removed and reserved

2 tablespoons olive oil

¼ teaspoon salt

⅛ teaspoon black pepper

2 tablespoons dry sherry

⅓ cup scallions, minced

1 celery stalk, minced

1 tablespoon fresh basil leaves, chopped

1 teaspoon fresh sage leaves, minced

2 tablespoons Parmesan cheese

2 tablespoons plain bread crumbs

2 to 3 tablespoons remaining liquid from cooked mushrooms

PREPARATION

1 In a large saucepan, sauté the mushrooms in 1 tablespoon of olive oil, and add the salt, pepper, and sherry. Cook until most of the liquid is absorbed and the mushrooms are soft.

2 Drain the mushrooms, set them aside, and reserve any remaining cooking liquid.

3 In the same saucepan, sauté the scallions and celery in 1 tablespoon of oil for 5 minutes. Add the basil, sage, and tofu, and continue to cook for 1 minute longer.

4 Turn off the heat, and add the remaining ingredients. Stir well.

5 Spoon the mixture into the bottoms of the mushrooms caps.

6 Place the mushrooms in a baking pan, and bake at 350°F for 10 minutes.

Recipe Tip

While large button mushrooms work well in this recipe, experiment with shiitake or portabello mushrooms, as well.

Tofu "Crab" Cakes

• • •

Crab cakes without the crab? These crispy patties mimic the texture of traditional crab cakes and are wonderful with a side of tartar sauce.

• • •

Serves 4

INGREDIENTS

12 ounces extra-firm tofu, frozen, thawed, and mashed

1 tablespoon yellow onion, minced

1 egg, beaten

¾ cup plain bread crumbs (with additional for cake coating)

¼ cup celery, minced

¼ teaspoon mustard powder

½ teaspoon sugar

½ teaspoon paprika

2 tablespoons mayonnaise or Tofu Mayonnaise (see recipe on page 212)

1 teaspoon vegetarian Worcestershire sauce

2 tablespoons wheat germ

¼ teaspoon salt

¼ teaspoon lemon pepper

2 tablespoons olive oil

➡

Tofu-Stuffed Mushrooms (see opposite page)

Tofu "Crab" Cakes (see opposite page)

PREPARATION

1 In a large bowl, combine the tofu with the rest of the ingredients, except the olive oil.

2 Form the mixture into small cakes approximately 2 inches across.

3 Roll each of the cakes in the additional bread crumbs.

4 In a large saucepan, heat the olive oil and sauté the cakes until golden. Make sure to turn the cakes during the cooking process.

5 Serve warm.

"Fish" Sticks

• • •

Kids love these baked goodies because they can eat them with their hands. Dip them in everything from tartar sauce to ketchup.

• • •

Serves 4

INGREDIENTS

16 ounces firm tofu, drained and pressed
1/3 cup apple or raspberry vinegar
1 tablespoon soy sauce
1/3 cup flour
1 teaspoon dried oregano
1 teaspoon dried basil
1 teaspoon salt
2 eggs, beaten
1½ cups bread crumbs
1 teaspoon vegetable oil

PREPARATION

1 Slice the tofu into sticks 3 inches long and ½ inch thick.

2 In a large bowl, combine the vinegar and soy sauce. Add the tofu and marinate it for at least 1 hour.

3 Put the flour, oregano, and basil in a dish. In a separate bowl, combine the salt and eggs. Place the bread crumbs in a third dish.

4 Remove the tofu from the marinade. Dip each piece of tofu in the flour mixture, then in the eggs, and finally in the bread crumbs.

5 Place the sticks on a lightly-oiled baking sheet and bake at 350°F for 20 minutes.

6 Serve hot.

Twice-Baked Parmesan Potatoes

• • •

There's really no comfort food quite like potatoes, and these have the added bonus of sautéed mushrooms, nutrition-packed tofu, and grated Parmesan cheese. They're so good you may just want to eat them as a meal.

• • •

Yields 4 potatoes

INGREDIENTS

4 ounces soft tofu, mashed
1 cup button mushrooms, sliced
4 large baking potatoes, scrubbed clean
1 tablespoon olive oil
1 tablespoon soy sauce
2 tablespoons grated Parmesan cheese

PREPARATION

1 Prick the potatoes with a fork, and bake at 375°F for about 1 hour.

2 In a medium-sized saucepan, sauté the mushrooms in oil for 3 minutes.

3 Add the soy sauce, stir, and remove from the heat.

4 Scoop out the center of each baked potato, leaving the skin to be used later.

5 In a large mixing bowl, mash the potato with the tofu.

6 Stir in the mushrooms, including the juice from the pan.

7 Spoon the mixture back into the potato skins and sprinkle the cheese on top.

8 Place the potatoes in a baking pan, and broil until the tops are golden brown.

Croatian Veggie Balls with Herbed Yogurt Sauce

• • •

This appetizer, accented with caraway and fennel seeds, is perfect for entertaining. You can also stuff them into a pita sandwich for a light and tasty snack.

• • •

Yields 24 balls

INGREDIENTS

MEATBALLS

36 ounces firm tofu, drained and pressed
2 large onions, diced
2 garlic cloves, minced
3 tablespoons vegetable oil
3 medium carrots, grated
Salt to taste
Pepper to taste
2 eggs, beaten
1¼ cups bread crumbs
1 cup almonds, lightly toasted and ground
2 tablespoons Dijon mustard
1 tablespoon sesame oil
¼ cup soy sauce
1 teaspoon fennel seeds, ground
⅛ teaspoon cayenne pepper
½ teaspoon caraway seeds, ground
2 teaspoons dried basil
¼ cup fresh parsley sprigs, chopped

SAUCE

4 eggs, beaten
2 cups plain yogurt
2 teaspoons caraway seeds, ground
1 tablespoon fresh dill sprigs, chopped
Salt to taste
Pepper to taste

PREPARATION

1 In a large saucepan, sauté the onions and garlic in the oil until the onions begin to turn golden.

2 Add the carrots, salt, and pepper, and continue to cook for about 5 minutes, stirring occasionally. Set aside to cool.

3 In a medium mixing bowl, combine the eggs, bread crumbs, almonds, mustard, sesame oil, and soy sauce.

4 Stir the herbs and spices into the mixture.

5 Add the tofu to the mixture, kneading it with your hands until well-blended.

6 Drain the sautéed vegetables, and stir them into the mixture. The mixture should now be moist and sticky.

7 Roll the mixture into 24 2-inch balls.

8 Place the balls on an oiled baking sheet, and bake at 350°F for 30 minutes, or until nicely browned.

9 In a small saucepan, combine the sauce ingredients.

10 Heat gently for about 15 minutes, stirring constantly until the sauce thickens. If the heat is too high or you don't stir enough, the eggs may curdle.

11 Serve the balls warm, with the sauce on the side for dipping.

5 Drain the balls and arrange them in a baking pan.

6 In a small mixing bowl, mix together the tomato juice, ketchup and oregano. Pour this sauce over the balls.

7 Top with a sprinkling of Parmesan, and bake at 350°F for 15 minutes, or until nicely browned.

Italian "Meat" Balls

• • •

Dip these convincing fakes in some warm marinara or alfredo sauce, or toss them into your favorite spaghetti dish for an old-fashioned meal.

• • •

Serves 2 or 3

INGREDIENTS

12 ounces firm tofu, drained and pressed
¼ cup walnuts, chopped
½ medium onion, minced
⅓ cup bread crumbs
1 egg, beaten
3 tablespoons fresh parsley sprigs, minced
½ teaspoon salt
Dash of pepper
Oil for deep-frying
¼ cup tomato juice
¼ cup ketchup
Dash of dried oregano
3 tablespoons Parmesan cheese

PREPARATION

1 In a large mixing bowl, stir together the tofu, walnuts, onion, bread crumbs, egg, parsley, salt, and pepper.

2 Using your hands, shape the mixture into ½-inch balls.

3 In a large saucepan, wok, or deep fryer, heat the oil to 350°F.

4 Carefully drop in the tofu balls, and deep-fry until they are cooked through and browned.

Zucchini Nut Balls

• • •

Full of spices, nuts, tofu, and veggies, these baked appetizers taste great dipped in our Sweet and Sour Sauce (see recipe on page 65).

• • •

Yields 24 balls

INGREDIENTS

24 ounces firm tofu, drained and pressed
2 cups zucchini, grated
6 large garlic cloves, minced
2 tablespoons vegetable oil
1 teaspoon dried mint
1 teaspoon salt
¼ teaspoon cayenne pepper
1 tablespoon fennel seeds, ground
4 teaspoons cumin seeds, ground
1 teaspoon cinnamon
1 teaspoon turmeric
2 tablespoons flour
½ cup cashews or walnuts, chopped

PREPARATION

1 In a large saucepan, sauté the zucchini and garlic in the oil, stirring often, until most of the moisture has evaporated.

2 Add the spices and cook for 1 minute, stirring constantly.

3 Transfer the mixture to a large bowl. Crumble in the tofu, flour, and nuts, stirring until well-blended.

4 Form the mixture into 24 balls. Place on an oiled baking sheet and bake at 350°F for 20 to 30 minutes, or until firm.

Tofu Samosas

• • •

These traditional Indian deep-fried treats are filled with well-seasoned peas, potatoes, onion, and tofu. Serve them hot with a mild mint sauce or fiery chutney.

• • •

Yields 4 to 6 samosas

INGREDIENTS

FILLING

8 ounces firm tofu, drained and cubed
1 teaspoon mustard seeds
1 teaspoon ginger root, grated
1 small yellow onion, chopped
2 tablespoons butter
1 cup frozen green peas, thawed
1 large potato, cooked and cubed
Juice of 1 lemon
½ teaspoon salt
1 teaspoon ground cumin
1 tablespoon garam masala
1 tablespoon curry powder
¼ cup fresh cilantro leaves, chopped
2 cups oil for deep-frying

DOUGH

2 cups flour
¼ teaspoon salt
¼ cup butter, melted
⅓ cup plain yogurt
2 tablespoons cold water

PREPARATION

1 In a large saucepan, sauté the mustard seeds, ginger, and onion in butter until the onions are golden brown.

2 Add the tofu, peas, potato, lemon juice, salt and spices. Sauté for another 3 to 5 minutes. Set aside to cool.

3 In a large mixing bowl, stir together all the dough ingredients. Knead for 5 to 10 minutes until the dough is smooth and pliable.

4 On a floured surface, roll the dough out to ⅛-inch thickness. Cut into 4-inch circles.

5 Place 2 tablespoons of filling in the center of each circle, leaving ½-inch edges.

6 Fold over the pastry and seal by crimping with a fork. Repeat this procedure until all the dough is used up.

7 In a large saucepan, wok, or deep fryer, heat the oil to 350°F.

8 Carefully drop in the balls, and deep-fry until cooked through and well browned.

9 Drain the samosas on paper towels. Serve hot.

Recipe Tip

If you prefer not to deep-fry the samosas, you can put them on a baking sheet and bake at 350°F for 20 minutes, or until golden brown.

Thai Cabbage Rolls

• • •

Also known as Phak Muan, these vegetarian rolls make a beautiful presentation, served with their own sweet sauce and garnished with toasted sesame seeds.

• • •

Yields 14 rolls

INGREDIENTS

CABBAGE ROLLS

2 ounces firm tofu, cut into 1-inch strips
Water for boiling
Dash of salt
14 cabbage leaves
½ cup button mushrooms, sliced
¼ cup bean sprouts, clean, with roots removed
¼ cup cooked carrot, cut into 1-inch strips
¼ cup kidney beans, cooked
¼ cup cucumber, cut into 1-inch strips
¼ cup green bell pepper, cut into 1-inch strips
1 teaspoon sesame oil
2 teaspoons sugar
½ teaspoon black pepper
2 teaspoons rice vinegar

SWEET SAUCE

¼ cup soy sauce
¼ cup sugar
2 teaspoons sesame oil
1 tablespoon rice vinegar
½ teaspoon salt
2 tablespoons toasted sesame seeds

PREPARATION

1 In a large saucepan, bring several cups of water to a boil with a dash of salt. Add the cabbage leaves, and cook for about 1 minute. Remove with a slotted spoon, and set aside.

2 Place the mushrooms and bean sprouts in the boiling water for 1 minute. Immediately remove with a slotted spoon and place in a large mixing bowl.

3 Mix these cooked vegetables with the carrots, kidney beans, cucumber, tofu, and bell peppers.

4 Season with the sesame oil, sugar, pepper, and vinegar. Mix well.

5 Place 2 tablespoons of the mixture onto each piece of cabbage. Fold in both ends and roll into a cylinder shape.

6 In a small saucepan, combine the sauce ingredients over medium heat until hot.

7 Serve the rolls on a plate, with the sweet sauce poured over the top.

Thai Baked Tofu Triangles

• • •

This fiery curry-flavored tofu is crispy on the outside and soft and creamy on the inside.

• • •

Yields 24 triangles

INGREDIENTS

24 ounces firm tofu, drained and pressed
⅓ cup Thai curry paste
3 tablespoons soy sauce

PREPARATION

1 Cut each tofu cake into three slices about ½-inch thick. Stack the slices, then cut through all the layers diagonally, making an "x." The resulting shapes will resemble triangles.

2 In a lightly-oiled baking dish, arrange the tofu triangles. Cover all of them with the curry paste and soy sauce.

3 Bake at 350°F for 45 minutes, turning twice during the baking process.

4 Serve hot.

Light Vegetable and Tofu Spring Rolls

• • •

For a fresh taste of Thailand, try these delicate spring rolls stuffed with tofu, shredded cabbage, carrots, scallions, and fresh basil leaves. Dunk them into the Spicy Peanut Sauce (see recipe on page 207) or a simple combination of soy sauce and sugar.

• • •

Yields 10 to 12 rolls

INGREDIENTS

4 ounces firm tofu, cubed
1½ cups Chinese or Napa cabbage, shredded
½ cup carrot, grated
⅓ cup scallion greens, finely diced
10 to 12 8-inch round rice papers
20 large fresh basil leaves

PREPARATION

1 In a large bowl, combine the tofu cubes, cabbage, carrot, scallions, and basil.

2 In a 10-inch pie plate filled with warm water, submerge each of the rice papers for 30 to 60 seconds, or until pliable.

3 Transfer to a flat space and blot dry.

4 Place about ⅓ cup of the vegetable mixture along the bottom third of one rice paper round.

5 Lift the bottom edge over the filling, fold the sides toward the center, and roll up tightly. Repeat with the remaining rice paper.

6 Serve the spring rolls immediately, seam-side down.

Chinese Sweet and Sour Tofu Balls

• • •

These tasty treats are usually made with meat or seafood, but our tofu balls offer a vegetarian option that's just as good as the original. Dip the flavorful nuggets into the savory-sweet sauce, and enjoy!

• • •

Yields 14 to 16 balls

INGREDIENTS

TOFU BALLS

12 ounces soft tofu, mashed
1 tablespoon creamy peanut butter
1 tablespoon soy sauce
½ cup flour
½ cup green bell pepper
¼ cup button mushrooms, sliced
¼ cup celery, sliced
4 scallions, finely chopped

SWEET AND SOUR SAUCE

1 cup unsweetened pineapple juice
6 tablespoons honey
6 tablespoons apple cider vinegar
2 tablespoons soy sauce
1½ tablespoons cornstarch
¼ teaspoon garlic powder

PREPARATION

1 In a large mixing bowl, stir together the peanut butter and soy sauce.

Chinese Sweet and Sour Tofu Balls
(see page 65)

2 Add the mashed tofu, stirring well.

3 Add the flour, green pepper, mushrooms, celery, and scallions, and stir until well-blended.

4 Form the mixture into 14 to 16 small balls, approximately 1½ inches in size.

5 On a lightly oiled baking dish, arrange the balls and bake at 350°F oven for 20 minutes.

6 Turn the balls over, and bake for another 20 minutes.

7 In a medium saucepan, whisk together all the sauce ingredients until thickened and well-blended.

8 Serve the tofu balls warm, with the sauce on the side for dipping.

Siu Mai

• • •

These steamed Chinese dumplings are stuffed with a delicious tofu, scallion, and water chestnut filling. Dipped into soy sauce, they provide an elegant start to a Chinese meal.

• • •

Yields 30 dumplings

INGREDIENTS

12 ounces firm tofu
2 scallions, finely chopped
¼ cup water chestnuts, coarsely chopped
1½ tablespoons soy sauce
1 tablespoon dry sherry
2 teaspoons cornstarch
2 teaspoons ginger root, grated
1½ teaspoons sesame oil
1 teaspoon sugar
¼ teaspoon ground white pepper
30 sui mai or wonton wrappers
Water for steaming

PREPARATION

1 In a medium-sized mixing bowl, mash the tofu with a fork until smooth. Stir in all the remaining ingredients, except the wrappers. Refrigerate the mixture for 30 minutes.

2 Place 1 heaping teaspoon of filling in the center of one wrapper. If you are using wonton wrappers, trim the edges to form circles.

3 Gather up and pleat the wrapper around the filling to form an open-topped pouch.

4 Repeat with the remaining wrappers and filling.

5 Fill a wok or cooking pot with water to just below the bottom of an inserted steaming rack. Bring to a boil over high heat.

6 Arrange the dumplings on the steaming rack so that they're not touching each other, and steam for 10 to 12 minutes, or until the filling is heated through. Don't try to squeeze them all in. You will probably have to repeat the steaming process several times to finish all the dumplings.

7 Serve hot.

Japanese Agedashi Tofu

• • •

These traditional Japanese deep-fried tofu squares are delicious in their simplicity. Serve them piping hot with soy sauce and finely diced scallions.

• • •

Serves 4

INGREDIENTS

24 ounces firm tofu, drained and pressed
1 egg, beaten
½ cup arrowroot or cornstarch
Oil for deep-frying
2 teaspoons fresh ginger root, grated
2 tablespoons leeks, minced

➡

PREPARATION

1 Cut each 12-ounce block of tofu lengthwise into halves, then crosswise into thirds.

2 Dip the tofu slices into the beaten egg, then roll them in cornstarch.

3 In a large saucepan, wok, or deep-fryer, heat the oil to 350°F.

4 Carefully drop the tofu blocks into the oil, and fry until golden brown.

5 Serve immediately, accompanied by a dipping sauce, ginger, and leeks.

2 In the same saucepan, cook the onion, stirring, until softened. Add the tomatoes, wine, vegetable stock, salt, and pepper, and bring to a boil.

3 Add the zucchini and simmer, covered, for 20 minutes.

4 Stir in the chickpeas, tofu, and mint. Simmer, uncovered, for 15 minutes, or until the sauce thickens slightly.

5 Serve warm in a large bowl with pita bread and crackers for dipping.

North African Tofu with Chickpeas

• • •

Feeling a little exotic? Serve this delightful tomato, zucchini, and chickpea sauce with a basket of warm pita bread. Finger food at its best.

• • •

Serves 4

INGREDIENTS

16 ounces firm tofu, drained and cut into 1-inch strips
2 tablespoons olive oil
1 medium onion, chopped
2 cups canned diced tomatoes, with liquid
1 cup dry white wine
1 cup vegetable stock (see recipe on page 81)
¼ teaspoon salt
⅛ teaspoon black pepper
1 medium zucchini, diced
2 cups chickpeas, cooked
1 tablespoon fresh mint leaves, minced
Pita bread or crackers

PREPARATION

1 In a large saucepan, sauté the tofu in oil until browned. Remove from the pan and set aside.

Mediterranean Banana Tortilla Wedges

• • •

Mediterranean cuisine is known for its delicious and surprising food combinations. These crispy tortilla wedges are filled with savory layers of banana, tofu, and fresh cilantro. Serve with a big bowl of chilled salsa.

• • •

Serves 4 to 6

INGREDIENTS

BANANA FILLING

1 yellow onion, sliced thin
1 teaspoon garlic, minced
¼ cup sherry
1 tablespoon ground cumin
1 teaspoon ground coriander
1 teaspoon dried oregano
1 teaspoon red pepper flakes
2 ripe bananas, cut into ½-inch slices
1 cup water
1 teaspoon salt

North African Tofu
with Chickpeas
(see opposite page)

Mediterranean Banana
Tortilla Wedges
(see opposite page)

TOFU FILLING

- 8 ounces firm tofu
- 1 bunch fresh cilantro leaves, stemmed and chopped
- ½ teaspoon salt
- 2 tablespoons vinegar
- 1 tablespoon light miso
- 3 tablespoons water
- 5 8-inch whole wheat tortillas

PREPARATION

1. In a large saucepan, sauté the onion and garlic in the sherry over medium heat until the onions are soft.

2. Add the cumin, coriander, oregano, pepper flakes, bananas, water, and salt. Stir well, reduce the heat to low, and cook until the liquid evaporates.

3. Transfer the mixture to a blender and purée until smooth. Pour the mixture into a bowl and set aside.

4. In a blender, combine the tofu, cilantro, salt, vinegar, and miso until creamy. Add water as needed to thin. Pour the filling into a bowl and set aside.

5. Place one tortilla on a lightly-oiled baking sheet, and spread half the banana mixture evenly over it.

6. Place another tortilla on top, and spread half the cilantro-tofu mixture evenly over a second tortilla.

7. Repeat the layering with four tortillas, and top with the fifth.

8. Slice the tortillas into eight pieces.

9. Bake at 400°F for 15 minutes, or until the edges are golden.

10. Serve warm with fresh salsa.

Baba Ganoush

• • •

This Middle Eastern favorite is almost identical to the more familiar hummus, except the central ingredient here is puréed eggplant in place of puréed chickpeas. Serve with warm pita triangles or corn tortilla chips for dipping.

• • •

Yields 2 cups

INGREDIENTS

- 4 ounces soft tofu, mashed
- 1 medium eggplant, peeled and cut into ½-inch cubes
- ¼ cup water
- ¼ cup tahini
- 2 tablespoons lemon juice
- 2 teaspoons garlic, minced
- ½ teaspoon black pepper
- ¼ teaspoon ground cumin
- Dash of salt
- 2 tablespoons toasted sesame seeds
- 1 tablespoon fresh parsley sprigs, chopped

PREPARATION

1. In a large saucepan, combine the eggplant and about ¼ cup water. Cook on medium-high heat until the eggplant has softened. Drain well.

2. In a blender, combine the cooked eggplant, tofu, tahini, lemon juice, and garlic and blend until smooth and creamy.

3 Stir in all the remaining ingredients.

4 Serve at room temperature.

Green Bean Pâté

• • •

Serve this elegant and colorful vegetable pâté with thinly sliced bread or toasted crackers. It makes a perfect garden party appetizer.

• • •

Yields 4 cups

INGREDIENTS

12 ounces extra-firm tofu, drained and mashed
4 cups water
3 cups fresh green beans, diced
1 large onion, finely chopped
1 cup leeks, finely chopped
2 shallots, finely chopped
2 teaspoons olive oil
1 tablespoon soy sauce
¼ teaspoon salt
Dash of ground black pepper
2 tablespoons miso
1 tablespoon vegetarian Worcestershire sauce
1 tablespoon tahini

PREPARATION

1 In a large saucepan, bring 4 cups of water to a boil.

2 Add the green beans, and cook for 15 to 25 minutes. The beans should be well-cooked, not crunchy.

3 Drain the green beans, and set aside.

4 In a medium saucepan, sauté the onion, leeks, and shallots in olive oil until the onions are translucent.

5 Add the tofu, soy sauce, salt, and pepper, and continue to cook for another 10 minutes.

6 Transfer the contents of the saucepan, as well as the green beans, to a blender, and mix until smooth.

7 Add the miso, Worcestershire sauce, and tahini, and continue blending.

8 Empty the mixture into a bowl and refrigerate overnight.

Tofu Guacamole

• • •

In Southwestern cuisine, guacamole is often used as a topping or filling for a variety of recipes. We think the flavor of our recipe can be appreciated by itself, served with plenty of warm tortilla chips for dipping.

• • •

Yields 2 cups

INGREDIENTS

4 ounces silken tofu
3 ripe avocados
2 tablespoons olive oil
5 tablespoons lemon juice
2 garlic cloves
1 teaspoon ground cumin
1 teaspoon salt
Hot pepper sauce, to taste
1 small tomato, chopped

PREPARATION

1 Cut open the avocados, remove the pits, and scoop out the flesh.

2 In a blender, mix the avocado and tofu until creamy.

3 Add the rest of the ingredients, except the tomato, and continue blending until smooth.

4 Stir in the chopped tomato just before serving.

5 Serve chilled.

Zippy Horseradish Dip

• • •

The distinctive flavors of fresh horseradish and black olives are surprisingly compatible. Serve with raw veggies or crackers.

• • •

Yields 2 cups

INGREDIENTS

8 ounces firm tofu, mashed
¼ cup horseradish, freshly grated
¼ cup olives, finely chopped
1 tablespoon vegetable oil
¼ teaspoon salt
1 teaspoon lemon juice
2 tablespoons fresh parsley sprigs, minced

PREPARATION

1 In a blender, purée all the ingredients except the parsley.

2 Transfer to a bowl, garnish with the parsley, and serve.

"I Love Olives" Dip

• • •

If you've got a craving for something salty, we're pretty sure this recipe will fit the bill. A rich blend of olives, capers, and tofu, this dip is great served with crunchy bagel chips or multi-grain crackers.

• • •

Yields 2 cups

INGREDIENTS

8 ounces firm tofu, boiled for 5 minutes and drained
4 garlic cloves, minced
¼ cup olive oil
Juice of 1 lemon
10 to 12 green olives, pitted and minced
⅛ cup capers, drained well

PREPARATION

1 In a saucepan, sauté the garlic in olive oil for 2 minutes.

2 Transfer the garlic, along with the tofu and lemon juice, to a blender, and mix until smooth.

3 Scoop the mixture into a bowl, and add the minced olives and capers. Stir well.

4 Chill before serving.

Tofu Bean Dip

• • •

Always popular at parties, this bean
dip is great with tortilla chips
or pita wedges.

• • •

Yields 3 cups

INGREDIENTS

8 ounces soft tofu
2 15-ounce cans of pinto beans, drained and
   rinsed
2 tablespoons olive oil
Juice of 1 lemon
2 teaspoons dried oregano
2 teaspoons ground cumin
1 teaspoon chili powder
½ teaspoon garlic salt
3 green onions, chopped

PREPARATION

1 In a blender, purée all the ingredients until
   creamy.

2 Serve chilled.

Sautéed Mushroom Dip

• • •

Serve this tasty recipe chilled as a dip
for raw veggies or warm as a
spread for slices of freshly
baked bread.

• • •

Yields 2 cups

INGREDIENTS

8 ounces soft tofu, drained and mashed
2 cups button mushrooms, sliced
1 tablespoon butter or margarine
½ cup sour cream or Tofu Sour Cream (see
   recipe on page 209)
1 teaspoon salt
2 tablespoons scallions, finely chopped

PREPARATION

1 In a saucepan, sauté the mushrooms in
   butter or margarine until soft.

2 Transfer the mushrooms to a large mixing
   bowl and combine with the tofu, sour
   cream, salt, and scallions.

3 Chill before serving, or heat up slowly in a
   saucepan to serve warm.

Roasted Red Pepper Dip

• • •

The sweet flavor of roasted red bell
peppers teams up with the kick of
hot red chili peppers for a
memorable appetizer.

• • •

Yields 1½ cups

INGREDIENTS

6 ounces silken tofu
1 tablespoon lemon juice
2 hot chili peppers, finely chopped
2 roasted red bell peppers, peeled, seeded, and
   diced
1 tablespoon shallots, minced
2 tablespoons fresh parsley sprigs, minced
¼ teaspoon dried tarragon

PREPARATION

1 In a blender, mix the tofu, lemon juice, and
   chilies until smooth.

2 Add the roasted peppers and shallots, continuing to blend. The texture will be
   chunky.

3 Stir in the parsley and tarragon.

4 Serve chilled.

Dill Dip

• • •

This wonderfully fresh dip is truly divine when served with sliced cucumbers and carrot sticks.

• • •

Yields 2½ cups

INGREDIENTS

16 ounces soft tofu, crumbled
1 tablespoon fresh dill sprigs
1 garlic clove, minced
1 tablespoon onion, minced
2 tablespoons lemon juice
¼ cup fresh parsley sprigs
½ teaspoon garlic powder
Salt to taste
Pepper to taste

PREPARATION

1 In a blender, mix all the ingredients until smooth.

2 Serve chilled.

Old-Fashioned Onion Dip

• • •

Always the favorite, onion dip is fabulous when teamed with raw vegetables, potato chips, or crackers. The tofu makes the dip extra creamy.

• • •

Yields 2 cups

INGREDIENTS

10 ounces extra-firm tofu, drained
3 tablespoons cream cheese
1 2-ounce package dry onion soup mix
2 garlic cloves, minced
3 scallions, chopped
⅓ cup milk

PREPARATION

1 In a blender, purée the tofu and cream cheese until smooth.

2 Add the dry soup mix and garlic, continuing to blend.

3 Add the scallions and milk, and blend thoroughly.

4 Serve chilled.

Peppery Parmesan Dip

• • •

This dip makes an elegant spread when paired with a platter of fresh cut vegetables and crispy melba toast.

• • •

Yields 1 cup

INGREDIENTS

8 ounces soft tofu, mashed
½ cup Parmesan cheese, freshly grated
2 tablespoons lemon juice
1 tablespoon tarragon
1 tablespoon white wine vinegar
½ teaspoon garlic, minced
¼ teaspoon coarsely ground black pepper

PREPARATION

1 In a blender, mix all the ingredients until smooth and creamy.

2 Serve at room temperature.

Recipe Tip

If the Peppery Parmesan Dip thickens while standing, stir in a little milk or water as needed.

Dill Dip (see opposite page)

Spinach and Water Chestnut Dip

• • •

Spinach works amazingly well in dips. This one adds the extra crunch of water chestnuts for a tasty accompaniment to crackers and crudités.

• • •

Yields 4 cups

INGREDIENTS

- 12 ounces soft tofu
- 1 10-ounce package frozen spinach, thawed and chopped
- 1 package dry vegetable soup mix
- 1 8-ounce can water chestnuts, chopped
- ⅔ cup scallions, chopped
- 1 cup sour cream or Tofu Sour Cream (see recipe on page 209)
- ½ cup mayonnaise or Tofu Mayonnaise (see recipe on page 212)

PREPARATION

1 In a large mixing bowl, stir together all the ingredients until well-blended.

2 Chill before serving.

Green Onion Dip

• • •

It's rare that green onions are given the spotlight in recipes, but they are front and center in this flavorful recipe. An ideal topper for a tray of crackers.

• • •

Yields 1¼ cups

INGREDIENTS

- 8 ounces silken tofu
- ½ cup green onions, chopped
- ½ cup fresh parsley sprigs
- 1 tablespoon lemon juice
- 1 tablespoon olive oil
- ¼ teaspoon salt

PREPARATION

1 In a blender, mix all the ingredients until well-blended.

2 Serve chilled.

Sun-Dried Tomato and Basil Dip

• • •

The intensity of sun-dried tomatoes and fresh basil leaves makes this dip ideal for slices of crusty Italian bread or a selection of crackers.

• • •

Yields 1 cup

INGREDIENTS

- 8 ounces silken tofu
- ¼ cup sun-dried tomatoes, marinated in olive oil, minced
- 2 garlic cloves, minced
- 1 tablespoon olive oil
- ¼ cup fresh basil leaves
- 2 tablespoons fresh lemon juice
- Salt to taste

PREPARATION

1 In a blender, mix all of the ingredients until smooth.

2 Serve chilled.

Garlic Dip with Capers

• • •

Capers are unique in their fragrance and tangy flavor. Teamed with pungent garlic cloves, they make a distinctive dip that's a real crowd-pleaser.

• • •

Yields 1¼ cups

INGREDIENTS

8 ounces soft tofu, drained
2 garlic cloves, minced
1 tablespoon capers, drained
1 tablespoon mustard
1 teaspoon dried tarragon
2 teaspoons fresh chives, minced

PREPARATION

1 In a blender, purée the tofu.

2 Add the garlic, capers, mustard, tarragon, and chives. Blend until smooth.

3 Chill before serving.

Hot and Spicy Curry Dip

• • •

Served with crackers or traditional Indian breads, this colorful dip may prove to be habit forming.

• • •

Yields 1 cup

INGREDIENTS

8 ounces soft tofu, drained
3 garlic cloves, minced
1 teaspoon cayenne pepper
2 tablespoons curry powder
Juice of 1 lemon
½ teaspoon salt

PREPARATION

1 In a blender, mix all the ingredients until creamy.

2 Serve chilled or at room temperature.

Jalapeño Dip

• • •

There are those of us who prefer a little bite to our food. This jalapeño-packed dip sizzles with peppery heat. Serve it with tortilla chips and plenty of cold beverages.

• • •

Yields 2 cups

INGREDIENTS

8 ounces soft tofu, drained
1 tablespoon olive oil
1 tablespoon lemon juice
1 cup fresh cilantro leaves
1 to 2 jalapeño peppers, chopped
1 garlic clove, minced
½ teaspoon salt

PREPARATION

1 In a blender, mix the tofu, oil, and lemon juice until smooth.

2 Add the cilantro, jalapeño peppers, garlic, and salt. Blend until creamy.

3 Serve chilled.

Sweet and Tangy Fruit Dip

• • •

Sweetened with honey and brown sugar, this delightful dip is a perfect partner for grapes and freshly sliced apples.

• • •

Yields 1¼ cups

INGREDIENTS

- 8 ounces soft tofu, drained
- ¼ cup vegetable oil
- 2 tablespoons lemon juice
- 2 tablespoons light brown sugar
- 1½ teaspoons honey
- ½ teaspoon salt

PREPARATION

1 In a blender, mix all the ingredients until creamy.

2 Store in the refrigerator until ready to use.

Creamy Citrus-Almond Dip

• • •

The flavors of oranges and almonds combine to create an elegant appetizer that's ideal for a cocktail party or small get-together. Serve with orange segments or apple slices.

• • •

Yields 1½ to 2 cups

INGREDIENTS

- 6 ounces soft tofu, drained
- 1 8-ounce package cream cheese
- 1 tablespoon almond extract
- ¼ cup orange juice
- ½ teaspoon grated orange rind
- 2 tablespoons vanilla soy milk
- 2 tablespoons honey
- 3 tablespoons slivered almonds, for garnish

PREPARATION

1 In a blender, mix all the ingredients, except the slivered almonds, until smooth.

2 Transfer the dip to a serving bowl, and garnish with the almonds.

3 Serve chilled.

Soups

Soup's on and tofu's in. Crumbled, cubed, blended,
or baked, tofu is the perfect blank
canvas for the rich and savory
soups enclosed within.

• • •

Gazpacho (see opposite page)

Basic Vegetable Stock

• • •

Some of the soup and entrée recipes in this book require a certain amount of vegetable stock. You may use a pre-packaged version, or follow this recipe for a fresh broth with an amazing depth of flavor. Store the stock in the refrigerator for a couple of days, or keep some in the freezer for future use.

• • •

Yields 6 to 8 cups

INGREDIENTS

2 tablespoons olive oil
2 large celery ribs with leaves, cut into 1-inch pieces
2 carrots, coarsely chopped
1 large onion, chopped
1 zucchini, peeled and sliced
3 cups tomatoes, coarsely chopped
2 leeks, white part only, chopped
3 green onions
3 garlic cloves, peeled
⅓ cup fresh parsley sprigs, chopped
¼ cup fresh basil leaves, chopped
1 teaspoon dried marjoram
½ cup button mushrooms, chopped
10 cups cold water
5 whole black peppercorns

PREPARATION

1 In a large saucepan, sauté the celery and carrot in the olive oil for 1 minute.

2 Add all the remaining ingredients, except the water and peppercorns, and continue to sauté for another 5 minutes.

3 Add the cold water and the peppercorns and bring the mixture to a boil.

4 Lower the heat and simmer, covered, for 2 hours.

5 Remove the cover and simmer for another 30 minutes.

6 Strain the stock through a fine strainer, and salt to taste.

Recipe Tip

For a spicy stock, add three chopped jalapeño chili peppers, seeds and stems removed, to the pan with the rest of the ingredients.

Gazpacho

• • •

We've added some tropical flair to this traditional Spanish soup with the addition of sweet pineapple. With its crunchy vegetables and chilled tomato juice, it's the perfect cool-down for a hot summer afternoon.

• • •

Serves 4 to 6

INGREDIENTS

4 ounces firm tofu, drained and cubed
4 garlic cloves, minced
1 cup canned unsweetened pineapple chunks, with juice
1½ cups cucumbers, peeled, seeded, and diced
1½ cups red bell peppers, diced
½ cup red onions, diced
1 cup tomatoes, diced
3 cups tomato juice
2 tablespoons red wine vinegar
Pinch of cayenne pepper
1 teaspoon ground cumin
¼ teaspoon salt
⅛ teaspoon black pepper
1 lemon, thinly sliced, for garnish

PREPARATION

1 In a blender, purée the garlic, half of all the diced vegetables, the pineapple and its juice, the vinegar, spices, and tomato juice until smooth.

2 Transfer the liquid to a bowl, and stir in the cubed tofu and the remaining vegetables.

3 Refrigerate the soup for 1 to 2 hours until cold.

4 Serve garnished with lemon slices.

Chilled Beet Soup (see above)

Chilled Beet Soup

• • •

Talk about incredible color! This gorgeous magenta soup will add color to any table. Its combination of sweet and savory flavors are best accented with a generous dollop of cool sour cream or yogurt.

• • •

Serves 4

INGREDIENTS

6 ounces silken tofu

3 to 4 cups water

4 medium beets, rinsed and trimmed

1 cup orange juice

1 tablespoon olive oil

¼ cup yellow onion, coarsely chopped

1 teaspoon grated orange rind

⅛ teaspoon ground nutmeg

Dash of salt

Dash of black pepper

Sour cream or plain yogurt, for garnish

PREPARATION

1 In a medium saucepan, bring the water and the beets to boil.

2 Reduce the heat to medium and cook until the beets are tender.

3 Drain the beets, rinse under cold water, then slip off the skins, and quarter.

4 In a blender, combine the beets with the remaining ingredients and blend until smooth.

5 Refrigerate in a covered container for at least 3 hours before serving.

6 Serve with a spoonful of sour cream or plain yogurt on top.

Recipe Tip

Purchase beets with green tops that are crisp and bright. You can refrigerate beets in a plastic bag for up to three weeks.

Chilled Cucumber Soup

• • •

The flavors of cool cucumbers, fresh dill, and mint. Could anything be more refreshing?

• • •

Serves 6

INGREDIENTS

12 ounces firm tofu
3 large cucumbers, peeled, seeded, and chopped
2 garlic cloves, minced
4 fresh mint leaves
2 dill sprigs
1 cup milk

1 tablespoon honey
3 whole scallions, thinly sliced
1 teaspoon salt

PREPARATION

1 In a blender, purée the cucumbers, garlic, mint, and dill.

2 Add the tofu, milk, and honey, and blend until smooth.

3 Transfer to a large bowl and chill for at least 1 hour.

4 Garnish with sliced scallions, and salt to taste.

Recipe Tip

Chilled Cucumber Soup should be served the day it is made.

Chilled Peaches and "Cream" Soup

• • •

If you've never enjoyed the pleasure of a fruit-based soup, this sweet recipe should win you over. On a sultry hot day, this peachy soup is a delightfully refreshing snack or meal.

• • •

Serves 6

INGREDIENTS

24 ounces soft tofu
6 ripe peaches
Water for blanching
1 cup orange juice
1 cup papaya juice
Fresh mint leaves

➡

PREPARATION

1 In a large saucepan, blanch the peaches in boiling water for 1 minute, then plunge them into a bowl of ice water. Using a sharp paring knife, remove the skins.

2 Slice the peaches and place them in a blender.

3 Add the tofu and fruit juices, and mix until smooth.

4 Transfer the soup to a large bowl and refrigerate for at least 2 hours, but no longer than 24 hours.

5 Serve cold, garnished with fresh mint leaves.

2 Stir in the chives and thyme.

3 Refrigerate in a covered container for at least 3 hours before serving.

Recipe Tip

Roasted Red Pepper Soup will keep for up to three days, covered and refrigerated. Since it thickens while standing, stir in water or vegetable stock as needed.

Roasted Red Pepper Soup

• • •

If you love to add roasted red bell peppers to your favorite sandwiches and entrées, just wait until you try them in this chilled soup!

• • •

Serves 4

INGREDIENTS

12 ounces soft tofu, mashed
2 roasted red bell peppers
1¼ cups vegetable stock (see recipe on page 81)
3 tablespoons red wine vinegar
1 tablespoon olive oil
2 garlic cloves, minced
1 teaspoon sugar
½ teaspoon black pepper
¼ teaspoon salt
2 tablespoons fresh chives, minced
1 tablespoon fresh thyme leaves, minced

PREPARATION

1 In a blender, purée the tofu, peppers, vegetable stock, vinegar, oil, garlic, sugar, pepper, and salt until smooth and creamy.

Soup with Chinese Greens and Tofu

• • •

This broth-based soup is filled with crunchy vegetables. Served with a side dish of rice, it makes a light and comforting meal.

• • •

Serves 6

INGREDIENTS

8 ounces extra-firm tofu, cubed
1 tablespoon vegetable oil
2 medium carrots, peeled and sliced
1 medium onion, chopped
2 garlic cloves, minced
2 teaspoons fresh ginger root, grated
6 cups water
¼ cup soy sauce
2 teaspoons rice vinegar
2 teaspoons sesame oil
½ teaspoon black pepper
2 cups bok choy or spinach, chopped
2 cups Chinese cabbage or Napa cabbage, chopped
1 cup snow peas, trimmed and halved

Soup with Chinese Greens and Tofu (see opposite page)

PREPARATION

1 In a large saucepan, sauté the carrots, onion, garlic, and ginger in oil.

2 After 5 minutes, add the water, soy sauce, rice vinegar, sesame oil, and pepper. Bring to a simmer over high heat.

3 Reduce the heat to medium-low, and continue to cook for 15 minutes.

4 Stir in the tofu, bok choy, cabbage, and snow peas, and cook for another 10 minutes.

5 Serve hot.

Recipe Tip

Add six to eight fresh shiitake mushrooms to the saucepan while cooking the onions.

Vichyssoise

• • •

This chilled French potato-leek soup makes an ideal first course—or, when paired with a basket of fresh baked bread, a fabulous main course.

• • •

Serves 4 to 6

INGREDIENTS

6 ounces soft tofu
4 leeks, finely chopped
1 medium onion, finely chopped
¼ cup olive oil
2½ cups potatoes, peeled and diced
1 tablespoon paprika
4 cups vegetable stock (see recipe on page 81)
3 tablespoons soy sauce
⅛ teaspoon black pepper
¼ cup fresh chives, chopped

PREPARATION

1 In a large saucepan, sauté the leeks and onion in oil over low heat until tender.

2 Add the potatoes, paprika, vegetable stock, soy sauce, and pepper.

3 Bring the soup to a boil, cover, and simmer for approximately 20 minutes, or until the potatoes are soft.

4 Transfer the liquid to a blender, add the tofu, and purée until smooth.

5 Refrigerate prior to serving. Garnish with chopped chives.

Mediterranean Tofu and Basil Soup

• • •

This light soup, seasoned with an abundance of fragrant fresh basil, is a flavorful start to an Italian entrée.

• • •

Serves 6

INGREDIENTS

12 ounces firm tofu, cubed
12 to 15 fresh basil leaves
2 tablespoons fresh oregano leaves, minced
2 tablespoons fresh thyme leaves, minced
1 tablespoon olive oil
2 medium carrots, chopped
2 celery stalks, chopped
½ small onion, chopped
1 medium leek, chopped
2 garlic cloves, minced
6 cups vegetable stock (see recipe on page 81)
Salt to taste
Pepper to taste

PREPARATION

1 In a large saucepan, sauté the onion, carrots, celery, leek, and garlic in oil until the onion is translucent.

2 Add the vegetable stock, herbs, and tofu, and reduce the heat to low.

3 Simmer for approximately 40 minutes.

4 Add the salt and pepper to taste, and serve hot.

Classic Miso Soup

• • •

You don't have to go to your local Japanese restaurant for this delicious brothy soup. This recipe is so easy, you'll find yourself making it frequently.

• • •

Serves 2

INGREDIENTS

2 ounces firm tofu, drained and cut into ¼-inch cubes
2¼ cups water
1 tablespoon sweet white miso
2 teaspoons dark miso
1 tablespoon instant wakame (seaweed) flakes or ½ cup spinach, chopped
1 scallion, thinly sliced

PREPARATION

1 In a medium-sized saucepan, bring the water to a boil.

2 Empty ½ cup of the hot water into a glass and add the miso pastes, stirring until blended. Set aside.

3 Add the tofu to the saucepan. Reduce the heat to medium, and continue to cook, covered, for 2 more minutes.

4 Just before serving, add the wakame or spinach to the soup and simmer for about 1 minute.

5 Turn off the heat and add the miso broth.

6 Serve immediately, and garnish with the scallions.

Hot and Sour Soup

• • •

This dark, rich Southeast Asian soup combines a touch of sweetness with the fiery punch of fresh chili peppers. This version offers a variety of surprising ingredients.

• • •

Serves 6 to 8

INGREDIENTS

12 ounces firm tofu, cubed
2 teaspoons vegetable oil
2 cups onions, thinly sliced
5 garlic cloves, minced
1 or 2 fresh chilies, seeded and minced
7 cups vegetable stock (see recipe on page 81)
1½ cups canned straw mushrooms
½ cup bamboo shoots, cut into strips
¾ cup canned pineapple chunks, in juice
1 cup fresh tomatoes, chopped
2 tablespoons fresh basil leaves, chopped
1 tablespoon fresh mint leaves, chopped
2 tablespoons fresh lime juice
¼ cup soy sauce
Basil leaves for garnish

PREPARATION

1 In a large saucepan, sauté the onions in the oil until softened.

2 Add the garlic and chilies and sauté for 1 minute, stirring to prevent sticking.

3 Add the vegetable stock, mushrooms, bamboo shoots, pineapple, and tomatoes, and bring to a boil.

4 Reduce heat and simmer for 5 minutes.

5 Add the basil, mint, lime juice, soy sauce, and tofu. Simmer for another 5 to 10 minutes, until the flavors are well blended.

6 Sprinkle with fresh basil leaves and serve.

Asian Noodle Soup

• • •

Are you crazy for those large bowls of noodle soup they serve at Asian restaurants? Now, with this simple recipe, you can make them yourself at home.

• • •

Serves 6

INGREDIENTS

12 ounces firm tofu, cubed
8 cups vegetable stock (see recipe on page 81)
8 ounces buckwheat, soba, or ramen noodles
½ cup oyster mushrooms, stems removed, cut into strips
½ cup snow peas, stems and strings removed, cut in half
½ cup carrots, coarsely shredded
2 scallions, chopped
¼ cup red bell pepper, diced
2 tablespoons soy sauce
1 garlic clove, minced
½ teaspoon red pepper flakes
⅛ teaspoon ground white pepper
2 teaspoons sesame oil

PREPARATION

1 In a large saucepan, bring the vegetable stock to a boil.

2 Add the noodles, vegetables, soy sauce, garlic, red pepper flakes, and white pepper.

3 Reduce the heat to medium; cover and cook until both the noodles and vegetables are tender.

4 Carefully stir in the tofu and sesame oil. Heat until the tofu is warm.

5 Put a generous amount of noodles in each bowl, and ladle the broth, tofu, and vegetables over them.

Recipe Tip

Asian Noodle Soup should be served the same day it is prepared. If left standing, the noodles will absorb a lot of the broth, and more will need to be added.

Tofu Wonton Soup

• • •

These little dumplings are usually filled with ground pork, but we've used tofu and finely diced vegetables for an equally delicious soup.

• • •

Serves 4 to 6

INGREDIENTS

8 ounces firm tofu, drained and mashed
1 egg, beaten
¼ cup onion, finely diced
¼ cup carrots, finely diced
½ cup spinach, chopped
½ teaspoon salt
½ teaspoon ground white pepper
1 tablespoon sesame oil
1 tablespoon cornstarch
1 package wonton wrappers
6 cups vegetable stock (see recipe on page 81)
2 tablespoons soy sauce
4 cups water
4 scallions, chopped

PREPARATION

1 In a small bowl, combine the egg, vegetables, salt, pepper, sesame oil, tofu, and cornstarch. Mix well.

2 Place 1 teaspoon of the tofu mixture in the center of each wonton wrapper.

3 Wet the edges of the wrapper and fold it, corner to corner. Pinch the three corners together so that the filled wonton resembles a triangle. Make sure there are no holes, so the filling doesn't come out.

4 In a large pot, bring the vegetable stock and soy sauce to a boil, then set aside.

5 In a separate pot, bring the water to a boil and drop in the wontons. Cook, uncovered, for 3 minutes.

6 Remove the wontons with a slotted spoon, and put approximately five into each serving bowl. Ladle the vegetable stock over the top.

7 Serve immediately, and garnish with the scallions.

Creamy Cauliflower and Potato Soup

• • •

A comforting first course, this Norwegian soup is wonderful served with a selection of crispy crackers.

• • •

Serves 4 to 6

INGREDIENTS

8 ounces soft tofu
3¼ cups water or vegetable stock (see recipe on page 81)
1 small head of cauliflower, chopped
2½ cups potatoes, peeled and cubed
1 medium onion, chopped
1 tablespoon margarine
Salt to taste
Pepper to taste
Fresh parsley sprigs for garnish

PREPARATION

1 In a large saucepan, bring the water or vegetable stock to a boil.

2 Add the cauliflower, potatoes, and onion. Reduce the heat to medium, cover, and cook until the vegetables are tender.

3 Transfer the entire contents of the saucepan to a blender, add the tofu, and mix thoroughly.

4 Return the soup to the saucepan, add the seasoning and margarine, and reheat.

5 Serve hot, garnished with chopped parsley.

Deep-Fried Tofu Soup

• • •

This delicately flavored broth is given a wonderful texture with crispy, chewy bits of deep-fried tofu.

• • •

Serves 2

INGREDIENTS

12 ounces firm tofu, drained and cut into 12 to 16 small rectangles
2 teaspoons leeks or scallions, minced
1½ teaspoons sugar
½ teaspoon salt
1 tablespoon sake or white wine
1 teaspoon fresh ginger root, grated
2 tablespoons soy sauce
¾ teaspoon sesame oil
3 to 4 tablespoons flour
1 egg, beaten
Oil for deep-frying
2 cups water
2 mushrooms, finely diced
2 cups cooked brown rice
¼ cup scallions, minced
Dash of red pepper flakes

PREPARATION

1 In a frying pan, heat the leeks, salt, sake, ginger, 1 tablespoon of the soy sauce, and 1 teaspoon of sugar in ¼ teaspoon of the sesame oil. Stir well.

2 Add the tofu and sauté for 10 minutes on each side.

3 Remove the tofu, reserving the liquid. Dust each piece of tofu with flour, and dip it in the beaten egg.

4 In a wok, frying pan, or deep-fryer, heat the oil to 350°F. Carefully add the tofu and deep-fry until golden brown.

5 In a large saucepan, bring the water, remaining liquid, mushrooms, ½ teaspoon of the sesame oil, 1 tablespoon of the soy sauce, and ½ teaspoon of the sugar to a boil.

6 Add the deep-fried tofu. Reduce the heat to medium, and cook, uncovered, for about 3 minutes.

7 Divide the cooked rice among 2 large serving bowls. Top with the tofu and a sprinkling of scallions and pepper flakes. Pour on the broth and serve steaming hot.

Cream of Mushroom Soup

• • •

This luscious soup proves that a little sweet wine is the perfect accent for the richness of fresh mushrooms. Use any combination of button, shiitake, porcini, or crimini mushrooms.

• • •

Serves 4 to 6

INGREDIENTS

12 ounces silken tofu
1 medium onion, chopped
5 garlic cloves, minced
1 tablespoon olive oil
8 ounces mushrooms, sliced thick
1 teaspoon dried thyme
½ cup sherry
1 cup water
1 teaspoon soy sauce
Pinch of salt

PREPARATION

1 In a large saucepan, sauté the onion and garlic in olive oil until the onion is translucent.

2 Add the mushrooms and thyme, and sauté for 5 minutes.

3 Add the sherry, and simmer for another 5 minutes.

4 In a blender, mix the tofu and water until smooth.

5 Slowly add the tofu mixture to the saucepan, stirring thoroughly.

6 Add the soy sauce and salt, and continue to simmer until the mushrooms are tender.

Recipe Tip

For some extra spice in your Cream of Mushroom Soup, add ¼ teaspoon of cayenne pepper.

Cream of Mushroom Soup (see above)

Pasta Fagiole

• • •

This hearty Italian soup is a very filling meal in itself. In addition to the traditional beans, vegetables, and pasta, we've added a little tofu to give it even more health appeal.

• • •

Serves 8

INGREDIENTS

6 ounces firm tofu, cubed
1 medium yellow onion, diced
1 small zucchini, diced
10 to 12 button mushrooms, sliced
4 garlic cloves, minced
1 tablespoon olive oil
7 cups water
1 14-ounce can stewed tomatoes
6 tablespoons canned tomato paste
¼ cup dry red wine
1 tablespoon dried oregano
2 teaspoons dried basil
1 teaspoon salt
½ teaspoon black pepper
½ cup small pasta
1 15-ounce can white beans, drained
½ cup fresh green beans, trimmed and cut into 1-inch pieces

PREPARATION

1 In a large saucepan, sauté the onion, zucchini, mushrooms, and garlic in oil.

2 Add the water, tomatoes, tomato paste, wine, oregano, basil, salt, and pepper. Bring to a simmer over high heat.

3 Reduce the heat to medium-low, and continue cooking for another 20 to 25 minutes, stirring occasionally.

4 Stir in the pasta, tofu, white beans, and green beans, and cook until the pasta is tender.

5 Remove from heat and let sit for 10 minutes before serving.

Curried Squash Bisque

• • •

Butternut squash melds surprisingly well with the rich flavor of curry in this indulgent winter soup.

• • •

Serves 6

INGREDIENTS

4 ounces soft tofu, drained
1 tablespoon vegetable oil
1 large yellow onion, diced
2 celery stalks, diced
2 large tomatoes, diced
4 garlic cloves, minced
2 teaspoons fresh ginger root, minced
1 tablespoon curry powder
2 teaspoons ground cumin
1 teaspoon ground coriander
1 teaspoon salt
½ teaspoon black pepper
4 cups butternut squash, peeled and diced
5 cups water
2 cups spinach, chard, or kale, coarsely chopped

PREPARATION

1 In a large saucepan, sauté the onion and celery for 5 minutes, or until the onions become translucent.

2 Add the tomatoes, garlic, and ginger and cook for another 5 minutes.

3 Stir in the curry powder, cumin, coriander, salt, and pepper. Cook for 1 minute more over low heat.

4 Add the squash and water and bring to a simmer over medium heat.

5 Reduce the heat to a low simmer, and cook until the squash is tender. Stir the soup occasionally.

6 Add the greens and cook for 10 more minutes.

7 In a blender, combine the soup with the tofu, and process until smooth.

8 Serve at once.

6 Add this mixture to the saucepan, stirring until the soup thickens.

7 Simmer for 1 minute.

8 Serve hot, and garnish with the scallions.

Creamy Eggplant Soup

• • •

Here's an unusual and hearty soup that is sure to warm the hearts of friends and family on a chilly day.

• • •

Serves 4 to 6

INGREDIENTS

16 ounces firm tofu, drained and cubed
1 yellow onion, chopped
1 garlic clove, minced
1 small eggplant, cubed
2 large potatoes, peeled and cubed
3 celery stalks, chopped
2 tablespoons margarine
1 teaspoon salt
1 teaspoon dried thyme
5 cups vegetable stock (see recipe on page 81)
1 cup milk
½ teaspoon ground white pepper
½ teaspoon brown sugar
3 tablespoons cornstarch
¼ cup scallion, finely chopped

PREPARATION

1 In a large saucepan, sauté the onion and garlic until light golden brown.

2 Add the eggplant, potatoes, celery, salt, and thyme and sauté for 2 minutes, stirring frequently.

3 Add the vegetable stock, pepper, and tofu.

4 Simmer for another 10 minutes, or until the vegetables are soft.

5 In a blender, combine the milk, sugar, and cornstarch, and blend until smooth.

Creamy Leek Soup

• • •

For a taste of Tuscany, try this delicious soup, delicately flavored with white wine.

• • •

Serves 6 to 8

INGREDIENTS

16 ounces soft tofu, drained and mashed
2 tablespoons olive oil
1 small yellow onion, chopped
3 garlic cloves, minced
4 leeks, chopped
4 cups water
1 cup dry white wine
2 large potatoes, peeled and cubed
½ teaspoon ground white pepper
1 teaspoon salt
¼ cup fresh parsley sprigs, chopped
2 cups milk
¼ cup scallions, chopped

PREPARATION

1 In a large saucepan, sauté the onion and garlic in olive oil until light golden brown.

2 Add the leeks, and sauté for 2 more minutes.

3 Add the water, wine, potatoes, tofu, pepper, salt, and parsley.

4 Simmer for 40 minutes, or until the vegetables are soft.

5 Pour the mixture into a blender and mix until smooth.

6 Return the soup to the saucepan and add the milk. Simmer over low heat for 5 minutes, stirring well.

7 Garnish with the scallions.

Apple and Acorn Squash Soup

• • •

The sweetness of acorn squash combines beautifully with the tartness of apples in this delightful fall dish.

• • •

Serves 6

INGREDIENTS

8 ounces soft tofu, mashed
1 cup onions, chopped
2 tablespoons vegetable oil
1 tablespoon curry powder
3 cups vegetable stock (see recipe on page 81)
2 large acorn squash, peeled, seeded, and cut into 1-inch cubes
2 apples, peeled, cored, and chopped
1 cup apple juice
1/4 teaspoon black pepper
Dash of salt

PREPARATION

1 In a large saucepan, sauté the onion in oil until translucent.

2 Add the curry powder, and stir well.

3 Stir in the vegetable stock, squash, and apples. Bring to a boil.

4 Reduce the heat to medium, cover, and cook until the squash and apples are very tender. Remove from the heat.

5 Empty the soup into a large mixing bowl.

6 In a blender, mix the tofu and 2 cups of the soup until smooth.

7 Pour the puréed mixture back into the saucepan.

8 Transfer the remaining unblended soup to the blender, and mix until smooth.

9 Empty that mixture into the saucepan, and stir well.

10 Add the apple juice, pepper, and salt.

11 Stir over medium heat until the soup is warmed through.

Tomato Bisque

• • •

A childhood favorite, tomato soup, grows up with this elegant and tasty recipe. Serve with a crusty grilled cheese sandwich.

• • •

Serves 4

INGREDIENTS

8 ounces soft tofu
1 1/2 cups water
2 medium onions, chopped
2 14-ounce cans diced tomatoes
1 tablespoon margarine
Salt to taste
Pepper to taste

PREPARATION

1 In a large saucepan, bring the water, onions, tomatoes, margarine, and seasonings to a boil.

2 Lower the heat, and simmer the mixture, uncovered, for 20 to 30 minutes.

3 In a blender, mix the tofu with several spoonfuls of the soup mixture.

4 Add the blender contents to the soup, stirring thoroughly until well-heated.

Zucchini Bisque

• • •

This soup is so rich and flavorful you won't miss the cream.

• • •

Serves 4 to 6

INGREDIENTS

8 ounces soft tofu
1 medium onion, chopped
2 cups zucchini, sliced
2 tablespoons olive oil
2½ cups vegetable stock (see recipe on page 81)
⅛ teaspoon ground black pepper
½ teaspoon ground nutmeg

PREPARATION

1 In a large saucepan, sauté the onion and zucchini in 1 tablespoon of the oil until tender.

2 Add the vegetable stock, pepper, and nutmeg, cover, and simmer for 20 minutes.

3 In a blender, combine the tofu and 1 tablespoon of olive oil and blend until smooth.

4 Add the tofu mixture to the saucepan, stirring well.

5 Serve warm.

Very Green Soup

• • •

This beautiful soup, full of healthy, tasty greens, will warm your body and lift your spirits!

• • •

Serves 4 to 6

INGREDIENTS

12 ounces firm tofu, cubed
6 cups vegetable stock (see recipe on page 81)
1 tablespoon ginger root, grated
1½ cups carrots, thinly sliced
1½ cups leeks, thinly sliced
2 cups bok choy, kale, or Chinese cabbage, chopped
4 cups fresh spinach, rinsed and chopped
Salt to taste
Scallions, chopped, for garnish

PREPARATION

1 In a large saucepan, bring the vegetable stock to a boil.

2 Add the ginger, carrots, leeks, and bok choy or other greens.

3 Lower the heat and simmer for about 10 minutes, or until the vegetables are tender.

4 Stir the spinach and tofu into the soup, and cook for another 5 minutes.

5 Add salt to taste, and garnish with the chopped scallions.

Recipe Tip

Add noodles of your choice for a more filling Very Green Soup.

3 Reduce the heat to low. Cover and simmer for 30 minutes, or until the vegetables are soft.

4 Add the tofu and simmer for 3 minutes.

5 Serve the soup hot or at room temperature with 1 tablespoon of sour cream in each bowl. Garnish with the scallions.

Lemon Rice Soup

• • •

When you're feeling under the weather, this soup's fragrant lemon aroma and rich nutrients will help get you back on your feet.

• • •

Serves 4 to 6

INGREDIENTS

16 ounces firm tofu, drained and cubed
4 cups vegetable stock (see recipe on page 81)
2 cups milk
1 cup cooked rice
1/4 cup fresh lemon juice, dissolved with 2 tablespoons cornstarch
1 teaspoon grated lemon rind
1/2 teaspoon salt
1/2 teaspoon ground white pepper
1/4 cup fresh parsley sprigs, chopped
1/4 cup scallions, chopped

PREPARATION

1 In a large saucepan, bring the tofu, vegetable stock, and milk to a boil.

2 Add the rice and simmer for 15 minutes.

3 Slowly add the lemon juice and cornstarch mixture, stirring constantly.

4 Add the grated lemon rind, salt, pepper, and parsley. Simmer for 5 more minutes.

5 Serve hot with the scallions as garnish.

Borscht

• • •

A slimmed-down version of a traditional Russian vegetable soup, this soup is a perfect dish to serve on a cold winter night.

• • •

Serves 6 to 8

INGREDIENTS

12 ounces firm tofu, drained and cubed
1 small red onion, chopped
2 tablespoons olive oil
2 large potatoes, peeled and cubed
4 beets, peeled and cubed
1 large carrot, peeled and cubed
1 teaspoon caraway seeds
6 cups water
1/4 cup fresh lemon juice
1 teaspoon salt
1/2 teaspoon black pepper
1 teaspoon dried dill
1 tablespoon honey
1 cup sour cream
1/4 cup scallions, chopped

PREPARATION

1 In a large saucepan, sauté the onion in the olive oil until light golden brown.

2 Add the potatoes, beets, carrot, caraway seeds, water, lemon juice, salt, pepper, dill, and honey. Bring to a boil.

Hot and Spicy Roasted Garlic and Red Pepper Soup

• • •

If you're a fan of roasted garlic and vegetables, you'll love this soup. We've added citrus peel for added aroma and taste appeal.

• • •

Serves 4

INGREDIENTS

8 ounces soft tofu, drained and cut into 1-inch strips
1 whole garlic head, separated into cloves
1 tablespoon vegetable oil
6 cups vegetable stock (see recipe on page 81)
1 lemon peel
½ orange peel
2 tablespoons fresh basil leaves
1 roasted red bell pepper, peeled and cut into 1-inch strips
2 teaspoons cayenne pepper

PREPARATION

1 In a baking dish, coat the garlic cloves with oil and bake at 375°F for about 20 minutes or until light brown. Remove from the oven and cool to room temperature.

2 Squeeze the garlic to release the cloves from their skins.

3 In a blender, mix the garlic and ¼ cup of the vegetable stock until smooth.

4 In a large saucepan, combine the rest of the vegetable stock, the lemon peel, the orange peel, and the basil. Bring the soup to a boil.

5 Add the garlic mixture, tofu, roasted pepper, and cayenne pepper to the mixture. Reduce the heat and simmer, uncovered, for 5 minutes.

6 Discard the citrus peels before serving the soup.

Hot Cucumber Soup

• • •

You may only be familiar with cucumbers in chilled soups, but as this recipe proves, they taste great in a warm soup, too.

• • •

Serves 4 to 6

INGREDIENTS

24 ounces firm tofu, cut into julienne strips
1½ cups vegetable stock (see recipe on page 81)
1½ cups cold water
2 teaspoons ginger root, grated
1¼ cups cucumbers, peeled, seeds removed, and cubed
¼ cup celery leaves
Salt to taste

PREPARATION

1 In a large saucepan, bring the vegetable stock, water, and ginger to a boil.

2 Add the tofu and cucumbers and cook for about 1 minute, or until the cucumbers become tender.

3 Add the celery leaves to the soup, and stir.

4 Add salt to taste. Serve hot.

Lentil Soup with Tofu

• • •

Serve this soup by itself or, with some added curry powder, as the first course of an Indian meal.

• • •

Serves 6

INGREDIENTS

8 ounces silken tofu, drained and cubed
6 cups water
1 cup dry lentils, washed and drained
½ teaspoon salt
1 medium onion, chopped
1 medium carrot, sliced
1 celery stalk, sliced
1 garlic clove, minced
2 tablespoons olive oil
1 cup peeled tomatoes
1½ teaspoons vinegar
¼ teaspoon dried basil
¼ teaspoon black pepper

PREPARATION

1 In a large saucepan, bring the water, lentils, and salt to a boil.

2 In a separate pan, sauté the onion, carrot, celery, and garlic in oil.

3 Once the onion is soft, transfer the mixture to the boiling lentils.

4 Add the tomatoes, reduce heat, and simmer for about 30 minutes.

5 Add the tofu, vinegar, basil, and pepper. Continue simmering until the lentils are soft. Serve hot.

Argentinean Carbonada

• • •

This traditional soup is usually made with meat, but our recipe is just as good with a simple tofu substitution. Accompany each steaming bowl with a big slice of warm cornbread.

• • •

Serves 4 to 6

INGREDIENTS

6 ounces extra-firm tofu, cubed
1 medium onion, chopped
2 celery stalks, chopped
3 garlic cloves, minced
2 teaspoons olive oil
1 teaspoon paprika
1 teaspoon dried dill
½ teaspoon dried oregano
1 bay leaf
4 cups vegetable stock (see recipe on page 81)
½ cup dry white wine
1 medium potato, diced
1 carrot, peeled and diced
1 green or red bell pepper, seeded and diced
½ cup cooked brown rice
1 medium tomato, chopped
1 tablespoon fresh lemon juice
Salt to taste
Pepper to taste

PREPARATION

1 In a large saucepan, sauté the onions, celery, and garlic in oil until the onions become translucent, stirring often to prevent sticking.

2 Add the paprika, dill, oregano, and bay leaf, and continue cooking for 1 more minute.

3 Stir in the vegetable stock, wine, potatoes, carrots, and bell peppers.

4 Bring to a boil, cover, and reduce the heat to simmer the vegetables and broth for 10 minutes.

➡

5 Add the tofu, rice, and tomatoes, and simmer until all of the vegetables are tender.

6 Add the lemon juice, salt, and pepper to taste.

Mediterranean Cilantro Soup

• • •

Cilantro, the fresh green leaves and stems of the coriander herb, is known for its rich aroma and mild licorice flavor. This soup makes cilantro the much-deserved center of attention.

• • •

Serves 4 to 6

INGREDIENTS

36 ounces firm tofu, finely cubed
3½ tablespoons olive oil
½ teaspoon salt
2 teaspoons fresh ginger root, grated
4½ tablespoons fresh cilantro roots and stems, minced
2 cups onions, finely diced
1½ cups celery, finely diced
4½ cups vegetable stock (see recipe on page 81)
1 cup cold water
½ cup fresh cilantro leaves, finely chopped

PREPARATION

1 In a large saucepan, cook the oil, salt, and ginger on high heat.

2 When a wisp of white smoke appears, add the cilantro stems and roots. Cook for 20 seconds.

3 Add the onions, stir, and cook until the onions become translucent.

4 Add the celery, stir, and cook for 1 more minute.

5 Add the vegetable stock and water, and mix well. Cover the saucepan and bring the soup to a boil.

6 Lower the heat to medium and cook another 10 minutes, or until the celery is tender.

7 Return to high heat and add the tofu. Bring the soup back to a boil for 2 to 3 minutes.

8 Turn off the heat, add the cilantro leaves, and mix well.

9 Serve immediately.

Tofu Gumbo

• • •

For a taste of the French Quarter, cook up a pot of this New Orleans classic.

• • •

Serves 4

INGREDIENTS

8 ounces firm tofu, cubed
2 tablespoons vegetable oil, plus extra for deep-frying
1 medium onion, chopped
1 small green bell pepper, chopped
1 cup okra, ends cut off, chopped
1 14-ounce can diced tomatoes
2 cups vegetable stock (see recipe on page 81)
1 bay leaf
3 tablespoons fresh parsley sprigs, chopped
Salt to taste
Pepper to taste

PREPARATION

1 In a large saucepan, deep-fry the tofu cubes in oil until golden brown. Drain well and set aside.

2 Sauté the onion, bell pepper, and okra in oil for 4 to 5 minutes, stirring occasionally.

3 Add the tomatoes, vegetable stock, and bay leaf to the mixture and bring to a boil. Lower the heat and simmer, covered, for 15 to 20 minutes.

4 Add the fried tofu, parsley, salt and pepper, and continue to cook for a couple of minutes longer. Serve immediately.

Recipe Tip

If you like your gumbo with a kick, add cayenne pepper powder and hot pepper sauce, to taste.

Veggie Tofu Soup with Red Chili and Ginger

• • •

Talk about your hot soup! This delicious recipe will raise your body and taste temperature.

• • •

Serves 4

INGREDIENTS

24 ounces firm tofu, cubed
2 tablespoons shallots, sliced
1 tablespoon coriander root, chopped
1 teaspoon black peppercorns
3 cups vegetable stock (see recipe on page 81)
¼ cup button mushrooms, sliced
¼ cup baby corn, sliced to ½-inch pieces
½ cup asparagus, sliced to ½-inch pieces
1 teaspoon salt
2 tablespoons soy sauce
2 tablespoons sugar
4 tablespoons tamarind juice
1 tablespoon scallions, chopped
1 tablespoon hot red chili pepper, shredded
2 tablespoons ginger root, shredded

PREPARATION

1 In a small, sturdy bowl, use a mortar to pound the shallots, coriander root, and pepper into a fine paste.

2 In a large saucepan, bring the vegetable stock and the ground paste to a boil, stirring well.

3 Add the tofu, mushrooms, corn, and asparagus, and bring to a full boil.

4 Add the salt, soy sauce, sugar, and tamarind juice. Simmer for another 15 minutes.

5 Serve hot and garnish with the scallions, chili pepper, and ginger shreds.

Corn Chowder (see opposite page)

Corn Chowder

• • •

This thick, hearty soup is a favorite throughout New England. Its lovely yellow color, accented with green and red bell peppers, makes it as pleasing to the eye as it is to the appetite.

• • •

Serves 6

INGREDIENTS

24 ounces firm tofu, cubed
1 large white onion, chopped
1 small red bell pepper, chopped
1 small green bell pepper, chopped
2 garlic cloves, minced
1 10-ounce package frozen corn, thawed
1 tablespoon vegetable oil
2 cups vegetable stock (see recipe on page 81)
¼ teaspoon dried thyme
4 medium red potatoes, diced
1½ cups milk
1 teaspoon salt
½ teaspoon ground black pepper

PREPARATION

1 In a large saucepan, sauté the onion, peppers, garlic, and corn until the onion is translucent.

2 Add the vegetable stock, thyme, and potatoes, and bring to a boil.

3 Reduce the heat to a simmer and cook for 15 minutes, or until the vegetables are very soft.

4 Add the milk and tofu, and simmer for another 15 minutes.

5 Season with salt and pepper. Serve immediately.

Cream of Celery Soup

• • •

Served hot for a winter meal or chilled for a refreshing break from summer heat, this soup puts the distinctive flavor of celery front and center.

• • •

Serves 6 to 8

INGREDIENTS

8 ounces soft tofu
1 celery head, leaves removed, chopped
1 medium onion, chopped
2 tablespoons vegetable oil
4 cups water or vegetable stock (see recipe on page 81)
½ teaspoon dried oregano
½ teaspoon dried tarragon
Salt to taste
Pepper to taste
Fresh parsley sprigs, for garnish

PREPARATION

1 In a large saucepan, sauté the celery and onion in oil until the onion is translucent.

2 Add the water or vegetable stock, seasonings, and herbs.

3 Bring to a boil, then lower the heat and cover. Simmer for 15 to 20 minutes.

4 In a blender, combine the contents of the saucepan with the tofu, and mix until smooth.

5 Pour the soup back into the saucepan to reheat, and serve with parsley sprigs.

Salads

No more boring iceberg lettuce and cucumber
salads for you. Re-invent the salad,
and let tofu turn it into a
refreshing, filling meal.

• • •

Mock Tuna Salad

• • •

Baking tofu gives it a wonderfully chewy texture that mimics good old-fashioned tuna fish. Served with an assortment of fresh vegetables, this salad makes a fresh and nutritious meal.

• • •

Serves 6

INGREDIENTS

8 ounces firm tofu, pressed and diced
1 large red onion, thinly sliced
½ cup red-wine vinaigrette salad dressing
10-ounce package frozen green beans
1 large head lettuce, torn in pieces
6 plum tomatoes, quartered
1 14-ounce can artichoke hearts, drained and cut into large, bite-sized pieces
1 15-ounce can great Northern beans, drained and rinsed
4 ounces black olives
1 garlic clove, minced
1 teaspoon Dijon mustard
¼ cup mixed fresh basil leaves and parsley sprigs, chopped

PREPARATION

1 On an oiled cookie sheet, bake the tofu at 350°F for 15 minutes or until firm.

2 Place the onion slices in a small bowl, pour the red wine dressing over them, and set aside to marinate for 15 minutes.

3 Blanch the green beans until they are bright green and tender-crisp. Drain and rinse them until they are at room temperature.

4 Drain the red onion, reserving the dressing in a small bowl.

5 In a deep bowl, arrange the lettuce to make a bed. Arrange the tofu to form a pie-wedge shape, then make another wedge of the tomato quarters, another each of the green beans, artichoke hearts, beans, and red onion. Arrange the black olives in a small mound in the center.

6 In a small bowl, combine the reserved dressing plus enough additional red wine dressing to make ½ cup. Add the garlic, mustard, and mixed herbs to the dressing. Whisk with a fork, and pour over the salad.

Taco Salad with Tofu

• • •

The chili powder and ground cumin spark this satisfying salad of sautéed onions, fresh tomatoes, and tofu.

• • •

Serves 6

INGREDIENTS

24 ounces extra-firm tofu, cubed
6 6-inch corn tortillas
2 tablespoons vegetable oil
¼ cup onion, chopped
2 garlic cloves, minced
1 ripe, medium tomato, chopped
1 tablespoon chili powder
1 teaspoon ground cumin
1 head romaine lettuce, shredded
8 ounces Cheddar cheese, shredded
⅓ cup Tofu Sour Cream (see recipe on page 209)
⅓ cup Tofu Guacamole (see recipe on page 71)
Salsa

PREPARATION

1 Bake the tortillas at 400°F for 3 to 5 minutes, or until crispy. Remove and cool.

2 In a medium saucepan, sauté the onion and garlic in oil until the onion is translucent.

3 Add the tomato, chili powder, cumin, and tofu, and cook for 8 to 10 minutes.

4 Place each tortilla on a plate, and divide the tofu mixture evenly among them.

5 Top with the lettuce, cheese, Tofu Sour Cream and Tofu Guacamole. Serve alongside your favorite salsa.

Garden Salad with Mandarin Oranges
(see opposite page)

Garden Salad with Mandarin Oranges

• • •

If you've never experienced the exquisite
flavor of fruit in your green salads, we
think this recipe will win you over.
Try sprinkling the salad with
sunflower seeds for added
taste and texture.

• • •

Serves 4 to 6

INGREDIENTS

12 ounces extra-firm tofu, drained and cubed
1 head red leaf lettuce, torn into small pieces
1 small red bell pepper, sliced
1 cucumber, peeled, thinly sliced
1 large tomato, thinly sliced
1 small red onion, thinly sliced
2 scallions, finely chopped
1 11-ounce can whole Mandarin orange
    segments, drained
¼ cup slivered almonds, toasted
¼ cup fresh orange juice
¼ cup canola oil
2 tablespoons fresh lemon juice
1 teaspoon salt
3 garlic cloves, minced
½ teaspoon mustard powder
1 teaspoon honey

PREPARATION

1 In a large salad bowl, arrange the lettuce
leaves, bell pepper, tofu, cucumber, tomato,
onion, scallions, orange segments, and
toasted almonds in layers.

2 In a small bowl, mix the orange juice,
canola oil, lemon juice, salt, garlic,
mustard, and honey.

3 Pour the dressing over the salad, and toss.
Chill before serving.

Tofu Tostada Salad with Parsley Dressing

• • •

This Southwestern-influenced salad is
robust enough to be a main course.
To turn up the heat a bit, add a
pinch or two of cayenne pepper
to the sautéing veggies.

• • •

Serves 4 to 6

INGREDIENTS

6 ounces extra-firm tofu, cut into 1-inch cubes
¼ cup barbecue sauce
1 tablespoon vegetable oil, plus extra
1 ear corn, kernels cut from the cob
½ red bell pepper, cut into strips
1 small zucchini, cut into strips
1 small red onion, sliced
1 fresh serrano chili, minced
4 corn tortillas
1 15-ounce can black beans, drained and
    rinsed
5½ cups romaine lettuce, shredded
1 medium tomato, cut into 8 slices
1 lime, quartered
Fresh cilantro leaves
Parsley Dressing (see recipe on page 205)

PREPARATION

1 On an oiled cookie sheet, place a single
layer of tofu cubes. Drizzle the cubes with
barbecue sauce, and bake at 400°F for 20
minutes.

2 Meanwhile, in a frying pan, sauté the corn,
pepper, zucchini, onion, and chili for 5
minutes.

3 Add the baked tofu, and mix lightly.
Remove from the heat.

4 Heat the tortillas in the oven until crispy.
Wrap them in a towel, and set aside.

5 In a small pot, heat the black beans.

6 Place the tortillas on a plate or platter. Cover them with the beans.

7 Toss the romaine lettuce with some of the Parsley Dressing, and place over the tortillas and beans.

8 Arrange the vegetable and tofu mixture over the salad. Garnish with cilantro leaves, tomato wedges, and limes.

Rosemary, Orange, and Broiled Tofu Salad

• • •

As the tofu soaks in this aromatic marinade, it captures the woody, pinelike taste of the rosemary and the contrasting orange flavoring, making this salad perfect for a hot summer evening.

• • •

Serves 4

INGREDIENTS

16 ounces firm tofu, drained and sliced into
  ¾-inch-thick slices
¼ cup soy sauce
1 cup orange juice
2 garlic cloves, minced
1 tablespoon dried rosemary
2 teaspoons mirin
2 teaspoons tahini
1 tablespoon light miso
2 teaspoons honey
1½ teaspoons sesame oil
4 cups mixed salad greens
16 cooked snow peas
½ cup mung bean sprouts
1 celery stalk, sliced
1 carrot, thinly sliced
¼ cup red radish, sliced

PREPARATION

1 In a shallow baking dish, combine the soy sauce, ½ cup of the orange juice, one of the minced garlic cloves, rosemary, and mirin. Stir well.

2 Cut each slice of tofu in half lengthwise to form strips, then place these in the baking dish with the marinade. Spoon the marinade over the strips, cover, and marinate for at least 30 minutes (or up to 24 hours in the refrigerator).

3 In a small bowl, whisk together the remaining orange juice, the remaining garlic, the tahini, miso, honey, and sesame oil to make the salad dressing. Set aside.

4 Broil the tofu, turning once, until the tofu has turned golden and the edges of the strips are beginning to crisp.

5 Meanwhile, toss the salad greens with the dressing, and arrange them, along with the snow peas, bean sprouts, celery, carrot, and radishes, on a serving platter. As soon as the tofu is cooked, place the strips on top of the salad and serve.

Mixed Salad Greens with Sweet 'N Spicy Tofu

• • •

The distinctive marinade, combining sweet, salty, and spicy, gives the tofu in this salad a real zing.

• • •

Serves 4

INGREDIENTS

12-ounces extra-firm tofu, frozen, thawed, and pressed
2 tablespoons soy sauce
2 tablespoons Dijon mustard
1 tablespoon sweet white miso
1 tablespoon maple syrup
1 tablespoon water
1 tablespoon sesame oil
¼ teaspoon chili oil (optional)
¾ to 1 pound mixed salad greens
Seasoned rice vinegar
20 strips roasted red bell pepper, about 2 inches long and ½ inch wide

PREPARATION

1 In a shallow bowl, use a fork to mash and mix the soy sauce, mustard, miso, maple syrup, water, sesame oil, and chili oil until thoroughly blended. Set aside.

2 With the long side of the tofu block facing you, cut the tofu into eight slices, each about ½ inch thick. Cut each slice into two triangles.

3 Dip the triangles into the sauce to coat all sides. Arrange the triangles on a broiling pan lined with aluminum foil.

4 With the top oven rack 5 to 6 inches from the broiling element, broil the tofu triangles for 3 minutes, or until lightly browned and slightly crusty on the first side.

5 Turn the triangles over, and brush with the remaining sauce. Broil until the second side is browned. Set aside to cool slightly.

6 Divide the mixed salad greens among four plates. Lightly pour the rice vinegar over the greens.

7 On top of the greens, arrange four tofu triangles per plate. Place five red pepper strips over each serving, and serve.

Spinach Salad with Tofu

• • •

We've added tofu to the traditional spinach salad for even more health appeal.

• • •

Serves 4

INGREDIENTS

12 ounces firm tofu, drained and cubed
1 pound fresh spinach leaves, washed, stems removed
1 small red onion, sliced
½ cup olive oil
3 garlic cloves, minced
3 tablespoons lemon juice
1 teaspoon honey
½ teaspoon salt
1 teaspoon mustard powder
½ teaspoon black pepper
3 scallions, chopped
½ cup pine nuts

PREPARATION

1 In a large salad bowl, arrange the spinach, red onion, and tofu in layers.

2 In a small bowl, mix the olive oil, garlic, lemon juice, honey, salt, mustard, pepper, and scallions.

3 Pour the dressing over the salad and toss.

4 Chill for 15 minutes, and garnish with the pine nuts before serving.

Tofu and Avocado Salad

• • •

Few things taste as fresh as avocado and tomato. Their flavors truly come to life with this tangy lime dressing.

• • •

Serves 4

INGREDIENTS

12 ounces extra-firm tofu, drained and cubed
1 head green leaf lettuce
2 tomatoes, cubed
2 avocados, seeded and cubed
1 green cayenne pepper, chopped
½ cup red onion, chopped

¼ cup fresh cilantro leaves, chopped
3 garlic cloves, crushed
Juice of 1 lime
½ cup olive oil
1 teaspoon salt
½ teaspoon black pepper
1 teaspoon paprika

PREPARATION

1 Place the lettuce leaves on a large serving platter, and arrange the tofu, tomatoes, avocados, cayenne pepper, red onion, and fresh cilantro leaves in layers.

2 In a small bowl, thoroughly mix the garlic, lime juice, olive oil, salt, and pepper.

3 Pour the dressing over the salad. Sprinkle with the paprika, and chill before serving.

Tofu and Avocado Salad (see above)

Mushroom, Watercress, and Tofu Salad

• • •

The slightly peppery taste of the watercress brings the mellow mushrooms and tofu to life.

• • •

Serves 4 to 6

INGREDIENTS

8 ounces firm tofu
3 to 4 tablespoons cider vinegar
1 teaspoon soy sauce
½ teaspoon mustard powder
1 small garlic clove, minced
Salt to taste
Pepper to taste
½ cup olive oil
2 bunches watercress
¼ pound button mushrooms, thinly sliced
½ tablespoon dried basil
½ tablespoon dried dill
½ tablespoon dried marjoram
½ tablespoon dried thyme

PREPARATION

1 In a bowl, mix the vinegar, soy sauce, dry mustard, garlic, salt, and pepper. Whisk in the oil, and set aside.

2 In another bowl, mash the tofu, and toss with the dressing.

3 Add the watercress, mushrooms, and herbs, toss again, and serve.

New Orleans Spicy Vegetables and Rice

• • •

For a taste of Louisiana cooking, try this fiery mixture of chopped vegetables and spices. Add some hot sauce for an extra kick.

• • •

Serves 6

INGREDIENTS

16 ounces firm tofu, cubed
1¼ cups olive oil
1 small onion, finely chopped
½ teaspoon hot red pepper flakes
½ teaspoon filé powder
½ teaspoon dried thyme
1 bay leaf
2 cups vegetable stock (see recipe on page 81)
1 teaspoon salt
1 cup basmati rice
⅛ teaspoon cayenne pepper
⅛ teaspoon allspice
⅛ teaspoon fennel seed, ground
⅓ cup cider vinegar
3 tablespoons mustard
1 teaspoon black pepper
2 celery ribs, chopped
1 small green bell pepper, chopped
1 small red bell pepper, chopped
4 scallions, minced
6 cups romaine lettuce, coarsely chopped
12 cherry tomatoes

PREPARATION

1 In a medium saucepan, sauté the onion in 2 tablespoons of the oil until tender.

2 Add the red pepper flakes, filé powder, thyme, and the bay leaf, and cook, stirring, for 2 to 3 minutes.

3 Stir in the stock, ¾ teaspoon of the salt, and the rice, and bring to a boil.

4 Reduce the heat to low, cover the pan, and cook for 20 minutes, or until the rice is tender and all the liquid is absorbed.

5 Remove from the heat, and let stand, covered, for 5 minutes. Remove the bay leaf. Transfer the rice to a large bowl, and let stand, stirring occasionally, until cool.

6 In a large frying pan, heat 2 tablespoons of the oil, and add the tofu, cayenne pepper, allspice, and fennel seed. Cook for 5 minutes, or until the tofu is browned on all sides. Add to the rice.

7 In a food processor or blender, combine the vinegar, mustard, remaining salt, and black pepper. Process for 1 minute.

8 With the machine still running, stream in the remaining 1 cup of olive oil. Pour over the rice mixture, and mix.

9 Add the celery, bell peppers, and scallions. Toss well to mix, and serve on top of the shredded lettuce. Garnish with the cherry tomatoes.

Tofu and Rice Salad with Peanut Sauce

• • •

The roasted tofu adds protein and texture to this rice and vegetable salad, while the cilantro and mint add a pungent bite to the peanut sauce.

• • •

Serves 4

INGREDIENTS

8 ounces extra-firm tofu, cubed
¼ cup hot water
3 tablespoons chunky peanut butter
2 to 3 tablespoons soy sauce
1 tablespoon rice vinegar
2 garlic cloves, minced pepper
1 jalapeño pepper, seeded and minced
1 teaspoon sesame oil
2 tablespoons fresh mint leaves, chopped
2 tablespoons fresh cilantro leaves, chopped
Rice, cooked to serve 4
1 red bell pepper, diced
3 whole scallions, trimmed and chopped
1 4-ounce can sliced water chestnuts, drained
1 head lettuce, torn in small pieces

PREPARATION

1 Place the tofu cubes on a lightly greased baking pan, and bake at 375°F for 15 minutes, or until lightly browned. Remove the pan from the oven, and let the tofu cool slightly.

2 Meanwhile, in a large mixing bowl, whisk the water, peanut butter, soy sauce, rice vinegar, garlic, jalapeño, sesame oil, mint, and cilantro.

3 Stir in the rice, bell pepper, scallions, water chestnuts, and tofu, coating the grains and vegetables completely with the dressing. Chill for 1 hour.

4 Fluff the rice salad before serving over a bed of lettuce. Garnish with any remaining sprigs of herbs.

Fried Tofu Salad with Brown Rice and Vegetables

• • •

A substantial dish for big appetites, this salad is packed with sweet and savory flavors.

• • •

Serves 4

INGREDIENTS

8 ounces firm tofu, diced

8 tablespoons vegetable oil plus extra for deep-frying

3 scallions, chopped

2 garlic cloves, minced

2 tablespoons parsley sprigs, chopped

½ teaspoon mustard powder

Juice of ½ lemon

3 tablespoons cider vinegar or wine vinegar

Brown rice, cooked to serve 4

1 tablespoon miso

2 tablespoons honey

3 tablespoons water

1 large potato, baked and chopped

2 small tomatoes, chopped

1 celery stalk, chopped

⅓ cup white cabbage, grated

½ raw beetroot, grated

⅓ cup alfalfa sprouts

PREPARATION

1 In a large frying pan, deep-fry the tofu in oil. Set aside.

2 In a bowl, combine the scallions, garlic, parsley, mustard powder, lemon juice, 4 tablespoons of the oil, and half the vinegar. Add the cooked rice, and mix well. Marinate in the refrigerator for 1 hour.

3 In a blender, combine the remaining 4 tablespoons of oil, the rest of the vinegar, the miso, honey, and water, and blend thoroughly. Set aside.

➤

Fried Tofu Salad with Brown Rice and Vegetables (see above)

4 In a large bowl, combine the potato, tomatoes, celery, cabbage, beetroot, sprouts, and fried tofu. Pour the miso dressing over the salad, and mix well.

5 Place the marinated rice in bowls, and top with the vegetables and tofu.

Greek-Asian Salad

• • •

East meets West to create a tantalizingly tasty tofu salad over a simple bed of lettuce.

• • •

Serves 6

INGREDIENTS

16 ounces firm tofu, cubed
¼ cup olive oil
2 tablespoons wine vinegar
2 tablespoons miso
¼ teaspoon black pepper
2 garlic cloves, minced
2 tablespoons fresh basil leaves, chopped
1 tablespoon fresh oregano leaves, chopped, or
  1 teaspoon dried
1 head lettuce, torn in small pieces
2 tomatoes, cubed
2 cucumbers, cubed
1 avocado, cubed
½ small red onion, chopped
½ cup black or oil-cured olives

PREPARATION

1 In a small bowl, blend the olive oil, vinegar, miso, black pepper, and garlic. Stir in the basil and oregano.

2 Add the tofu cubes to the bowl, and marinate for at least 1 hour.

3 In a salad bowl, arrange the lettuce, and toss in the marinated tofu, along with the tomatoes, avocado, onion, and olives.

Mediterranean Salad

• • •

Celebrate the arrival of spring with the fresh flavors of artichokes and asparagus in this surprisingly filling salad.

• • •

Serves 4

INGREDIENTS

8 ounces firm tofu, cubed
Brown rice, cooked to serve 4
6-ounce can pimentos, chopped
3 slices onion
1 tablespoon fresh parsley sprigs, chopped
Salt to taste
¾ cup olive oil
4 tablespoons cider vinegar
16-ounce can artichoke hearts, chopped
1 pound fresh asparagus

PREPARATION

1 In a large bowl, mix the rice and pimentos. Set aside.

2 In another bowl, mix the onion slices, parsley, and salt with the olive oil. Leave to marinate for 30 minutes. Remove the onion slices and mix in the vinegar.

3 Stir half of this vinaigrette into the rice and pimentos.

4 Marinate the artichoke hearts in the remaining vinaigrette for 15 minutes.

5 When ready to serve, add the artichoke hearts with their dressing to the rice, along with the cubes of tofu. Decorate with the asparagus.

Rice and Bulgur Salad

• • •

Bulgur, a cracked wheat grain often used in Middle Eastern dishes, makes a hearty base for salads. Here it is paired with brown rice and a great-tasting tofu dressing.

• • •

Serves 4

INGREDIENTS

12 ounces soft tofu
2 tablespoons vegetable oil
1 onion, finely chopped
1 cup brown rice, cooked
2½ cups vegetable stock (see recipe on page 81)
4 teaspoons soy sauce
2 garlic cloves, minced
⅔ cup bulgur wheat
2 tablespoons lemon juice
Salt to taste
2 tablespoons cider vinegar
1 tablespoon sesame oil
2 tablespoons fresh parsley sprigs, chopped
3 scallions
1 head lettuce, separated into large leaves

PREPARATION

1 In a saucepan, sauté the onion in the vegetable oil until lightly browned.

2 Stir in the cooked rice, then add the stock and 2 teaspoons of the soy sauce, and bring to a boil. Lower the heat, cover, and simmer for 15 minutes.

3 Add the garlic, bulgur, lemon juice, and salt to the rice, and simmer for about 10 minutes longer, or until the liquid is absorbed, and both the rice and bulgur are tender.

4 In a blender, add the tofu, vinegar, sesame oil, the rest of the soy sauce, and parsley, and blend thoroughly. Add the scallions.

5 Pour the dressing over the rice and wheat, and stir well. Chill in the refrigerator, and serve piled on lettuce leaves.

Fast and Fabulous Quinoa Salad with Tofu

• • •

Quinoa, an ancient grain first used by the Incas, is rich in nutrients and amino acids. Its earthy taste blends well with the nuts and sweet raisins.

• • •

Serves 4

INGREDIENTS

8 ounces extra-firm tofu, diced
Quinoa, cooked to serve 4
½ cup pine nuts
¾ cup golden raisins
½ cup scallions, chopped
⅓ cup olive oil
¼ cup rice vinegar
2 tablespoons soy sauce
¼ teaspoon black pepper
1 head lettuce, separated into large leaves
½ teaspoon ginger root, grated
Paprika to taste
Parsley sprigs for garnish

PREPARATION

1 In a large serving bowl, add all of the ingredients, and toss.

2 Cover the bowl, and chill in the refrigerator for 1 hour.

3 Arrange the salad on the lettuce leaves, sprinkle with paprika, and garnish with the parsley.

3 Add the dressing to the tofu mixture, and toss thoroughly.

4 Chill, covered, for at least 1 hour, and serve.

Curried Rice Salad with Tofu and Fruit

• • •

The sweetness of apples and raisins harmonizes deliciously with the kick of curry and other spicy ingredients in this rice salad.

• • •

Serves 6

INGREDIENTS

4 ounces firm tofu, diced
Brown rice, cooked to serve 6
1/3 cup scallions, minced
1 Red Delicious apple, unpeeled, cut into 1/2-inch pieces
1 cup golden raisins
2 celery ribs, finely chopped
5 radishes, chopped
1 1/2 tablespoons mustard
3 tablespoons cider vinegar
2 teaspoons curry powder
1/2 cup corn oil
1/2 cup Tofu Mayonnaise (see recipe on page 212)
2 teaspoons sugar
1/2 teaspoon salt

PREPARATION

1 In a large bowl, combine the tofu, rice, scallions, apple, raisins, celery, and radishes.

2 In a small bowl, combine the mustard, vinegar, curry powder, oil, Tofu Mayonnaise, sugar, and salt. Whisk until well-blended.

Pasta Salad with Dill

• • •

A favorite at potlucks, this flavorful pasta salad uses tofu to cut down on fat. You'll find, however, that it tastes as good as the salad you gobbled down as a kid.

• • •

Serves 4

INGREDIENTS

10 ounces silken tofu
2 tablespoons lemon juice
1/2 cup Tofu Mayonnaise (see recipe on page 212)
1 medium red onion, thinly sliced
4 plum tomatoes, diced
3/4 cup sweet pickles, diced
2 medium green bell peppers, diced
12 ounces ziti pasta, cooked al dente
1/4 cup fresh dill sprigs, chopped
Salt to taste
Pepper to taste

PREPARATION

1 In a food processor or blender, add the tofu, lemon juice, and Tofu Mayonnaise, and blend until smooth. Set aside.

2 In a serving bowl, place the onions, tomatoes, sweet pickles, and bell peppers, and toss.

3 Combine the pasta with the vegetables and the tofu dressing. Add the dill and toss gently but thoroughly. Season to taste with salt and pepper, and serve.

Tofu-Bell Pepper Salad over Asian Noodles

• • •

Serve this chilled salad by itself or accompanied by an Asian-style rice dish.

• • •

Serves 4

INGREDIENTS

8 ounces firm tofu, drained and diced
¾ cup all-purpose flour
2 tablespoons vegetable oil
¼ pound button mushrooms
8 ounces rice noodles, cooked
½ pound scallions, chopped
1 red bell pepper, sliced julienne
1 yellow bell pepper, sliced julienne

2 tablespoons soy sauce
¼ cup rice vinegar
2 teaspoons sesame oil
1 tablespoon olive oil
⅛ teaspoon hot pepper sauce

PREPARATION

1 Gently place the tofu, along with ½ cup of the flour, in a paper bag. Shake to coat the tofu completely. Set aside.

2 In a frying pan, sauté the mushrooms in vegetable oil for 2 to 3 minutes.

3 Add the cooked noodles, scallions, red bell pepper, yellow bell pepper, and tofu. Cook for 5 minutes, then remove from the heat.

4 In a bowl, combine the rest of the flour, soy sauce, rice vinegar, sesame oil, olive oil, and hot pepper sauce.

5 Pour the combination over the noodle mixture, and chill before serving.

Tofu-Bell Pepper Salad over Asian Noodles (see above)

Mock Chicken Salad with Curry

• • •

The sweetness of raisins complements the warm flavor of curry in this mouth-watering recipe. Wonderful in a sandwich or served by itself on a bed of lettuce, it's sure to become one of your favorites.

• • •

Serves 4 to 6

INGREDIENTS

16 ounces extra-firm tofu, diced
⅓ cup walnuts, finely chopped
⅔ cup golden raisins
2 teaspoons poultry seasoning
1 tablespoon lemon juice
½ cup plain, low-fat yogurt
¼ cup Tofu Mayonnaise (see recipe on page 212)
2 teaspoons curry powder
Salt to taste
Pepper to taste
4 to 6 pitas
Lettuce leaves

PREPARATION

1 In a large bowl, combine the tofu, walnuts, and raisins.

2 In a small bowl, combine the poultry seasoning, lemon juice, yogurt, Tofu Mayonnaise, curry powder, salt, and pepper. Stir this mixture into the tofu mixture.

3 Serve in pita pockets with lettuce.

Tofu-Bean Salad

• • •

We think this simple salad is a perfect accompaniment to any Latin-American meal. The subtle flavors of kidney beans and parsley combine with the richness of sliced olives to create a deliciously fresh dish.

• • •

Serves 4 to 6

INGREDIENTS

12 ounces extra-firm tofu, cubed
2 15-ounce cans kidney beans, drained and rinsed
1 4-ounce can sliced black olives, drained
½ cup fresh parsley sprigs, chopped
2½ tablespoons olive oil
1 tablespoon lemon juice
Salt to taste
Pepper to taste

PREPARATION

1 In a large bowl, combine all of the ingredients and mix well.

2 Chill, covered, in the refrigerator for at least 2 hours before serving.

Warm Vegetable Salad in Peanut-Chili Sauce

• • •

We realize that looking at these ingredients, you may be a little skeptical, but we assure you that once you taste the sweet undertones and the kick of the chili pepper, this veggie-packed salad will win you over.

• • •

Serves 4 to 6

INGREDIENTS

8 ounces firm tofu, chopped into bits
3½ tablespoons peanut butter
3 teaspoons fresh green chili, minced
1½ tablespoons sugar
1½ tablespoons soy sauce
⅓ cup water
¾ cup coconut cream
1 tablespoon grated lemon rind
1 tablespoon olive oil
1 garlic clove, minced
½ medium onion, chopped
¼ to ½ cup cashews
¾ to 1 pound mixed lettuce
Red cabbage, sliced very thin
Carrot, sliced long and thin
Button mushrooms
Asparagus, blanched
Green beans, blanched
Avocado
Snow peas
Bean sprouts

PREPARATION

1 In a saucepan, mix together the peanut butter, chili, sugar, 1 tablespoon of the soy sauce, water, coconut cream, and lemon rind. Bring to a boil, then simmer for a few minutes. Keep warm.

2 In a large frying pan, sauté the garlic and onion in oil. Add the tofu, and the rest of the soy sauce. Sauté until the tofu has browned.

3 Add the cashews, and sauté for 1 minute longer.

4 Add in the chili/peanut sauce, and mix well.

5 In a salad bowl, mix the salad ingredients together to suit your taste. Put some of the salad on each plate, and place the tofu sauce mixture on top. Serve warm.

Cole Slaw Salad

• • •

Great by itself, or as a side for sandwiches and meals, no summertime picnic is complete without this slaw.

• • •

Serves 4 to 6

INGREDIENTS

8 ounces soft tofu, drained and mashed
½ cup canola oil
Juice of 1 lemon
1 tablespoon honey
1 teaspoon salt
½ teaspoon black pepper
1 small green cabbage, thinly shredded
1 large carrot, peeled and shredded
4 scallions, chopped
¼ cup fresh parsley sprigs, chopped
1 small onion, finely chopped
½ cup raisins (optional)
1 teaspoon paprika

PREPARATION

1 In a blender, blend the tofu, oil, lemon, honey, salt, and pepper until very creamy and smooth.

2 In a large salad bowl, arrange the cabbage, carrot, scallions, parsley, onion, and raisins in layers.

3 Pour the tofu mixture over the salad, and toss. Sprinkle with the paprika.

4 Chill for 30 minutes before serving.

A-Taste-of-the-East Noodle Salad

• • •

The wondrous blend of spices and
seasonings in this colorful dish will
make it a sure-fire hit at your
next family gathering.

• • •

Serves 4

INGREDIENTS

12 ounces firm tofu, frozen, thawed, and cubed
1 tablespoon olive oil
5 tablespoons soy sauce
16 ounces linguine, cooked al dente
¼ cup fresh cilantro leaves, chopped
2 tablespoons fresh mint leaves, chopped
2 tablespoons fresh basil leaves, chopped
1 carrot, grated
1 radish, grated
1 red bell pepper, minced
1 bunch scallions, finely chopped
2 tablespoons ginger root, grated
1 garlic clove, minced
1 small serrano chili, minced
⅛ teaspoon red chili flakes, if desired
2 tablespoons toasted sesame seeds
1 teaspoon sesame oil
2 tablespoons peanut butter
1 tablespoon tamarind paste
1 teaspoon sugar
2 tablespoons roasted peanuts, chopped

PREPARATION

1 In a frying pan, sauté the tofu in oil for 3
to 4 minutes on each side. Pour 2 tablespoons of the soy sauce on just before
removing the tofu from the heat. Set aside.

2 In a large serving bowl, combine the linguine, cilantro, mint, basil, carrot, radish,
pepper, and scallions. Mix well.

3 In a food processor or blender, blend the
ginger, garlic, chili, chili flakes, sesame
seeds, sesame oil, peanut butter, tamarind,

sugar, and remaining soy sauce. Toss with
the linguine and vegetables.

4 Let the salad marinate for 30 minutes.
Garnish with the tofu and peanuts before
serving.

Spicy Vietnamese Salad with Pickled Ginger Dressing

• • •

The unripe, green papaya is the real star
of this unusual Asian salad. The ginger
dressing adds just the right hint
of sweetness and spice.

• • •

Serves 6

INGREDIENTS

12 ounces firm tofu, frozen, thawed, and cubed
1 teaspoon paprika
⅛ teaspoon black pepper
⅛ teaspoon white pepper
Pinch cayenne pepper
½ teaspoon powdered garlic
½ teaspoon dry thyme leaves
½ teaspoon ground cumin
½ teaspoon chili powder
½ teaspoon salt
1 teaspoon vegetarian Worcestershire sauce
1 tablespoon soy sauce
1 medium unripe green papaya, peeled, seeded,
   and grated
1 carrot, grated
2 scallions, finely chopped
¼ cup fresh cilantro leaves, coarsely chopped
2 tomatoes, chopped into ½-inch cubes
¼ cup chopped roasted peanuts

GINGER DRESSING

> ¼ cup pickled ginger
> 1 tablespoon peanut oil
> 1 teaspoon honey
> ½ teaspoon Thai chili paste
> 2 scallions, finely chopped
> 1 tablespoon water
> ¼ teaspoon salt

PREPARATION

1 In a large bowl, toss the tofu with the paprika, black pepper, white pepper, cayenne, garlic, thyme, cumin, chili powder, salt, Worcestershire sauce, and soy sauce.

2 Place the tofu cubes on an oiled cookie sheet, and bake at 400°F for 20 minutes. Let the cubes cool.

3 In a blender, combine the dressing ingredients, and blend well. Set aside.

4 In a medium-sized bowl, mix the papaya and carrot with the dressing. Toss well.

5 Place the salad on a platter, and top with the tofu. Sprinkle with the scallions, cilantro, tomatoes, and peanuts.

Tofu Waldorf Salad (see above)

Tofu Waldorf Salad

• • •

Here's a great way to sneak in a healthy dose of tofu. This salad is so sweet and delicious, you may even want to serve it as a dessert.

• • •

Serves 6

INGREDIENTS

> 16 ounces extra-firm tofu, diced
> 1 cup Tofu Mayonnaise (see recipe on page 212)
> 1 tablespoon honey
> 3 celery stalks, chopped
> ¼ cup dark raisins
> ¼ cup golden raisins
> 3 Red Delicious apples, cored and chopped
> 1 orange, peeled, sectioned, and cut into chunks
> ½ cup chopped walnuts

PREPARATION

1 In a blender, mix the Tofu Mayonnaise and honey until smooth.

2 Place the tofu and the rest of the ingredients in a salad bowl, mix well, and pour the mayonnaise dressing over them.

3 Toss gently, and chill for 1 hour before serving.

Greek Salad with "Insteada Feta"
(see opposite page)

Sweet Potato and Cucumber Salad

• • •

When a few common ingredients come together in a surprising way, the result is a dish that is uncommonly good!

• • •

Serves 2

INGREDIENTS

6 ounces firm tofu, mashed
1 sweet potato, cut into ¼-inch cubes
1 cucumber, cut into julienne sticks
3 Chinese cabbage or lettuce leaves, cut into thin strips
½ cup Caesar Dressing (see recipe on page 201)

PREPARATION

1 In a steamer insert, steam the potato cubes until tender.

2 In a salad bowl, combine the potato cubes with the rest of the ingredients. Toss lightly, and serve.

Greek Salad with "Insteada Feta"

• • •

We've made this salad favorite even healthier by substituting tofu for the feta. Top with garlicky croutons, and enjoy!

• • •

Serves 6

INGREDIENTS

16 ounces firm tofu, cubed
1 cup canned garbanzo beans, drained
½ cup black olives, pitted and sliced
½ cup parsley sprigs, chopped
½ medium red onion, peeled and sliced
2 large tomatoes, diced
1 small cucumber, seeded and diced

DRESSING

⅓ cup olive oil
2 tablespoons red wine vinegar
2 garlic cloves, minced
1 teaspoon Dijon mustard
2 teaspoons honey
1 tablespoon dried oregano
1 teaspoon cayenne pepper
½ teaspoon salt
¼ teaspoon white pepper

PREPARATION

1 Place the tofu, beans, olives, parsley, and vegetables in a salad bowl, and toss.

2 In a small mixing bowl, whisk together all the dressing ingredients, and pour over the salad. Toss lightly and serve.

Carrot and Raisin Salad

• • •

This salad-bar favorite tastes better than ever—and is even more healthy, thanks to the addition of tofu.

• • •

Serves 4

INGREDIENTS

8 ounces silken tofu
2 tablespoons lemon juice
2 tablespoons sugar
1 teaspoon salt
1 teaspoon ginger root, grated
1 tablespoon celery, finely chopped
1 pound carrots, grated or thinly sliced
¼ cup raisins
¼ cup chopped walnuts

PREPARATION

1 In a blender, add the tofu, lemon juice, sugar, salt, ginger, and celery, and blend until smooth.

2 In a salad bowl, combine the carrots, raisins, and walnuts.

3 Add the tofu combination to the bowl, mix well, and serve.

Avocado-Raisin Salad

• • •

Now, this is an attractive dish! The rich green of the broccoli and avocado slices contrasts with the red of the bell peppers and shredded cabbage. Throw in some raisins and sunflower seeds, and you've got a delicious and memorable salad.

• • •

Serves 4 to 6

INGREDIENTS

4 ounces soft tofu
Juice of ½ lemon
3 tablespoons safflower oil
½ teaspoon dried dill
½ teaspoon mustard powder
1 medium bunch broccoli, cut into bite-sized pieces
1 red bell pepper, cut into julienne strips
1 cup red cabbage, finely shredded
1 medium avocado, quartered and thinly sliced
½ cup raisins
¼ cup toasted sunflower seeds

PREPARATION

1 In a blender, blend the tofu until smooth and creamy.

2 In a small bowl, combine the tofu, lemon, oil, dill, and mustard. Stir well, and set aside.

3 In a steamer insert, steam the broccoli until crisp-tender. Place in a serving bowl along with the pepper, cabbage, avocado, raisins, and sunflower seeds. Mix well.

4 Add the dressing to the salad, and toss well. Serve immediately.

Oriental Slaw

• • •

Traditional cole slaw receives an Asian infusion with the inclusion of Napa cabbage and an assortment of fresh herbs.

• • •

Serves 4 to 6

INGREDIENTS

4 ounces soft tofu
1 garlic clove, minced
1-inch piece fresh ginger root, chopped
¼ cup fresh cilantro leaves, chopped
2 tablespoons fresh mint leaves, chopped
¼ small sweet onion, chopped
3 tablespoons rice vinegar
3 tablespoons sugar
2 tablespoons vegetable oil
⅛ to ¼ teaspoon dried red pepper flakes
½ pound Napa or green cabbage, shredded
¼ pound red cabbage, shredded
1 carrot, shredded
1 tablespoon toasted sesame seeds

PREPARATION

1 In a blender or food processor, combine the garlic, ginger root, cilantro, mint, and onion. Blend briefly.

2 Add the rice vinegar, sugar, oil, tofu, and red pepper flakes. Blend until smooth.

3 In a salad bowl, toss the contents of the blender along with the cabbage and carrot. Top with the sesame seeds, and serve.

Chilled Bell Pepper and Tofu Salad

• • •

If fresh bell peppers are your thing, try this easy salad recipe. It's divine served by itself as a colorful side, or as a quick sandwich filling for lunch.

• • •

Serves 4

INGREDIENTS

8 ounces firm tofu, cubed
1 tablespoon olive oil
3 red or green bell peppers, seeded and sliced in half-rings
½ teaspoon dried basil
1 garlic clove, minced
5 scallions, chopped
2 teaspoons soy sauce
¼ cup water
1 tablespoon vinegar

PREPARATION

1 In a saucepan, sauté the peppers, basil, and garlic in oil for 5 minutes.

2 Add the scallions, tofu, soy sauce, and water. Bring to a boil, lower the heat, and simmer for about 10 minutes, or until the water has evaporated.

3 Add the vinegar, and remove from the heat.

4 Refrigerate for at least 1 hour before serving. Serve chilled.

Thai Salad

• • •

The tofu absorbs all the wonderful flavors of this elegant and tasty salad.

• • •

Serves 4 to 6

INGREDIENTS

12 ounces firm tofu, drained and cubed
¼ cup soy sauce
Juice of 2 limes
2 tablespoons sugar
½ head of lettuce, cubed
1 large carrot, shredded
1 cucumber, peeled and cut into julienne strips
2 red cayenne peppers, sliced
¼ cup fresh basil leaves, chopped
¼ cup fresh mint leaves, chopped
4 scallions, chopped
¼ cup fresh cilantro leaves, chopped
¼ cup unsalted roasted peanuts, crushed

PREPARATION

1 In a large salad bowl, mix the tofu, soy sauce, lime juice, sugar, lettuce, carrot, cucumber, cayenne peppers, basil, mint, scallions, and cilantro. Toss gently but thoroughly.

2 Garnish with the peanuts before serving.

Lunch
AND
Dinner

Okay, so you've made a stir-fry or a sloppy joe with
tofu, and your creativity is zapped. Well,
fear not, because these recipes will cure
you forever of not knowing
what to do with tofu.

• • •

Curried Tofu Sandwich

• • •

This flavorful taste of India is a wonderfully simple lunch recipe you can whip up in minutes.

• • •

Serves 2

INGREDIENTS

12 ounces extra-firm tofu
2 to 3 tablespoons curry powder
1 tablespoon vegetable oil
3 tablespoons soy sauce
4 slices of your favorite bread, toasted
Dijon mustard to taste
Bean sprouts
Tomatoes, chopped
Carrots, shredded
Cucumbers, sliced
Lettuce

PREPARATION

1 Pour the curry powder onto a plate.

2 Cut the tofu along the long side, making two slices, and dip the tofu sides into the curry powder until completely covered.

3 In a frying pan, sauté the tofu slices in the oil for 2 to 3 minutes.

4 Flip the tofu slices, and pour the soy sauce onto the tofu (make sure the tofu doesn't burn).

5 Place each slice of tofu on a slice of toasted bread, and add the rest of the ingredients to the sandwich.

Sloppy Joes

• • •

The tofu perfectly captures the singular, all-American flavor of the classic sloppy joe. You'll never miss the meat!

• • •

Serves 6

INGREDIENTS

12 ounces firm tofu, crumbled
6-ounce can tomato paste
½ cup water
1 teaspoon oregano
¼ cup ketchup
1 tablespoon vinegar
¼ teaspoon cayenne pepper
3 tablespoons soy sauce
1 tablespoon olive oil
2 garlic cloves, minced
1 onion, chopped
1 green bell pepper, chopped
Salt to taste
6 large hard rolls, halved
Lettuce, shredded

PREPARATION

1 In a medium-sized bowl, mix the tomato paste, water, oregano, ketchup, vinegar, cayenne, and one tablespoon of the soy sauce. Set aside.

2 In a large frying pan, sauté the garlic, onion, and pepper in the oil until the onion is translucent.

3 Add the tofu and the rest of the soy sauce, and cook until the tofu browns.

4 Stir the sauce from the bowl into the vegetables and tofu. Bring the mixture to a boil, and add salt if desired.

5 Once the sauce is thick (add a little water if it is too thick), spoon onto the rolls, and garnish with the lettuce. Serve immediately.

3 Warm the pitas, then cut around the outer edge of each pita to separate it into two disks. Cut off the edges to make each disk into a square.

4 Spread ¼ of the tofu mixture on each square.

5 Press the pepper, carrot, and cucumber into the spreaded tofu.

6 Roll up each square, and cut into four or five sections.

Herbed Tofu Roll-Ups

• • •

Chock full of herbs and fresh vegetables, these succulent mini-sandwiches make an unusual and richly satisfying lunchtime meal.

• • •

Serves 8 to 10

INGREDIENTS

16 ounces firm tofu
2 tablespoons lemon juice
1 teaspoon mustard
2 tablespoons red wine vinegar
1 tablespoon vegetable oil
2 tablespoons fresh mint leaves, minced
2 tablespoons chives, minced
2 tablespoons fresh parsley sprigs, minced
⅓ cup olives, chopped
Pepper to taste
Salt to taste
2 large pitas
1 small red bell pepper, thinly sliced
½ carrot, thinly sliced or grated
⅓ cucumber, sliced lengthwise

PREPARATION

1 In a large mixing bowl, mash the tofu, and add the lemon juice, mustard, vinegar, and oil. Mix well.

2 Add the mint, chives, parsley, and olives. Season with pepper and salt, and set aside.

Tofu Falafel with Tahini Sauce

• • •

You will be surprised and thrilled by the rich flavor of this traditional Arabic fare. But beware—though these sandwiches are high in protein, they are also high in fat.

• • •

Serves 8 to 10

INGREDIENTS

16 ounces firm tofu, mashed
4 cups canned chickpeas, drained and rinsed
1 cup water
3 garlic cloves
⅓ cup soy sauce
1 teaspoon salt
¼ teaspoon black pepper
1 medium onion, finely chopped
6 cups bread crumbs
½ cup unbleached white flour
Vegetable oil, for frying
8 to 10 pitas
2 tomatoes, chopped
Lettuce, chopped

TAHINI SAUCE

3 garlic cloves, minced
½ cup tahini
¼ cup lemon juice
2 tablespoons soy sauce

PREPARATION

1 In a blender, mix the chickpeas, water, and garlic, until creamy.

2 Pour the resulting mixture into a large mixing bowl, and mix in the tofu, soy sauce, salt, pepper, onion, and bread crumbs, until all the ingredients are moist.

3 Form 1½-inch balls, and roll them in the flour.

4 In a large frying pan or deep fryer, heat ½ inch oil to 350°F. Fry the balls, turning each one until golden all around.

5 Meanwhile, in a blender, combine the sauce ingredients, and blend until smooth. Set aside.

6 Cut the pitas in half, and open the pockets carefully.

7 Place two to three balls in each pocket, and pour 1 tablespoon of the Tahini Sauce over the balls. Top with tomatoes and lettuce, and serve.

Tofu Barbecue Sandwich

• • •

This sandwich is perfect for the health-conscious vegetarian who still yearns for the hot, smoky taste of barbecued pork.

• • •

Serves 4

INGREDIENTS

12-ounce extra-firm tofu, drained
2½ tablespoons Dijon mustard
2½ tablespoons ketchup
2 tablespoons soy sauce
1 garlic clove, minced
2 teaspoons blackstrap molasses
2 teaspoons sesame oil
¼ teaspoon cayenne pepper or ground chipotles to taste
Pepper to taste
Whole wheat buns or bread of choice

PREPARATION

1 In a large, shallow mixing bowl, combine all the ingredients, except the tofu. Mix well, and set aside.

2 With the longer side facing you, cut the tofu block into nine slices, each just less than ½-inch thick.

3 Dip the tofu slices into the sauce, and place on a broiling pan.

4 Broil the tofu for 5 minutes, or until lightly browned.

5 Flip the slices, and coat the other side with the remaining sauce.

6 Broil for 5 more minutes, or until deeply browned.

7 Serve over buns with onions and tomatoes, if desired.

Recipe Tip

Use chipotles or chipotle paste, if you can find it, to give this recipe more of a smoky flavoring. Chipotles can be found whole or ground in gourmet shops and Hispanic groceries.

Thai Burgers with Peanut-Cilantro Sauce

• • •

Turn your grill into a Bangkok barbecue. There's a touch of Thailand in every bite of these delectable burgers, smothered in a pleasing, peanuty sauce.

• • •

Serves 6 to 8

INGREDIENTS

12 ounces firm tofu, drained
2 cups cooked black beans, drained
¾ cup quick-cooking oats, uncooked
½ cup red onions, finely chopped
½ cup carrots, grated
1 teaspoon ginger root, grated
2 teaspoons soy sauce
2 teaspoons brown sugar, packed
2 garlic cloves, minced
1 to 2 teaspoons red pepper flakes, to taste
Vegetable oil, for brushing
Flour for dusting
1 cucumber, peeled and sliced

PEANUT CILANTRO SAUCE

3 tablespoons crunchy peanut butter
3 tablespoons lemon juice
¼ cup fresh cilantro leaves, minced

PREPARATION

1 In a large mixing bowl, mash the tofu.

2 Add the beans, oats, onions, carrots, ginger, soy sauce, sugar, garlic, and pepper flakes. Mix well, then mash until the mixture reaches a uniform consistency and holds together.

3 Form the mixture into six to eight patties.

4 Brush both sides of the patties with oil, and dust with flour.

5 Prepare the grill by brushing the rack with oil. Cook the patties for 4 minutes on each side.

6 Meanwhile, prepare the sauce by blending the peanut butter and lemon juice in a small bowl. Mix in the cilantro.

7 Serve the patties on toasted buns, and top with the Peanut Cilantro Sauce and cucumber slices.

Mock Egg Salad Sandwich

• • •

You don't have to worry about your diet with this terrific tofu translation of an egg salad sandwich. This culinary treat tastes better than the real thing.

• • •

Serves 4

INGREDIENTS

16 ounces firm tofu, drained and crumbled
1 large celery stalk, finely diced
1 scallion, finely chopped
4 tablespoons Tofu Mayonnaise (see recipe on page 212)
1 to 2 teaspoons Dijon mustard, to taste
1 teaspoon curry powder
½ teaspoon turmeric
¼ teaspoon cumin
Salt to taste
Pepper to taste
Bread of your choice
Alfalfa sprouts or shredded lettuce

PREPARATION

1 In a large bowl, combine the tofu, celery, and scallion. Mix well.

2 In a smaller bowl, combine the Tofu Mayonnaise, mustard, curry powder, turmeric, and cumin, and mix well.

3 Pour the contents of the smaller bowl into the tofu mixture, and stir well. Season with salt and pepper.

4 Top the bread of your choice with the Mock Egg Salad along with the sprouts or shredded lettuce.

7 Bake at 350°F for 15 minutes, then flip the patties, and bake for 10 minutes longer.

8 Serve the burgers on buns with your favorite toppings, and a generous helping of Hot and Sweet Dragon Sauce.

"Tastes Just Like Chicken" Burgers

• • •

These patties taste super slathered with tangy Hot and Sweet Dragon Sauce.

• • •

Serves 4

INGREDIENTS

8 ounces firm tofu, pressed
½ cup scallions, minced
1½ tablespoons olive oil
2 cups green cabbage, finely grated
1 cup carrots, grated
½ cup whole wheat flour
1½ tablespoons soy sauce
2 teaspoons baking powder
½ teaspoon poultry seasoning
Hot and Sweet Dragon Sauce (see recipe on page 203)

PREPARATION

1 In a frying pan, sauté the scallions in oil for 2 minutes.

2 Add the cabbage and carrots, and sauté for 5 minutes, or until soft. Set aside.

3 In a blender, mix the tofu until creamy.

4 Add the flour, soy sauce, baking powder, and poultry seasoning. Process until smooth.

5 Add the sautéed vegetables to the blender, and blend until the vegetables are slightly chopped.

6 Spoon ⅓ of a cup of the mixture onto an oiled baking sheet. Flatten the dollops into neat patties.

Tofu-Spinach Burgers

• • •

Tasty, nutritious, quick, and easy, these burgers are a lifesaver for those super-busy days when you don't even have time to think, let alone cook dinner for the family.

• • •

Serves 6

INGREDIENTS

12 ounces firm tofu, crumbled
10-ounce package chopped frozen spinach, thawed and squeezed
1½ cups crushed crackers (water crackers, matzoh, or soda crackers)
¼ medium onion, chopped
2 scallions, sliced
4 garlic cloves, minced
1 tablespoon dried tarragon
1 teaspoon dried sage
1 teaspoon dried thyme
½ teaspoon salt
½ teaspoon pepper
3 ounces Cheddar cheese, shredded (optional)

PREPARATION

1 In a blender or food processor, combine all the ingredients except the cheese, and process until the mixture reaches a uniform consistency and holds together.

2 Form into six patties, and broil for 5 minutes on each side, until slightly brown. Top with cheese, if desired.

Mushroom-Tofu Burger

• • •

If you're just wild about mushrooms, you'll want to make these enticing burgers a household staple.

• • •

Serves 8

INGREDIENTS

12 ounces firm tofu, mashed
1 medium yellow onion, finely chopped
2 scallions, peeled and minced
⅛ teaspoon salt
Vegetable oil for frying
1 cup dry shiitake mushrooms, soaked in very hot water until soft
2 cups Portobello mushrooms, stemmed and chopped
⅓ cup toasted wheat germ
⅓ cup bread crumbs
4 tablespoons soy sauce
1 teaspoon liquid smoke flavoring
1 teaspoon garlic powder
¾ cup quick-cooking oats

PREPARATION

1 In a frying pan, sauté the onions, scallions, and salt in oil for 5 minutes.

2 Stem the softened shiitake mushrooms, add to a food processor with the Portobello mushrooms, and mince.

3 Add the minced mushrooms to the frying pan, and cook for 10 minutes, stirring occasionally.

4 In a large bowl, mix the onions and mushrooms with the mashed tofu. Add the remaining ingredients, and mix well.

5 Measure out eight ½-cup portions, and form into patties.

6 Place the patties on an oiled baking sheet, and bake at 375°F for 25 minutes, flipping once after 15 minutes.

7 After baking, grill each patty in an oiled frying pan for a few minutes on each side. Serve with your favorite toppings.

Spicy Orange Teriyaki Cutlets

• • •

Marinating tofu is a simple and tasty way of adding tofu, infused with distinctive flavors, to your diet. We've selected one basic marinade recipe here, and added three variations. Also, check out the marinades for our shish kebobs (pages 178-179). Marinate the tofu for at least 1 hour. For more intense flavor, marinate the tofu in the refrigerator overnight.

• • •

Serves 6

INGREDIENTS

24 ounces extra-firm tofu, frozen, thawed, and sliced into cutlets
½ cup soy sauce
½ cup brown sugar
2 teaspoons soybean oil
2 garlic cloves, minced
1 teaspoon ginger root, minced
2 tablespoons brown rice vinegar
¼ cup orange juice
¼ teaspoon dry sherry
Pepper to taste
8-ounce can sliced water chestnuts

PREPARATION

1 In a large bowl, combine the soy sauce, brown sugar, oil, garlic, ginger, vinegar, orange juice, sherry, and pepper. Mix well.

2 Pour half of the marinade into the bottom of a 9 by 13-inch glass baking dish.

3 Place the tofu slices in the marinade. Cover the tofu with the remaining marinade, and marinate for at least 1 hour.

4 In a frying pan, sauté the tofu and water chestnuts in a couple of tablespoons of the remaining marinade until the tofu is browned on both sides. Serve warm.

Spicy Peanut Marinade

INGREDIENTS

2 teaspoons toasted sesame oil
1 tablespoon onion, grated
1 garlic clove, minced
2 teaspoons chili powder
1 cup unsweetened peanut butter
Soy sauce, to taste
1 tablespoon brown rice syrup
Juice of 1 lemon
Water

Note: Bring the ingredients to a boil, reduce heat, and simmer, uncovered, for 10 minutes. Place the tofu pieces in a shallow dish and spoon the hot marinade over them, covering them completely. Allow the tofu to marinate at least 1 hour.

Moroccan Marinade

INGREDIENTS

½ cup soy sauce
3 tablespoons lemon juice
3 tablespoons molasses
1 teaspoon cumin powder
1 teaspoon coriander powder
1 teaspoon pepper
1 teaspoon cinnamon
3 tablespoons sesame oil
1½ teaspoons jerk seasoning
1 generous pinch saffron

Note: Mix the ingredients in a blender until smooth. Marinate the tofu in the liquid for at least 1 hour before sautéing.

Lemon-Ginger Marinade

INGREDIENTS

2 tablespoons soy sauce
1 teaspoon toasted sesame oil
2 tablespoons fresh lemon juice
1 tablespoon ginger root, minced

Fishless Filet of Tofu with Mustard-Dill Sauce

• • •

There's nothing fishy about this quick and easy entrée. This sauce, traditionally used with salmon, works just as well with tofu.

• • •

Serves 4

INGREDIENTS

16 ounces extra-firm tofu, cut into ¼-inch thick slices
¼ cup mustard
1 teaspoon mustard powder
1 tablespoon honey
2 tablespoons white wine vinegar
2 tablespoons mayonnaise or Tofu Mayonnaise (see recipe on page 212)
1 tablespoon dried dill
1 tablespoon canola oil
4 plum tomatoes, sliced
Fresh parsley sprigs

PREPARATION

1 In a small bowl, combine the mustard, dry mustard, honey, vinegar, mayonnaise, and dill. Mix well, and set aside.

2 In a frying pan, sauté the tofu slices in the oil until golden on both sides.

→

3 Drain the tofu on paper towels, and arrange the slices in rows on a serving plate.

4 Spoon the mustard-dill dressing over the tofu slices.

5 Garnish with the tomatoes.

Blackened Tofu

• • •

You can serve these super-spicy tofu slices with rice, or as a sandwich filling topped with a favorite sauce.

• • •

Serves 4

INGREDIENTS

24 ounces firm tofu, pressed and cut into ½-inch thick slices
1 teaspoon salt
1 tablespoon sweet paprika
1 teaspoon onion powder
1 teaspoon garlic powder
1 teaspoon cayenne pepper to taste
¾ teaspoon white pepper
¼ teaspoon black pepper
½ teaspoon dried thyme
½ teaspoon dried oregano
6 to 8 tablespoons butter, melted

PREPARATION

1 In a bowl, combine the salt, paprika, onion powder, garlic powder, cayenne, white pepper, black pepper, dried thyme, and dried oregano. Mix well.

2 Brush each piece of tofu with the melted butter, then dredge each slice with the spice mixture, patting it firmly into the tofu.

3 Pour a teaspoon of melted butter onto each slice of tofu, then place it, butter side down, in a hot frying pan. Stand back, and fry for 2 minutes. Then turn each slice over, and fry for 2 minutes longer.

4 Keep the tofu slices in a warm oven until they are all ready to serve.

Tofu Cutlets with Piquant Sauce

• • •

Sun-dried tomatoes step in for the anchovies in this Provencal-inspired tapenade sauce.

• • •

Serves 4

INGREDIENTS

16 ounces firm tofu, cut into 8 ½-inch slices
2 tablespoons capers
6 oil-cured black olives, pitted
3 oil-packed sun-dried tomatoes, cut into pieces
¼ cup fresh parsley sprigs
2 tablespoons fresh lemon juice
¼ cup plus 2 tablespoons olive oil

PREPARATION

1 In a blender or food processor, blend the capers, olives, tomatoes, parsley, and lemon juice until the mixture is chopped fine.

2 While processing, add the ¼ cup olive oil in a stream, and blend the sauce until emulsified.

3 Meanwhile, in a frying pan, sauté the tofu in the remaining 2 tablespoons of olive oil until golden brown.

4 Serve the tofu topped with the sauce.

Tofu Steak

• • •

Smothered in a delicious pepper and tomato sauce, this tofu recipe creates a sumptuous, meatless meal, rich enough to call "steak."

• • •

Serves 4

INGREDIENTS

12 ounces extra-firm tofu, frozen and thawed
½ cup all-purpose flour
½ teaspoon salt
⅛ teaspoon pepper
¼ teaspoon paprika
¼ teaspoon dried thyme
2 tablespoons olive oil
1½ tablespoons soy sauce
1 small onion, sliced
1 garlic clove, minced
½ teaspoon salt
1½ cups red and green bell peppers, thinly sliced
1½ cups canned chopped tomatoes
½ cup water
2 teaspoons vegetable broth powder
Brown or white rice, cooked to serve 4

PREPARATION

1 In a paper bag, mix the flour, salt, pepper, paprika, and thyme. Shake well to mix.

2 Slice the tofu into 1½-inch strips, and place in the paper bag. Shake gently to coat the tofu.

3 In a frying pan, cook the tofu strips in 1 tablespoon of the olive oil. When the tofu strips are evenly browned, sprinkle with the soy sauce. Remove the pieces and set aside.

4 In a frying pan, sauté the onions, garlic, and salt in the remaining olive oil until the onions are translucent.

5 Add the peppers, and cook for 5 minutes longer.

6 Add the tomatoes, water, and broth powder. Simmer for 10 minutes.

7 Add the tofu, heat through, and serve with rice.

Goat Cheese and Tofu Filos

• • •

Mild, creamy, and sweet, this pastry dish has a distinctive flavor dinner guests will relish.

• • •

Serves 6

INGREDIENTS

16 ounces firm tofu, crumbled
8½ tablespoons olive oil
1 cup red onion, sliced
6 garlic cloves, finely chopped
¾ cup button mushrooms, sliced
¼ cup dry white wine
2 pounds of spinach, washed and stemmed
1 tablespoon fresh parsley sprigs, chopped
1 tablespoon fresh marjoram sprigs, chopped
Salt to taste
Pepper to taste
2 eggs, beaten
1 ounce Parmesan cheese, grated
16 frozen filo pastry sheets, thawed
⅓ cup pine nuts, toasted and coarsely chopped
2 cups goat cheese, crumbled

PREPARATION

1 In a large frying pan, sauté the onion in 1 tablespoon of oil until it begins to soften.

2 Add half the garlic, and cook for 3 to 4 minutes. Remove from the heat, and transfer to a bowl.

➡

3 Using the same frying pan, sauté the mushrooms in 1 tablespoon of oil until they are golden brown.

4 Add the remaining garlic, and sauté for 1 minute longer.

5 Add the wine, and cook until the pan is nearly dry. Add the mixture to the sautéd onions in the bowl.

6 Using the same frying pan, sauté the spinach in 1 tablespoon of oil until wilted. Let the wilted spinach cool, then squeeze the moisture out of the spinach until it is moist but not wet. Coarsely chop the spinach, and add it to the onions and mushrooms, along with the herbs. Season with salt and pepper to taste.

7 In another bowl, place the tofu, eggs, and Parmesan cheese. Mix thoroughly.

8 Unfold the filo dough onto a counter, and cover with a damp towel to keep the dough from becoming dry and brittle.

9 In an oiled 9 by 13-inch baking dish, lay down a sheet of filo, brush it lightly with some of the reserved oil, and sprinkle it with some of the nuts. Continue layering this way with seven more sheets of filo, using half the chopped nuts.

10 Spread the tofu mixture on the filo, followed by the vegetables. Sprinkle the goat cheese over the vegetables. Layer on eight more sheets of filo, lightly brushing each with oil, and sprinkling with the rest of the nuts.

11 Brush the top layer thoroughly with the remaining oil.

12 Refrigerate the filo for 10 minutes to chill the top layer. Cut the filo into six squares, and cut each square into two triangles.

13 Bake at 375°F for 35 to 40 minutes until golden.

Baked Tofu with Basil-Mint Sauce

...

Cooking this meal will fill the kitchen with the pleasantly sharp aromas of the basil and mint—a real summertime treat.

...

Serves 6

INGREDIENTS

16 ounces firm tofu, cut into ¼-inch slices
2 large garlic cloves
¼ teaspoon salt, plus extra to taste
2 cups fresh basil leaves, plus extra for garnish
¼ cup fresh mint leaves
½ cup plus 2 tablespoons olive oil
¼ cup Romano cheese, grated
¼ cup Jarlsberg cheese, shredded
2 medium scallions, chopped
Pepper to taste
½ teaspoon ground allspice
¼ cup vegetable stock (see recipe on page 81)
2 large tomatoes, seeded and diced

PREPARATION

1 In a blender or food processor, mince the garlic and ¼ teaspoon of the salt to a paste. Add the basil and mint, and coarsely chop.

2 With the blender or processor running, slowly add ½ cup of the oil. Then mix in the cheeses.

3 Meanwhile, in a large frying pan, sauté the scallions in 2 tablespoons of the oil for 3 minutes. Add the tofu slices, and sprinkle with salt, pepper, and allspice.

4 Cook the tofu for 2 minutes on each side.

5 Transfer the tofu to a glass baking dish.

6 Add the vegetable stock to the basil-mint mixture, and blend briefly. Drizzle the mixture over the tofu, and top with the tomatoes.

7 Bake at 400°F for 15 minutes, and garnish with the basil leaves. Serve immediately.

Baked Tofu with Basil-Mint Sauce (see opposite page)

Fried Tofu in Mushroom Sauce

•••

Serve these toasty and tasty fried
tofu slices with pasta.

•••

Serves 4

INGREDIENTS

12 ounces firm tofu, cut into ½-inch slices
1 egg
1 tablespoon whole wheat flour
1 teaspoon water
¼ teaspoon salt
3 tablespoons vegetable oil
¼ pound button mushrooms, sliced
2 teaspoons miso, dissolved in 1 cup water
4 teaspoons soy sauce
4 tablespoons cornstarch or arrowroot,
   dissolved in ¼ cup water

PREPARATION

1 In a bowl, blend the egg, flour, water, and
salt until smooth.

2 Dip the tofu in the resulting batter. In a
frying pan, sauté the slices in 1½ tablespoons of oil until golden on both sides.
Set aside.

3 In a saucepan, sauté the mushrooms in the
rest of the oil until tender.

4 Add the miso mixture to the mushrooms,
and bring to a boil.

5 Add the soy sauce and cornstarch to the
mushroom mixture, lower the heat, and
stir until the sauce thickens.

6 Add the tofu to the sauce, and simmer for
2 minutes before serving.

Stuffed Eggplant

•••

Versatile and nutritious, the eggplant is
one of the most pleasurable vegetables
to work with. The filling for this recipe
complements the eggplant perfectly.

•••

Serves 4

INGREDIENTS

8 ounces firm tofu, drained and mashed
2 cups water
1 large eggplant
2 tablespoons olive oil
1 small yellow onion, chopped
2 garlic cloves, crushed
1 cup mushrooms, chopped
1 teaspoon salt
½ teaspoon black pepper
¼ cup fresh parsley sprigs chopped
1 tablespoon lemon juice
¼ cup bread crumbs
¼ cup Parmesan cheese, grated
1 teaspoon paprika

PREPARATION

1 In a deep saucepan, bring the water to a
boil. Cook the eggplant in the boiling water
for 3 minutes.

2 Drain, and cut the eggplant in half lengthwise. Remove the eggplant pulp down to
½ inch. Chop the pulp, and set aside.

3 In a frying pan, sauté the onion and garlic
in oil until golden.

4 Add the chopped eggplant pulp, mushrooms, tofu, salt, pepper, parsley, lemon
juice, and bread crumbs. Stir well, and
cook for 3 to 5 minutes.

5 Stuff the eggplant shells with the mixture,
and place them in an oiled 9 by 13-inch
baking dish. Sprinkle with the Parmesan
cheese and paprika.

6 Bake the eggplant, uncovered, at 350°F for
30 minutes, or until the top is golden.

Jammin' Jambalaya with Tofu

• • •

The next time you're craving some down-home Cajun cooking, try this Louisiana favorite.

• • •

Serves 4 to 6

INGREDIENTS

12 ounces firm tofu, frozen, thawed, and diced
2 tablespoons olive oil
1 green bell pepper, seeded and diced
1 onion, diced
1 tomato, diced
8 button mushrooms, sliced
1 cup eggplant, diced
1 cup zucchini, diced
½ cup celery, diced
2 garlic cloves, minced
1½ cups canned crushed tomatoes
¾ cup vegetable stock (see recipe on page 81)
½ cup okra, chopped
10 broccoli florets
1 tablespoon dry red wine
1 tablespoon dried oregano
1 tablespoon fresh parsley sprigs, minced
2 teaspoons fresh thyme leaves
1 to 2 teaspoons hot pepper sauce
½ teaspoon black pepper
¼ teaspoon white pepper
¼ teaspoon salt
⅛ teaspoon cayenne pepper
4 cups brown rice, cooked
½ cup scallions, chopped

PREPARATION

1 In a large saucepan, sauté the pepper, onion, tomato, mushrooms, eggplant, zucchini, celery, and garlic in oil for 10 minutes, or until the vegetables are tender yet crisp.

2 Lower the heat, and stir in the remaining ingredients, except for the rice.

3 Simmer, uncovered, for 20 minutes, stirring frequently.

4 Serve over the rice, and garnish with the scallions.

Stuffed Peppers with Tofu, Fruit, and Nuts

• • •

This pleasant pepper plate contains a lot less fat than the beef-stuffed version, and tastes great.

• • •

Serves 4

INGREDIENTS

4 ounces firm tofu, diced
4 green bell peppers
1 cup brown rice, uncooked
2 cups water
¼ cup port wine
½ cup dried cranberries or currants
¼ to ½ cup chopped nuts (pine nuts, walnuts or almonds)
3 to 5 tablespoons Parmesan cheese, grated
1 teaspoon salt
1 teaspoon black pepper

PREPARATION

1 Cut off the tops of the peppers, and remove the seeds and membranes.

2 In a steamer insert, steam the peppers until barely tender, about 5 minutes. Set aside to cool.

3 In a saucepan, combine the rice and water. Cover, bring to a boil, then lower the heat, and simmer for 45 minutes, or until the rice is tender.

4 Meanwhile, in a small frying pan, heat the wine to a simmer over medium-low heat, and add the tofu. Simmer until the wine is absorbed or evaporated.

5 In a mixing bowl, stir together the hot rice, dried fruit, nuts, Parmesan cheese, salt, pepper, and tofu.

6 Stuff the peppers, and bake at 350°F for 15 minutes, or until the filling is hot and the peppers are tender.

PREPARATION

1 In a covered soup pot on high heat, cook the onions in the water, stirring frequently, for 5 minutes.

2 Add the celery, and continue to cook, covered, stirring frequently, for 5 minutes. Add more water if the vegetables begin to stick.

3 Add the mushrooms, lower the heat, and cook for 5 minutes, or until the mushrooms begin to release their juices.

4 Stir in the bay leaves, ginger, and tomatoes, and cook for 5 minutes.

5 Stir in the tahini or peanut butter, add the tofu, and simmer on very low heat for 6 to 8 minutes longer.

6 Add the soy sauce, discard the bay leaves, and serve over noodles or rice.

Mushroom and Tofu Stew

• • •

This potpourri of tastes is fiber- and protein-packed. Serve over noodles or rice.

• • •

Serves 4 to 6

INGREDIENTS

12 ounces firm tofu, pressed and diced
4 cups onions, chopped
½ cup water
3 cups celery, sliced
4 cups button mushrooms, sliced
2 bay leaves
1 tablespoon ginger root, grated
2 cups undrained canned whole tomatoes, chopped
2 tablespoons tahini or peanut butter
Soy sauce to taste
Rice or noodles, cooked to serve 4 to 6

Stuffed Tofu

• • •

If you want to try your hand at stuffing tofu, this is where you should start. Even if your tofu wedges don't entirely hold together, your dinner mates will be too impressed by the flavor to notice.

• • •

Serves 4

INGREDIENTS

• 2 12-ounce blocks firm tofu, pressed

FILLING

5 dried shiitake mushrooms
1 cup hot water
¼ cup toasted walnuts, chopped
1½ teaspoons ginger root, grated
1½ tablespoons scallions, chopped
1½ tablespoons green bell pepper, finely chopped
1 teaspoon molasses
Pinch of five-spice powder
Salt to taste
Cayenne pepper to taste

SAUCE

- ¼ cup soy sauce
- ¼ cup rice wine or dry sherry
- 1 cup reserved mushroom water (from step 1)
- 1 tablespoon peanut oil
- 1½ teaspoons ginger root, grated
- 1½ teaspoons cornstarch
- ½ cup water
- ¼ teaspoon hot chili paste (optional)

PREPARATION

1 In a bowl, soak the mushrooms in the hot water for 20 minutes. Drain, save the water, and squeeze any excess water from the mushrooms.

2 Trim off the stems, and chop the caps into ¼-inch pieces.

3 In a bowl, combine the mushrooms with the remaining filling ingredients, saving half of the ginger.

4 Cut each block of tofu in half so you have four square slices. Then slice each square diagonally to make eight triangles.

5 Cut a slit in the tofu along the long diagonal side. Spoon about ⅛ of the mushroom filling into each wedge.

6 Meanwhile, in a bowl, prepare the sauce by mixing together the soy sauce, rice wine, and reserved mushroom liquid.

7 In a saucepan, sauté the reserved ginger in oil for 30 seconds, then pour the sauce into the pan.

8 Carefully add the stuffed tofu, and heat to a simmer. Simmer for 20 minutes, turning the tofu once. Remove the tofu to a platter.

9 In a bowl, mix the cornstarch with the water. Then whisk the mixture into the simmering sauce. Add chili paste if desired.

10 Remove the sauce from the heat as soon as it thickens. Pour the hot sauce over the stuffed tofu, and serve immediately.

Tofu Moussaka

• • •

Even if you've never tried the traditional meat version of this baked Greek dish, you'll have a hard time believing anything could taste any better than this.

• • •

Serves 6

INGREDIENTS

- 16 ounces firm tofu
- 2 medium eggplants
- 2 tablespoons canola oil
- 2 large onions, chopped
- 2 garlic cloves, minced
- 1 medium carrot, diced
- 1 celery stalk, diced
- 3 tablespoons tomato paste
- 1 cup dry red wine
- 1 teaspoon dried basil
- ¼ teaspoon cinnamon
- 1 cup cottage cheese
- 2 tablespoons lemon juice
- 1 egg
- 8 tablespoons Parmesan cheese
- ¼ teaspoon nutmeg
- ½ teaspoon salt
- 1 cup whole wheat bread crumbs
- ½ cup fresh parsley sprigs, chopped
- 3 to 4 plum tomatoes, thinly sliced

PREPARATION

1 Cut the eggplants diagonally into ⅓-inch thick slices, and brush lightly with 1 tablespoon of the oil (use more if necessary).

2 On an oiled baking sheet, broil the eggplant slices for 3 minutes on each side, or until lightly browned.

3 In a saucepan, sauté the onion in the rest of the oil until tender. Add the garlic, carrot, and celery. Sauté for 10 minutes, stirring often, until the onion is golden brown.

4 Stir in the tomato paste. Stir the mixture over high heat for 2 minutes.

➡

5 Add the wine, basil, and cinnamon. Cover and simmer for 2 minutes.

6 In a food processor, combine the tofu, cottage cheese, lemon juice, egg, 4 tablespoons of the Parmesan cheese, nutmeg, and salt. Process until smooth. Set aside.

7 Sprinkle some of the bread crumbs to cover the bottom of an oiled 9 by 11-inch baking dish. Add a layer of eggplant slices. Spoon half the vegetable mixture on top of the eggplant, and spread evenly. Sprinkle with more bread crumbs and 2 tablespoons of Parmesan.

8 Repeat layers, using the rest of the eggplant, vegetable mixture, bread crumbs, and cheese. Sprinkle with parsley, and add the tomato slices in a layer, overlapping to cover.

9 Top with the tofu mixture, and sprinkle lightly with additional nutmeg.

10 Bake at 375°F for 1 hour. Allow to cool before serving.

Spanish Paella

• • •

Paella is a well-known Spanish meal, made with chicken, sausage, shellfish, and vegetables. Experiment with different kinds of packaged seasoned tofu, which are becoming more readily available as tofu gains popularity.

• • •

Serves 6

INGREDIENTS

12 ounces smoked tofu, cubed
¼ cup vegetable oil
2 tablespoons olive oil
3 tablespoons garlic cloves, minced
1 red bell pepper, diced
1 large onion, diced
1 large carrot, diced
1 teaspoon dried paprika
½ teaspoon fennel seeds (optional)
1 teaspoon ground cumin
½ teaspoon salt
½ teaspoon black pepper
¼ teaspoon cayenne pepper (optional)
¼ teaspoon crushed saffron
2 cups uncooked basmati or other white rice
3½ cups boiling water
2 bay leaves
1 cup fresh or frozen peas
1 cup fresh or frozen corn
12 cherry tomatoes, quartered
Fresh parsley sprigs, chopped, for garnish
Fresh cilantro leaves, chopped, for garnish
Black olives, sliced, for garnish

PREPARATION

1 In a large frying pan, fry the tofu in vegetable oil until golden brown.

2 Remove the tofu from the pan, drain on a paper towel, and set aside.

3 In a saucepan, heat 1 tablespoon of olive oil over medium-high heat, and add 1 tablespoon of garlic. Cook, stirring, until golden.

4 Add the bell pepper, and cook for another 2 minutes. Remove from the saucepan, and set aside.

5 Add the remaining olive oil and garlic to the saucepan, along with the onion and carrot. Cook, stirring, for 2 minutes.

6 Add the paprika, fennel, cumin, salt, black pepper, cayenne, and saffron. Stir for 1 minute.

9 Mix in the rice, boiling water, bay leaves, and tofu. Stir well.

10 Cover, lower the heat, and simmer for 15 minutes.

11 When the liquid has been absorbed, remove from the heat. Add the peppers, peas, and corn to the top of the rice.

12 Replace the cover, and let the paella sit for 5 minutes. Remove the cover, and fluff the paella with a fork. Remove and discard the bay leaves.

13 Serve and garnish with tomatoes, parsley, cilantro, and/or olives.

To-Foo Yung

• • •

Here's another delicious classic, updated to include the nutritional benefits of tofu.

• • •

Serves 6

INGREDIENTS

32 ounces firm tofu
2 tablespoons sesame oil
1 cup snow peas, cut into 1-inch pieces
1 cup button mushrooms, sliced
8 scallions, cut into 1½-inch pieces
8-ounce can water chestnuts, sliced
2 cups fresh bean sprouts
2 tablespoons soy sauce
¾ cup unbleached white flour
2 teaspoons baking powder
Rice or noodles, cooked to serve
Mushroom Gravy (recipe follows)

MUSHROOM GRAVY

2 cups cold water
4 tablespoons soy sauce
1 teaspoon sesame oil
2 tablespoons cornstarch
½ cup mushrooms, diced small

PREPARATION

1 In a large frying pan or wok, sauté the snow peas, mushrooms, scallions, and water chestnuts in oil over low heat for about 5 minutes.

2 When the vegetables are tender, mix in the bean sprouts.

3 Remove from the heat and set aside.

4 In a blender, blend all but 4 ounces of the tofu and the soy sauce until smooth and creamy.

5 Pour the tofu mixture into a large bowl, and mix in the rest of the tofu (mashed), the flour, and the baking powder.

6 Add the vegetables and mix well.

7 On an oiled baking sheet, make six to eight 5-inch rounds (about ½ inch in thickness).

8 Bake at 325°F or 30 minutes. Flip the patties, and bake 15 minutes longer.

9 To prepare the gravy, mix all of the ingredients in a saucepan, and cook over low heat until thickened. Keep warm until ready to serve.

10 Serve hot over rice or noodles with the Mushroom Gravy.

Southern Fried Tofu with Tofu-Enhanced Mashed Potatoes

• • •

Looking for some homemade country cooking without all the fat? Read on. Serve with cornbread and coleslaw for a complete Southern meal.

• • •

Serves 6

INGREDIENTS

24 ounces firm tofu, frozen, thawed, and cubed
½ cup unbleached flour
½ teaspoon salt
⅛ teaspoon pepper
¼ teaspoon dried paprika
¼ teaspoon dried thyme
2 teaspoons canola oil
1 small yellow onion, chopped
1 celery stalk, sliced
1 carrot, peeled and sliced
1 garlic clove, minced
2 cups water
½ teaspoon salt
⅓ cup cold water
1 tablespoon soy sauce
1 tablespoon vegetable broth powder
3 tablespoons quick-cooking flour

TOFU-ENHANCED MASHED POTATOES

8 ounces soft tofu
8 cups potatoes, peeled and quartered
Water for boiling
½ cup potato cooking water
1 teaspoon salt
¼ teaspoon black pepper
1 tablespoon olive oil

PREPARATION

1 For the mashed potatoes, place the potatoes in a large pot, and cover with water. Bring the water to a boil, and cook, covered, for 30 minutes, or until the potatoes are very soft.

2 Drain well, and reserve ½ cup of the water.

3 In a blender, purée the soft tofu until creamy and smooth.

4 In a large mixing bowl, mash the potatoes, and add the tofu, ½ cup of the potato cooking water, salt, pepper, and olive oil. Keep warm or covered until served.

5 For the fried tofu, mix the unbleached flour, salt, pepper, paprika, and thyme in a small bowl.

6 Place the mixture in a paper bag with the tofu cubes, and shake to coat the tofu.

7 Remove the tofu carefully from the bag. In a frying pan, sauté the tofu in 1 teaspoon of canola oil until browned.

8 Remove the tofu from the pan, and set aside.

9 In a saucepan, sauté the onion in the remaining teaspoon of canola oil until golden. Add the celery, carrot, garlic, water, and salt. Bring to a boil, reduce heat, and simmer for 10 minutes.

10 In a small bowl, mix the cold water, soy sauce, broth powder, and quick-cooking flour. Whisk it into the mixture, and let it simmer for another 2 to 3 minutes, stirring constantly.

11 Add the tofu cubes, and heat through. Serve with the mashed potatoes.

Baked Tofu with Tri-Colored Peppers

• • •

This colorful collage of vegetables, tofu, and herbs tastes as wonderful as it looks.

• • •

Serves 4

INGREDIENTS

16 ounces firm tofu, drained
2 tablespoons olive oil
2 medium onions, thinly sliced
1 teaspoon fresh thyme leaves, chopped
1 tablespoon fresh marjoram leaves, chopped
¼ cup fresh parsley sprigs, chopped
3 bell peppers, red, yellow, and green, thinly sliced
1 cup mushrooms, thinly sliced
1 garlic clove, minced
Salt to taste
Pepper to taste
½ cup dry white wine
20 black olives, halved and pitted
¼ cup Parmesan cheese, grated

SAUCE

2 tablespoons olive oil
2 tablespoons red wine vinegar
1 tablespoon tomato paste
1 teaspoon Dijon mustard
2 garlic cloves, minced
Pepper to taste
½ teaspoon soy sauce

PREPARATION

1 Cut the tofu into triangles, and place them in an ungreased pie plate. Bake at 375°F for 20 minutes, or until they're slightly firm. Pour off any excess liquid.

2 Meanwhile, in a large frying pan, sauté the onions in oil on high heat for 2 minutes. Add the herbs, peppers, mushrooms, and garlic, and sauté for 2 minutes longer.

3 Lower the heat to medium, and cook until the onions have softened, stirring occasionally.

4 Season with salt and pepper. Add the wine and olives, and simmer for 10 minutes, or until the vegetables are coated with a syrupy sauce.

5 Spread the vegetables in a lightly oiled casserole dish and place the tofu triangles into the vegetables.

6 Whisk the sauce ingredients together, then pour it over the vegetables and tofu.

7 Cover the dish, and bake at 375°F for 25 minutes, or until heated through. Serve with Parmesan grated over the top.

Stuffed Summer Squash

• • •

This is a delicious way to use some of those squash and zucchini your garden won't stop growing.

• • •

Serves 6

INGREDIENTS

8 ounces soft tofu
1 tablespoon low-fat milk
1½ cups basmati rice, cooked
¼ cup fresh spinach, minced
2 tablespoons onion, minced
2 tablespoons green bell pepper, minced
3 tablespoons Parmesan cheese, grated
¼ teaspoon salt
⅛ teaspoon cayenne pepper
3 large yellow squash or zucchini, halved lengthwise and seeded
1 teaspoon corn oil
¼ cup water
1 tablespoon lemon juice
Fresh chives, for garnish

PREPARATION

1 In a large bowl, combine 4 ounces of the tofu with the milk. Then add the rice, spinach, onion, green pepper, Parmesan, salt, and cayenne.

2 Spoon the mixture into the squash halves.

3 Arrange the squash halves in a lightly oiled baking dish. Add the water, and cover tightly.

4 Bake at 350°F for 30 minutes, or until the squash is tender.

5 Meanwhile, in a small bowl, mix together the lemon juice and remaining tofu.

6 When the squash is done, top each with some of the tofu mixture and chives, and serve immediately.

Tofu with Snow Peas in Lemon-Lime Vinaigrette

• • •

This vinaigrette turns your tofu into a tangy entrée. Serve over brown rice, and enjoy!

• • •

Serves 4

INGREDIENTS

16 ounces firm tofu, cubed
3 tablespoons lemon juice
2 teaspoon grated lime rind
2 scallions, minced
2 teaspoons Dijon mustard
1¼ teaspoons salt
½ cup olive oil
Pepper to taste
2 tablespoons corn oil
Boiling water for blanching
¼ pound snow peas, cut in half
Cold water

PREPARATION

1 In a small bowl, combine the lemon juice, grated lime rind, scallions, mustard, 1 teaspoon of the salt, and olive oil. Whisk briskly, and set aside.

2 Season the tofu with salt and pepper.

3 In a frying pan, sauté the tofu in the corn oil until golden on both sides.

4 Meanwhile, blanch the snow peas for 5 seconds in boiling water. Drain and refresh the peas with cold water.

5 Transfer the tofu to serving plates, sprinkle them with the snow peas, and spoon the vinaigrette over them.

Tofu Stroganoff

• • •

With its creamy sauce, brimming with mushrooms and tofu, this delicious dish gives you another good excuse to enjoy lots of noodles.

• • •

Serves 4

INGREDIENTS

4 ounces firm tofu, mashed
1½ cups Tofu Sour Cream (see recipe on page 209)
¼ cup dry sherry
2 tablespoons soy sauce
¼ teaspoon black pepper
1 tablespoon fresh parsley sprigs, minced
2 teaspoons thyme
8 ounces wide egg noodles
2 tablespoons olive oil
1 red bell pepper, finely chopped
4 cups button mushrooms, sliced
½ cup scallions, chopped
Paprika, for garnish

PREPARATION

1 In a blender, combine the Tofu Sour Cream, tofu, sherry, soy sauce, and pepper. Process until smooth. Stir in the parsley and thyme, and set aside.

2 Bring a large pot of water to a boil. Add the noodles, mixing occasionally. Cook until tender.

3 Meanwhile, in a frying pan, sauté the bell pepper in oil until tender. Add the mushrooms and scallions, stirring occasionally, for about 10 minutes or until the mushrooms are softened.

4 Reduce the heat, and add the Tofu Sour Cream mixture. Stir gently until the mixture is heated through.

5 When the noodles are done, drain well. Spoon them onto individual serving plates, and top with the stroganoff mixture.

Vegetable-Tofu Medley with Spicy Peanut Sauce

• • •

Make sure this recipe is on hand when asparagus is in season. This light meal captures the essence of its delectable taste.

• • •

Serves 4

INGREDIENTS

12 ounces firm tofu, pressed and cubed
1½ cups Spicy Peanut Sauce (recipe on page 207)
2 cups broccoli florets
2 cups asparagus, halved
2 carrots, cut into strips
1 red bell pepper, finely chopped
2 medium scallions, finely chopped
Lettuce leaves
Toasted sesame seeds, for garnish

PREPARATION

1 Marinate the tofu cubes in the Spicy Peanut Sauce for at least 30 minutes in the refrigerator.

2 Meanwhile, in a steamer insert, steam the broccoli, asparagus, and carrots until tender.

3 Drain the vegetables, and transfer them into a large bowl. Add the bell pepper and scallions, and toss. Add the tofu and peanut sauce, and toss again.

4 Place a layer of lettuce on serving plates, and top with the vegetable-tofu mixture. Garnish with sesame seeds.

Beans and Greens Medley with Sweet Potatoes

• • •

You will enjoy charming guests with this impressive looking (as well as tasting) gourmet-style stew.

• • •

Serves 4 to 6

INGREDIENTS

8 ounces firm tofu, frozen, thawed, and crumbled
¼ cup olive oil
1 medium onion, chopped
3 garlic cloves, minced
1 bay leaf
½ teaspoon dried paprika
½ teaspoon salt
⅛ teaspoon black pepper
2 tablespoons white wine vinegar
1 cup water
4 cups escarole, chopped
4 cups kale, chopped
1 sweet potato, peeled and diced
2 cups canellini beans, cooked
1 pound fresh spinach, stemmed and coarsely chopped

PREPARATION

1 In a large saucepan, sauté the onion and garlic in oil, stirring, for 5 minutes.

2 Add the bay leaf, paprika, salt, pepper, vinegar, water, escarole, and kale. Cover and cook over medium heat for 5 minutes, or until the greens wilt.

3 Add the sweet potato and tofu, cover, and cook at a slow boil for 30 minutes, or until the vegetables are tender. Stir occasionally.

4 Remove the bay leaf. Add the beans and spinach, and cook, stirring, until the spinach is wilted. Serve hot with fresh-baked bread.

Mushroom-Tofu Stuffed Potatoes

• • •

Stuff yourself with these simple yet elegant potatoes.

• • •

Serves 4

INGREDIENTS

4 ounces soft tofu, mashed
4 large baking potatoes, well scrubbed
1 tablespoon olive oil
1 cup mushrooms, sliced
1 tablespoon soy sauce
2 tablespoons Parmesan cheese, grated
Tofu Sour Cream (see recipe on page 209)

PREPARATION

1 Stab the potatoes with a fork, and bake at 400°F for 45 to 60 minutes, or until soft.

2 Meanwhile, in a frying pan, sauté the mushrooms in oil for 2 minutes.

3 Add the soy sauce, remove from the heat, and set aside.

4 When the potatoes are done, carefully scoop out the centers, and place in a bowl. Mash with the tofu, combining well.

5 Add the mushrooms, including the pan juices. Mix well.

6 Fill each potato skin with the stuffing, and arrange the stuffed potatoes in a baking pan. Sprinkle the potatoes with Parmesan, and broil until browned. Serve with tofu sour cream.

South African Tofu Melange

• • •

This aromatic "everything-but-the-kitchen-sink" meal features a delicious custard topping that complements all those spices.

• • •

Serves 6

INGREDIENTS

24 ounces firm tofu, frozen, thawed, and crumbled

3 cups onions, chopped

2 teaspoons garlic, minced

2 tablespoons peanut or vegetable oil

1 tablespoon cumin

1 tablespoon coriander

¼ teaspoon fennel

5 whole cloves, ground

1 teaspoon cinnamon

2 teaspoons turmeric

½ teaspoon black pepper

2 tablespoons white vinegar

3 tablespoons soy sauce

⅓ cup chutney (peach, apricot, or mango) plus extra for serving

1½ cups whole wheat bread chunks

1¼ cups milk

1 tablespoon dark sesame oil

½ cup raisins or currants

½ cup almonds, coarsely chopped

3 bay leaves

1 egg

Brown rice, cooked to serve 6

PREPARATION

1 In a covered saucepan, cook the onions and garlic in the oil on medium heat for 20 to 30 minutes, or until soft. Stir occasionally.

2 Then, add the cumin, coriander, fennel, cloves, cinnamon, turmeric, and black pepper, and sauté for 2 minutes, stirring constantly.

3 Mix in the vinegar, soy sauce, and chutney, and remove the pan from the heat. Set aside.

4 In a large mixing bowl, soak the bread in ½ cup of the milk for a few minutes, and then mash it with a fork.

5 Stir in the crumbled tofu, and drizzle on the sesame oil. Mix well.

6 Add the raisins, almonds, and onion-spice mixture. Stir well.

7 Spread the mixture in an 8 by 12-inch baking dish, and tuck the bay leaves in, leaving the stems sticking out.

8 Whisk the egg and ¾ cup of the milk together to make a custard. Pour the custard over the top of the mixture.

9 Bake, covered, at 350°F for 15 minutes. Then uncover, and bake for 15 minutes longer, or until the custard is set. Remove the bay leaves after baking.

10 Serve over brown rice with more chutney on the side.

Acorn Squash with Tofu and Vegetables
(see opposite page)

Cabbage, Tofu, and Squash Stir-Fry
(see opposite page)

Acorn Squash with Tofu and Vegetables

• • •

Serve up this great combination at your next small dinner party. The results are worth the effort.

• • •

Serves 8

INGREDIENTS

16 ounces firm tofu, frozen, thawed, and cubed
1 tablespoon mild barley miso
⅓ cup white wine
2 tablespoons ginger root, grated
1 cup onions, chopped
3 garlic cloves, minced
3 tablespoons tomato paste
2 acorn squash, seeded and quartered
Vegetable oil, for brushing and cooking
Water for baking
¼ teaspoon crushed red pepper
2 cups carrots, sliced
2 tablespoons balsamic vinegar
2 cups mushrooms, sliced
1 teaspoon garlic powder
1 15-ounce can garbanzo beans, drained and rinsed
2 tablespoons Dijon mustard
¼ cup dry sherry
1 tablespoon molasses
⅓ cup nutritional yeast flakes
⅓ cup scallions, sliced

PREPARATION

1 In a small mixing bowl, blend the miso and wine. Add the ginger, onions, garlic, and tomato paste, and blend well.

2 Place the tofu in a shallow pan, and pour the marinade over the tofu. Cover and refrigerate for at least 1 hour (for best results, refrigerate overnight).

3 Cut the squash into quarters, and brush lightly with the vegetable oil.

4 Place the squash, cut side down, in a shallow baking pan with 2 inches of water. Bake at 350°F for 45 minutes, turning every 15 minutes.

5 In a large saucepan, sauté the red pepper in oil for 1 minute. Add the carrots, vinegar, mushrooms, and garlic powder, and sauté for 5 minutes.

6 Add the beans, mustard, sherry, molasses, yeast, and scallions, and cook for 3 minutes.

7 Add the marinated tofu, and lower the heat. Simmer for 5 minutes, gently turning the mixture.

8 Transfer the mixture to a casserole dish, cover it, and bake for 30 minutes while the squash bakes.

9 Place the squash on dinner plates, cut side up, and top with the casserole filling.

Cabbage, Tofu, and Squash Stir-Fry

• • •

Stir-frying the cabbage and squash releases their natural sweetness, creating a satisfying contrast with the fresh ginger.

• • •

Serves 4

INGREDIENTS

12 ounces firm tofu, pressed and diced
2 tablespoons miso
¼ cup water
2 teaspoons ginger root, minced
1 teaspoon sesame oil
2 tablespoons safflower oil
2 medium onions, sliced
1 tablespoon sesame seeds
2 cups butternut squash, peeled and finely diced
4 cups purple cabbage, shredded
Brown rice, cooked to serve 4

PREPARATION

1 In a small bowl, combine the miso, water, 1 teaspoon of the ginger, and the sesame oil. Set aside.

2 In a wok or large frying pan, stir-fry the onion in 1 tablespoon of the safflower oil until the onion slices begin to brown.

3 Add the remaining teaspoon of ginger and the tofu, and stir-fry for 3 minutes.

4 Add the sesame seeds, squash, and the remaining safflower oil, and stir-fry for 10 minutes, or until the squash is tender. Add a little water if the squash begins to stick.

5 Add the cabbage and more water, if necessary, and cook, stirring, for 3 minutes.

6 Stir the miso mixture, and mix it into the vegetables. Cook for 10 minutes, stirring, and serve over the cooked rice.

Stir-Fry with Spinach and Tofu

• • •

Served on a bed of freshly cooked rice, this light and easy stir-fry makes a quick, yet nourishing, supper.

• • •

Serves 4

INGREDIENTS

16 ounces firm tofu, cubed
3 tablespoons low-sodium soy sauce
1 tablespoon red wine vinegar
1 teaspoon toasted sesame oil
3 tablespoons almonds, sliced
2 tablespoons safflower or canola oil
1 tablespoon ginger root, minced
1 pound spinach, washed well, cut into ½-inch strips
Brown or white rice, cooked to serve 4

PREPARATION

1 In a small bowl, combine the soy sauce, vinegar, and sesame oil, and mix well. Set aside.

2 In a wok, stir-fry the almonds in the sesame oil for about 1 minute, or until they turn golden. Remove from the wok, and set aside.

3 Add the safflower or canola oil to the wok, and add the ginger. Stir-fry for 30 seconds. Add the tofu, and stir-fry until the cubes are golden on each side. Remove the tofu, and place in a covered bowl.

4 Add the spinach to the wok, and stir-fry until just wilted. Drizzle with the soy sauce mixture.

5 To serve, divide the rice among four plates, and top with spinach. Place the tofu on top of the spinach, and sprinkle with almonds. Serve immediately.

Tofu-Spinach Eggplant Rolls

• • •

This mouth-watering entrée requires a little forethought, since the eggplant needs to be salted and drained, but once you bite into these rolls, you'll feel you're eating a gourmet creation.

• • •

Serves 8

INGREDIENTS

16 ounces firm tofu, crumbled
1 large eggplant
1½ teaspoons salt
8 ounces spinach, washed and trimmed
6 tablespoons vegetable oil
2 tablespoons all-purpose flour
1 cup milk, hot, but not boiling
1 bay leaf
⅛ teaspoon black pepper
¼ cup onion, minced
1 cup Parmesan cheese, grated
¼ cup heavy cream
½ teaspoon nutmeg, grated

PREPARATION

1 Peel the eggplant, and cut lengthwise into eight slices, each ¼-inch thick.

2 Sprinkle the eggplant slices with 1 teaspoon of the salt, and let them sit on a rack (this removes the bitter taste). After 1 hour, rinse the eggplant slices, and pat them dry.

3 Meanwhile, in a frying pan, sauté the spinach in 1 tablespoon of the oil. Let the spinach cool, and squeeze out any remaining liquid. Chop and set aside.

4 In a saucepan, heat 2 tablespoons of the oil over moderate heat, stir in the flour, and cook over low heat, stirring, for 3 minutes.

5 Remove the pan from the heat, and add the hot milk. Whisk vigorously until the mixture is thick and smooth.

6 Add the bay leaf, the remaining ½ teaspoon of salt, and pepper, and simmer for 10 minutes. Take out the bay leaf, and remove the sauce from the heat.

7 In a small frying pan, sauté the onions in 2 tablespoons of the oil until softened. Add the tofu, spinach, ¼ cup of the Parmesan, cream, and nutmeg. Combine the mixture well.

8 In a large frying pan, heat the remaining 2 tablespoons of oil over moderately high heat. Add the eggplant slices in batches, and cook them for 2 minutes on each side, or until they are soft. Add more oil if needed.

9 Transfer the cooked slices to paper towels to drain.

10 Place 2 tablespoons of the tofu mixture on a short end of each slice, and, starting with the filled end, roll up the slices.

11 In a large oiled baking dish, arrange the rolls with the seam side down. Pour the creamy sauce over the rolls, sprinkle them with the remaining ¾ cup of Parmesan, and bake at 350°F for 15 minutes, or until the cheese is lightly browned.

Chinese Tofu with Red Pepper Sauce (see opposite page)

Potato, Veggie, and Tofu Stir-Fry

• • •

In this hearty yet light stir-fry, the potatoes add a welcome surprise for your palate.

• • •

Serves 4

INGREDIENTS

8 ounces firm tofu, cut into ½-inch strips
1 large carrot, cut into matchstick julienne
3 small new red potatoes, halved, cut into ¼-inch slices
1 tablespoon cornstarch
3 tablespoons soy sauce
2 tablespoons vegetable stock (see recipe on page 81)
3 tablespoons corn oil
1 red bell pepper, seeded and cut into ½-inch squares
1 yellow bell pepper, seeded and cut into ½-inch squares
1 zucchini, cut into ¼-inch diagonal slices
1 large garlic clove, minced
2 scallions, minced
2 teaspoons ginger root, minced

PREPARATION

1 In a steamer insert, steam the julienned carrot for 2 minutes. Add the potatoes to the steamer, and steam for another 2 minutes.

2 Drain the steamed vegetables and rinse with cold water.

3 In a bowl, combine the cornstarch with the soy sauce and stock, and set aside.

4 In a wok or large frying pan, heat 2 tablespoons of the oil over high heat. Add the carrot and potatoes. Reduce heat to medium-high, add the peppers and zucchini, and stir-fry for 1 minute, or until the vegetables begin to soften.

5 Transfer the vegetables to a plate with a slotted spoon.

6 Return the wok or frying pan to medium-high heat, and add the remaining oil. Add the tofu, garlic, scallions, and ginger, and stir-fry for 30 seconds, or until the tofu browns.

7 Stir the cornstarch mixture into the wok or frying pan.

8 Return the vegetables to the wok, and bring to a simmer, stirring constantly, for 30 seconds. Serve immediately.

Chinese Tofu with Red Pepper Sauce

• • •

This popular Chinese dish is not shy about shouting "hot!" Serve with plenty of rice.

• • •

Serves 4

INGREDIENTS

24 ounces firm tofu, cut into 1-inch cubes
1 tablespoon corn oil
1½ teaspoons sesame oil
1 garlic clove, crushed
¼ cup leeks, minced
½ teaspoon red chili peppers, minced
4 mushrooms, diced
½ cup water
1½ teaspoons sake
2½ teaspoons soy sauce
½ teaspoon salt
Hot red pepper sauce to taste
2 teaspoons ketchup
2 teaspoons cornstarch, dissolved in 2 tablespoons water
1 tablespoon scallion greens, minced

PREPARATION

1 In a wok or frying pan, sauté or stir-fry the garlic, leeks, and red peppers in both oils over high heat for 15 seconds.

2 Reduce the heat to medium, and add the mushrooms, sautéing for 1 minute.

3 Add the water, sake, soy sauce, salt, and hot pepper sauce, and bring to a boil for 30 seconds.

4 Add the tofu, and return the mixture to a boil. Stir in the dissolved cornstarch, and simmer until thick. Serve hot, garnished with the scallion greens.

Sweet and Sour Tofu

• • •

Pineapples make an easy base for this yummy, Asian-style sauce. The sauce can also be used for dipping eggrolls or marinating tofu.

• • •

Serves 4 to 6

INGREDIENTS

12 ounces firm tofu, cubed

8 ounces spaghetti, cooked

¼ cup canola oil

1 medium onion, chopped

1 medium green bell pepper, seeded and cut into strips

1 cup mushrooms, sliced

1 broccoli stalk, cut into small florets, stalk peeled and finely chopped

1 celery stalk, cut into ½-inch slices

1 teaspoon ginger root, grated

1 garlic clove, minced

4 ounces snow peas, strings removed, cut in half diagonally

Sweet and Sour Tofu (see above)

SAUCE

- 1 cup canned pineapple chunks, in juice
- 2 tablespoons lemon juice
- 2 tablespoons maple syrup
- ¼ cup soy sauce
- 2 tablespoons arrowroot powder
- 2 tablespoons dark sesame oil
- 2 tablespoons rice vinegar
- 2 teaspoons Dijon mustard
- 2 teaspoons ginger root, finely grated
- 1 garlic clove, minced
- ⅛ teaspoon crushed red pepper flakes

PREPARATION

1. In a large mixing bowl, toss the cooked spaghetti and with 1 tablespoon of the canola oil to coat the noodles well.

2. In a large frying pan, heat 1 tablespoon of the canola oil over medium heat, swirling to coat the sides of the pan. Add the spaghetti, and press down with a spoon to form a pancake-shaped form.

3. Cook for 5 minutes, or until golden brown on the bottom. Carefully turn the pancake, and cook until the other side is browned. Set aside in a warm oven.

4. In a bowl, whisk together the sauce ingredients, and set aside.

5. In a frying pan, heat the remaining canola oil over medium-high heat, and sauté the onion, pepper, mushrooms, broccoli, celery, ginger, and garlic for 3 minutes.

6. Add the tofu and snow peas, and sauté for 2 minutes more.

7. Stir in the sauce, and simmer, stirring often, until the mixture is thickened. Remove from the heat.

8. Transfer the noodle pancake to a serving dish, spoon the vegetables and sauce over it, and serve hot.

Veggies, Tofu, and Black Bean Sauce

• • •

A thick, sweet, and pungent sauce coats the tofu and vegetables in this scrumptious meal.

• • •

Serves 4

INGREDIENTS

- 12 ounces extra-firm tofu, frozen, thawed, and cubed
- ¼ cup hoisin sauce
- 3 tablespoons honey
- 2 tablespoons soy sauce
- ½ cup dry sherry
- 1 teaspoon toasted sesame oil
- 1 tablespoon fermented Chinese black beans, minced
- 2 small garlic cloves, minced
- 1 teaspoon Thai chili paste
- 1 teaspoon canola oil
- 2 cups broccoli florets
- ¼ cup water
- 4 bunches baby bok choy, chopped into 1-inch pieces
- Vegetable oil for cooking

PREPARATION

1. In a bowl, combine the hoisin sauce, honey, soy sauce, 2 tablespoons of the sherry, sesame oil, black beans, garlic, and Thai chili paste. Set aside.

2. In a large frying pan, sauté the tofu in the canola oil for 5 minutes.

3. Add 3 tablespoons of the sauce from step 1, and cook for another 3 minutes. Remove the tofu from the pan, and set aside.

4. In a frying pan or wok, sauté or stir-fry the broccoli in ¼ cup of water until it turns bright green. Add the bok choy and the rest of the sherry, and cook for 3 minutes.

5. Add the tofu and the remaining sauce. Serve hot.

Spinach-Tofu Souffle

• • •

This is a super-quick, healthful meal that's perfect for the family cook who is also the family chauffeur, tutor, referee, etc....

• • •

Serves 6

INGREDIENTS

- 8 ounces firm tofu
- ½ cup onion, chopped
- 4 tablespoons vegetable oil
- 3 tablespoons unbleached white flour
- 1 cup reserved spinach juice (if less than 1 cup, add milk or water)
- 1 teaspoon salt
- ¼ teaspoon black pepper
- ¼ teaspoon nutmeg
- 10-ounce package frozen chopped spinach, thawed
- 2 tablespoons fresh lemon juice

PREPARATION

1 In a frying pan, sauté the onion in 3 tablespoons of oil until tender.

2 Stir in the flour, spinach juice, ¼ teaspoon of the salt, a dash of the pepper, and the nutmeg.

3 Add the thawed spinach to the sauce. Cook on low heat for 5 minutes.

4 Meanwhile, in a blender, mix the tofu, lemon juice, 1 tablespoon of the oil, and the rest of the salt and pepper, until smooth.

5 Add the tofu mixture to the spinach and sauce.

6 Pour the mixture into an oiled 8-inch round pan, and bake at 350°F for 30 minutes. Serve immediately.

Broccoli and Tofu in Sweet and Spicy Peanut Sauce

• • •

What a fetching combination of flavors! Adjust the sweetness of the sauce to fit your taste by adding more or less honey and ginger.

• • •

Serves 4

INGREDIENTS

- 16 ounces firm tofu, cubed
- 2 broccoli stalks, chopped (florets and stalks)
- 2 tablespoons peanut oil
- ½ cup peanut butter
- 1 cup hot water
- ¼ cup vinegar
- 4 tablespoons soy sauce
- 3 tablespoons molasses
- Cayenne pepper to taste
- 1 teaspoon honey, or to taste
- 1 teaspoon ginger root, grated, or to taste
- Brown or white rice, cooked to serve 4

PREPARATION

1 In a wok or large frying pan, stir-fry the tofu and broccoli in the peanut oil for 5 minutes.

2 In a bowl, mix the peanut butter and hot water. Add the vinegar, soy sauce, molasses, cayenne pepper, honey, and ginger.

3 Pour the sauce on the broccoli and tofu, and simmer for 2 to 3 minutes.

4 Serve over the rice.

Phat Thai with Mushrooms

• • •

Go Thai with this exotic-tasting noodle dish, a popular meal in Asia and in restaurants worldwide.

• • •

Serves 4

INGREDIENTS

8 ounces firm tofu, diced
4 cups rice noodles or fettuccine noodles
Cold water for soaking noodles
2 tablespoons vegetable oil
4 teaspoons garlic, minced
½ cup turnip, peeled and diced
1 cup mushrooms, coarsely chopped
2 tablespoons scallions, sliced
1 dried red chili pepper, finely chopped
2 teaspoons rice vinegar
3 tablespoons sugar
4 teaspoons fresh paprika, chopped
4 tablespoons tamarind juice
1½ cups water
1 cup roasted peanuts, chopped
2 cups bean sprouts
Juice of 1 lime
1 cup garlic cloves, cut into ½-inch pieces
Pinch of salt
Pinch of pepper
1 lime, peeled and cut into wedges
1 carrot, shredded

PREPARATION

1 In a medium-sized mixing bowl, soak the rice or fettuccine noodles in cold water for 20 minutes, or until slightly limp; drain.

2 In a saucepan, sauté the garlic and turnips in oil for 5 minutes.

3 Add the mushrooms, scallions, chili pepper, and tofu, and cook, stirring, for 2 minutes.

4 In a small bowl, combine the vinegar, sugar, paprika, and tamarind juice. Add to the saucepan along with the noodles and water. Continue to cook and gently toss until most of the water is absorbed.

5 Stir in ½ cup of the roasted peanuts, bean sprouts, lime juice, and chives, and season to taste with salt and pepper.

6 Place a serving of Phat Thai in the center of each plate. Arrange some of the lime sections, carrot shreds, and reserved peanuts on top.

Vegetable Lasagna with Tofu (see below)

Vegetable Lasagna with Tofu

• • •

You'd be hard pressed to tell the difference between this tofu lasagna and one made with ricotta cheese. For a totally cheese-less lasagna, try soy mozzarella, now available in most supermarkets.

• • •

Serves 8 to 10

INGREDIENTS

12 ounces firm tofu, crumbled
8-ounce package uncooked lasagna noodles
1 to 2 tablespoons vegetable oil
8 scallions, chopped
1 cup mushrooms, sliced
10-ounce package frozen chopped spinach, defrosted and drained
1 garlic clove, minced
48-ounce jar spaghetti sauce
1 egg

½ teaspoon dried oregano
½ teaspoon salt
¼ teaspoon pepper
½ teaspoon garlic powder
8-ounce package mozzarella cheese

PREPARATION

1 In a deep saucepan, cook the lasagna noodles according to the instructions on the box. Drain, and set aside.

2 In a saucepan, sauté scallions, mushrooms, spinach, and garlic in oil for 5 minutes. Mix in the spaghetti sauce, and set aside.

3 In a large mixing bowl, combine the tofu, egg, and seasonings. Mix well.

4 Cover the bottom of a 9 by 13-inch baking dish with some of the sauce mixture.

5 Top with three lasagna noodles, followed by the sauce, the tofu mixture, and a sprinkling of cheese. Repeat in layers until all of the ingredients are gone.

6 Ladle any remaining sauce over the top of the lasagna.

7 Cover the dish with aluminum foil, and bake at 350°F for 45 minutes.

8 Remove the foil, and top with any remaining cheese. Bake, uncovered, for an additional 15 minutes.

9 Allow to stand for 10 minutes before serving.

Recipe Tip

For a slightly more cheesy lasagna filling, substitute 8 ounces of mozzarella cheese for the same amount of tofu.

Corn and Zucchini Tamale Pie

• • •

This pie tastes best with the corn kernels right off the cob, though you can always substitute the canned variety for speed's sake.

• • •

Serves 4

INGREDIENTS

6 ounces extra-firm tofu, frozen and drained
6 ears fresh corn
1 teaspoon salt
2 tablespoons flour
4 tablespoons yellow cornmeal
½ teaspoon baking powder
1 teaspoon sugar
⅓ cup mild green chilies, chopped
1 cup zucchini, grated
⅛ teaspoon black pepper
Vegetable oil for baking

PREPARATION

1 Scrape the corn cobs with a corn scraper, or hold each cob at one end, and run the tip of a knife between each row of kernels, slicing down to the end of the ear. Continue until all the rows have been prepared.

2 Using the back of the knife, push or scrape the kernels downward; the flesh and "milk" will spurt out. Go back and forth, and up and down the ear until it is finished.

3 In a food processor or blender, blend the tofu until smooth.

4 In a large bowl, mix the scraped corn and tofu with the remaining ingredients.

5 Fill an oiled 9-inch round pie pan with the mixture, and bake at 375°F for 25 minutes.

Corn and Zucchini Tamale Pie (see above)

Tofu Enchiladas

• • •

You can raise the temperature of these enchiladas from mild to wild with your choice of salsas.

• • •

Serves 8

INGREDIENTS

16 ounces firm tofu
⅔ cup plain yogurt
¼ teaspoon salt
½ teaspoon turmeric
¼ teaspoon dried paprika
1 tablespoon cumin
1 cup button mushrooms, finely chopped
3 to 4 scallions, finely chopped
8 tortillas
Salsa
¾ cup black olives, chopped
¾ cup onions, chopped

PREPARATION

1 In a large bowl, mash the tofu, and mix in the yogurt, salt, turmeric, paprika, cumin, mushrooms, and scallions.

2 Brush each tortilla with a little of the salsa, and spoon the tofu mixture into the center of the tortillas.

3 Cover the bottom of a baking sheet with a thin layer of salsa.

4 Fold the tortillas over twice to form a rolled pancake shape, and place each filled tortilla on the baking sheet.

5 When all the tortillas have been filled, spoon the remaining salsa over them. Also top with any remaining filling.

6 Garnish with the olives and onions.

7 Bake the enchiladas at 350°F for 30 to 35 minutes.

Classic Chili Con Tofu

• • •

The meat traditionally found in this Southwestern-style dish is replaced by frozen tofu crumbles that give the chili a rich texture.

• • •

Serves 6

INGREDIENTS

16 ounces extra-firm tofu, frozen, thawed, drained, and crumbled
¼ teaspoon soy sauce
2 tablespoons peanut butter
2 garlic cloves, minced
¼ teaspoon cumin
¼ teaspoon powdered ginger
1 tablespoon vegetable oil, plus extra for baking
1 red bell pepper, roasted, peeled, seeded, and diced
1 small hot chili, seeded and diced
1 teaspoon chili powder
1 red onion, diced
1 carrot, diced
1 cup winter squash, diced
2 celery stalks, diced
1 cup pinto beans, cooked
1 cup red kidney beans, cooked
1 to 2 cups vegetable stock (see recipe on page 81)
Salt to taste
¼ cup fresh parsley sprigs, minced

PREPARATION

1 In a medium-sized mixing bowl, combine the soy sauce, peanut butter, garlic, cumin, and ginger.

2 Stir the crumbled tofu into the peanut butter mixture until the sauce is completely absorbed.

3 On an oiled baking sheet, spread the tofu, and bake at 375°F for 20 minutes. Stir well, and bake another 10 minutes. Set aside.

Classic Chili Con Tofu (see opposite page)

4 Heat the 1 tablespoon of oil in a soup pot over medium heat. Add the peppers, chili, chili powder, and onion, and cook, stirring, for 3 to 4 minutes.

5 Add the remaining vegetables and sauté 2 to 3 minutes more.

6 Add the beans and enough stock to just cover the ingredients. Bring to a boil, season to taste with salt, and stir in the baked tofu.

7 Cover and simmer over low heat for 10 to 15 minutes longer. Serve hot.

Traditional Tamale Pie

• • •

This is a deliciously spicy casserole featuring distinctive South-of-the-Border flavors.

• • •

Serves 8

INGREDIENTS

CHILI

16 ounces firm tofu, frozen, thawed, and crumbled
1 tablespoon vegetable oil
1 teaspoon garlic, minced
1¼ cups onions, finely chopped
¼ cup carrots, finely chopped
2 cups chopped canned tomatoes
3 cups pinto beans, cooked
¼ cup ketchup or tomato sauce
1½ cups fresh or frozen corn
3 teaspoons fresh paprika
1 teaspoon ground cumin
2 to 3 teaspoons chili powder to taste
⅛ to ¼ teaspoon cayenne pepper
½ teaspoon salt

CORNBREAD

3 ounces soft tofu
1 cup yellow cornmeal
1 cup whole wheat flour
1 teaspoon baking powder
1 teaspoon baking soda
Pinch of salt (optional)
¼ cup honey
2 cups low-fat milk
1 teaspoon sunflower oil

PREPARATION

1 In a large saucepan, sauté the garlic, onions, and carrots in oil. When the onions begin to soften, add the tofu and sauté 4 minutes longer.

2 Add the tomatoes, beans, tomato sauce, and corn. Mix well.

3 Stir in the spices, cover, and simmer over medium-low heat for 30 minutes, or until the chili is heated through.

4 In a medium-sized mixing bowl, combine all the dry ingredients for the cornbread.

5 In a blender, combine the tofu with the liquid ingredients until creamy.

6 Stir the liquid ingredients into the dry ingredients until mixed, but lumpy.

7 Place the chili in a casserole dish, and spread the batter on top.

8 Bake uncovered at 375°F for 40 minutes.

Tofu Burritos

• • •

This perennial favorite is always a big hit at the dinner table.

• • •

Serves 8

INGREDIENTS

16 ounces firm tofu, drained and crumbled
2 cups hot salsa
2 cups black beans, cooked
1 cup refried beans
¼ cup mild green chilies, chopped
8 flour tortillas, warmed
1 cup radish sprouts
½ cup tomatoes, chopped

PREPARATION

1 In a medium-sized mixing bowl, combine the tofu and 1 cup of the salsa. Let this mixture marinate at room temperature for 30 minutes.

2 Meanwhile, in a saucepan, heat the beans and chilies.

3 To assemble the burritos, place a large spoonful of the tofu-salsa mixture in the lower corner of a tortilla. Layer the beans, sprouts, tomato, and salsa over the tofu.

4 Roll the tortilla away from you, folding in the two sides, and tucking the top edge under as you roll.

5 On a baking sheet, bake the burritos at 350°F for 10 to 15 minutes. Serve with more salsa, if desired.

Tex-Mex Tofu and Vegetables

• • •

This easy-to-prepare combination will serve you well as a hearty, tasty everyday main dish.

• • •

Serves 4

INGREDIENTS

16 ounces firm tofu, diced
½ cup salsa
1 tablespoon miso
1 tablespoon arrowroot or cornstarch, dissolved in 1 cup water
1 teaspoon sesame oil
1 leek or onion, diced
2 carrots, diced
2 ears of corn, kernels cut off the cob (see page 159 for instructions)
½ teaspoon cayenne pepper, or chili powder, or to taste
⅓ cup scallions, chopped
Brown or white rice, cooked to serve 4

PREPARATION

1 In a small bowl, mix the salsa, miso, and dissolved arrowroot or cornstarch. Set aside.

2 In a saucepan, sauté the onion, carrots, and corn in oil until the onion is translucent. Stir in the spices and tofu.

3 Pour the salsa sauce over the vegetables and tofu. Stir until the sauce becomes thick.

4 Simmer on low heat for 15 minutes.

5 Add the scallions, and serve over the rice.

Mexican Stew

• • •

This veggie and bean melange is a zesty
fiesta for your taste buds.

• • •

Serves 6

INGREDIENTS

8 ounces firm tofu, frozen, thawed, and finely
   diced
1 cup dry red beans
1 cup onions, chopped
2½ tablespoons fresh garlic, minced
1 tablespoon vegetable oil
¼ cup jalapeño peppers, seeded and diced
½ cup carrots, thinly sliced
½ cup celery, thinly sliced
2 red bell peppers, seeded and diced
3 tablespoons fresh cilantro leaves, minced
6 cups water or vegetable stock (see recipe on
   page 81)
3 cups whole-kernel corn (fresh or frozen)
2 teaspoons cumin
2 teaspoons coriander
½ teaspoon cayenne pepper (optional)
1 cup crushed tortilla chips
Salsa and nonfat, plain yogurt, for garnish

PREPARATION

1 Soak the beans in a covered bowl of water
overnight. Drain, rinse, and set aside.

2 In a large saucepan, sauté the onion and
garlic in oil for 5 minutes, or until the
onions are soft.

3 Add the jalapeños, carrots, celery, and
bell peppers, and continue cooking for 3
minutes, stirring frequently.

4 Add the cilantro, water or stock, corn,
cumin, coriander, tofu, and beans.

5 Cover and cook on low heat for up to 2
hours, or until the beans are tender and
the stew is thick.

6 Add the cayenne pepper, and top with the
crushed tortilla chips, salsa, and yogurt to
serve.

Tofu with Spicy Mexican Mole Sauce

• • •

This dark Mexican sauce, made with the
unusual combination of spices and
unsweetened chocolate, is usually
served over poultry or beef.
Here the fragrant sauce works
just as well with tofu.

• • •

Serves 6

INGREDIENTS

48 ounces firm tofu
3 tablespoons vegetable oil
2 medium onions, minced
1 small green bell pepper, minced
3 garlic cloves, minced
5 ripe, medium tomatoes, diced
2 mild chilies, minced
1 teaspoon cinnamon
¼ teaspoon dried thyme
2 cups vegetable stock (see recipe on page 81)
¼ cup fresh cilantro leaves, chopped
⅓ cup unsweetened cocoa powder
1 teaspoon salt

PREPARATION

1 In a large saucepan, sauté the onions and
green pepper over high heat in 1 tablespoon of the oil until the onions are
browned.

2 Add the garlic, and sauté for 30 more
seconds.

3 Lower the heat to medium-low, and add
the tomatoes, chilies, cinnamon, and
thyme.

4 Stir for 5 minutes longer, or until the mixture reaches the consistency of a paste.

5 Add the stock and cilantro, and simmer on
very low heat for 30 minutes.

6 Stir in the cocoa until it is combined, and
simmer for another 10 minutes. Season
with salt.

7 Meanwhile, cut the tofu blocks into six slices each.

8 In a frying pan, lightly brown both sides of the slices in the rest of the oil.

9 Place three slices of tofu on a plate, and cover with the mole sauce.

Recipe Tip

If you wish, reserve some of the Mexican Mole Sauce, and pour it over a side dish of Spanish rice.

Tofu Tacos

• • •

Say "adios!" to the meat, and "hola!" to a hot, spicy, and delicious taco.

• • •

Yields 12 tacos

INGREDIENTS

12 ounces firm tofu, cubed
6-ounce can tomato paste
¾ cup water
2 teaspoons chili powder
½ teaspoon hot pepper sauce
¼ teaspoon ground cumin
¼ teaspoon black pepper
2 tablespoons olive oil
2 small zucchini, cut lengthwise into
  ¼-inch-thick slices
2 cups mushrooms, sliced
2 carrots, coarsely shredded
1 small onion, cut into strips
1 teaspoon garlic, minced
3 plum tomatoes, cut into ½-inch cubes
12 taco shells
1 head lettuce, shredded
12 ounces Cheddar cheese, shredded

PREPARATION

1 In a small bowl, combine the tomato paste, water, chili powder, hot pepper sauce, cumin, and pepper. Mix well, and set aside.

2 In a frying pan, sauté the zucchini, mushrooms, carrots, onion, and garlic in oil. Stir occasionally until the vegetables are tender but not browned.

3 Add the contents of the bowl to the frying pan, and cook for 3 minutes.

4 Stir in the tofu cubes and tomatoes. Reduce the heat to low, cover, and heat through, for 5 minutes.

5 Meanwhile, place the taco shells on a baking sheet. Heat them at 350°F until just warm.

6 Spoon about ½ cup of the vegetable-tofu mixture into each of the taco shells. Also stuff with the lettuce and cheese.

Tofu-Stuffed Chilies

• • •

These "no problema" poblanos are quick and rewarding; simply sauté, mix, stuff, and serve.

• • •

Serves 8

INGREDIENTS

8 ounces tofu, drained and crumbled
8 large poblano chilies, roasted and peeled
1 tablespoon peanut oil
1 cup golden raisins
½ cup toasted pumpkin or sunflower seeds
1 cup corn kernels, cooked
1 cup Monterey Jack cheese, shredded
2 cups feta cheese

PREPARATION

1 Cut a slit in the side of each poblano and remove the seeds. Set aside.

2 In a frying pan, sauté the tofu in the peanut oil until browned. Set aside in a large bowl.

3 Add the rest of the ingredients (except the poblanos) to the tofu, and mix well.

4 Stuff the resulting mixture into the poblanos.

5 On a baking sheet, cook the poblanos at 350°F for 15 minutes, or until the cheese melts. Serve hot.

Tofu, Potato, and Tomato Wraps

• • •

Tortillas are making a comeback as "wraps." Try this deep, rich, and surprising filling the next time you're looking for something different in your tortillas.

• • •

Yields 12 wraps

INGREDIENTS

24 ounces firm tofu
1 pound boiling potatoes, diced
2 medium tomatoes
1 medium onion, minced
1 garlic clove, minced
1 serrano pepper
¼ cup vegetable oil
2 teaspoons soy sauce
1 teaspoon cumin
2 tablespoons fresh cilantro leaves, chopped
12 flour tortillas
Salsa
1 package alfalfa sprouts
1 head lettuce, shredded

PREPARATION

1 On an oiled baking sheet, arrange the diced potatoes and the tomatoes. Broil for 5 to 10 minutes, or until the potatoes are tender and the tomatoes blister on all sides. Turn the tomatoes often.

2 In a blender, purée the tomatoes with ¼ of the onion, the garlic, and serrano pepper. Set aside.

3 In a frying pan, heat 2 teaspoons of the oil, and add the tomato purée.

4 Cook for 5 minutes, then add the tofu, mashing it thoroughly with the back of a spoon.

5 Add the soy sauce and cumin, and continue to cook for another 5 minutes. Stir frequently.

6 Place the mixture in a bowl. Set aside.

7 In a frying pan, sauté the rest of the onion in 1 tablespoon of oil until it begins to brown.

8 Add the potatoes, and sauté for another 5 minutes.

9 Stir in the tomato mixture, remove from the heat, and add the cilantro.

10 Heat the tortillas briefly in a dry frying pan, and then fill them with 2 heaping tablespoons of the mixture, and fold.

11 Heat the remaining oil in the frying pan, and sauté the tortilla wraps gently on both sides until just crisp. Drain on paper towels, and serve immediately, garnishing with salsa, sprouts, and lettuce.

Vegetable Chop Suey

• • •

This Chinese-American dish features a medley of crisp vegetables enhanced by a simple, thick sauce.

• • •

Serves 6

INGREDIENTS

12 ounces firm tofu, cubed
⅔ cup onion, chopped
3 garlic cloves, minced
2 teaspoons ginger root, grated
1 tablespoon sesame oil
½ cup carrots, sliced
½ cup celery, sliced
2 cups zucchini, sliced
1 cup green bell peppers, sliced
⅔ cup red cabbage, shredded
⅔ cup mushrooms, sliced
1 cup tomatoes, sliced
⅔ cup mung bean sprouts
⅔ cup green beans, sliced
⅔ cup pea pods
⅔ cup bamboo shoots

⅔ cup water chestnuts, sliced
1 cup water
2 tablespoons soy sauce
2 tablespoons cornstarch or arrowroot
White or brown rice, cooked to serve 6

PREPARATION

1 In a wok or large frying pan, stir-fry the onion, garlic, and ginger root in the sesame oil over medium-high heat, until the onion is tender.

2 Add the carrots and celery, and stir-fry for 2 minutes.

3 Add the zucchini, bell peppers, cabbage, mushrooms, and tofu, and stir-fry for 2 minutes longer.

4 Add the tomatoes, bean sprouts, green beans, pea pods, bamboo shoots, and water chestnuts, and stir-fry for 3 minutes.

5 In a small bowl, combine the water, soy sauce, and cornstarch or arrowroot. Pour the mixture into the vegetables. Cook, stirring constantly, until the sauce is thickened, and all the vegetables are tender-crisp. Serve over the cooked rice.

Satay with Tofu (see below)

Satay with Tofu

• • •

This Indonesian dish usually consists of strips of marinated meat or seafood grilled on skewers and dipped in peanut sauce. Here, the tofu steps in admirably to capture the exotic taste of the peanut sauce.

• • •

Serves 4 to 6

INGREDIENTS

16 ounces extra-firm tofu, frozen, thawed, and cubed
3 tablespoons soy sauce
2 teaspoons sesame oil
1 garlic clove, crushed
1 yellow and 1 red bell pepper, cut in squares
8 to 12 fresh bay leaves
Sunflower oil, for grilling

SAUCE

2 scallions, finely chopped
2 garlic cloves, minced
¼ teaspoon chili powder
1 teaspoon sugar
1 tablespoon white vinegar
2 tablespoons soy sauce
3 tablespoons crunchy peanut butter

PREPARATION

1 Soak 8 to 12 wooden skewers in water for 20 minutes, then drain. This will prevent them from burning on the grill.

2 In a large bowl, combine the tofu with the soy sauce, sesame oil, and garlic. Cover and marinate for 20 minutes.

3 In another bowl, mix the sauce ingredients together until well blended, but still chunky.

4 Drain the tofu, and thread the cubes onto the soaked skewers with the pepper squares and bay leaves.

5 Brush the satays with oil. Broil or grill, turning the sticks occasionally, until the ingredients are browned and crisp. Serve hot with the sauce.

Curried Tofu and Vegetables

• • •

Traditional Indian spices are a perfect accent to the understated taste of tofu, potatoes, and eggplant.

• • •

Serves 4 to 6

INGREDIENTS

24 ounces firm tofu, pressed and diced
2 potatoes, diced
2 cups eggplant, diced and peeled
2 tablespoons safflower or peanut oil
1 onion, sliced
1 garlic clove, minced
1 teaspoon ginger root, minced
1 tablespoon curry powder
¼ cup peanuts
½ cup raisins
Salt to taste
1 cup plain, low-fat yogurt
2 tablespoons fresh cilantro leaves, chopped
3 to 4 cups cooked brown rice or couscous
Chutney

PREPARATION

1 In a steamer insert, steam the potatoes and eggplant for 15 minutes.

2 Meanwhile, in a saucepan or wok, sauté or stir-fry the onion, garlic, and ginger in oil for 2 minutes.

3 Add the tofu and curry powder. Sauté or stir fry for 10 minutes, stirring gently.

4 Add the steamed potatoes and eggplant, peanuts, and raisins, and sauté or stir-fry another 5 minutes.

Curried Tofu and Vegetables (see above)

5 Season to taste with salt, then remove from the heat. Let the mixture cool for 3 to 5 minutes.

6 Stir in the yogurt and the cilantro. Serve over hot cooked grains, with chutney on the side.

Recipe Tip

For the Curried Tofu and Vegetables, you can substitute 1 chopped zucchini and ¾ pound of cauliflower for the potatoes and eggplant. Simply sauté the zucchini and cauliflower, and add to the mixture.

Hearty Indian Stew

• • •

You'll love this spicy stew on a cold winter's night. Serve with a garnish of soy yogurt and chopped cilantro.

• • •

Serves 4

INGREDIENTS

8 ounces firm tofu, frozen, thawed, drained, and diced
½ tablespoon margarine or butter
1 tablespoon safflower oil
2 garlic cloves, minced
1½ tablespoons ginger root, minced
1 teaspoon cumin
½ teaspoon ground coriander
¼ teaspoon ground cloves
½ teaspoon ground cardamom
¼ teaspoon mustard powder
½ teaspoon turmeric
½ stick cinnamon

1 teaspoon salt
3 cups vegetable stock (see recipe on page 81)
3 tablespoons fresh lime juice
1 tablespoon honey
3 carrots, sliced diagonally
1½ cups button mushrooms, sliced
2 cups cauliflower florets
1 medium russet potato, diced

PREPARATION

1 In a large saucepan, melt the margarine or butter over medium heat, and add the oil. Sauté the garlic and ginger, stirring, for 1 minute.

2 Add the cumin, coriander, cloves, cardamom, mustard, turmeric, cinnamon, and salt. Stir and cook for 2 minutes.

3 Add the stock, lime juice, tofu, and honey, and cook 3 to 4 minutes longer.

4 Add the carrots, mushrooms, cauliflower, and potato, and cook, covered, for 25 minutes, or until tender. Discard the cinnamon stick, and serve warm.

Saag Tofu

• • •

In this recipe, tofu takes the place of paneer, a fresh cheese used in Indian cooking.

• • •

Serves 4

INGREDIENTS

12 ounces firm tofu, cubed
6 tablespoons vegetable oil
1 teaspoon garam masala or curry powder
1 teaspoon salt
1-inch piece of ginger root, peeled and chopped
3 garlic cloves
1 green chili
4 tablespoons water
1 pound fresh spinach, washed and chopped
4 tablespoons milk
Basmati or other rice, cooked to serve 4

PREPARATION

1 In a frying pan, deep-fry the tofu in 3 tablespoons of the oil until golden brown.

2 Sprinkle the tofu with the garam masala and half the salt. Set aside.

3 In a blender or food processor, add the ginger, garlic, chili, and water, and process until smooth.

4 In a saucepan, heat the rest of the oil, and add the contents of the food processor. Stir for about 30 seconds, then add the spinach and the remaining salt.

5 Stir for a minute, then cover the saucepan, and leave to simmer for 5 to 10 minutes.

6 Add the tofu cubes and milk to the saucepan, stir gently, and leave to simmer 5 to 10 minutes more, stirring once or twice.

7 Serve over the rice.

Mattar Tofu

• • •

A very popular dish in Indian restaurants—we've made it dairy free without sacrificing flavor.

• • •

Serves 4

INGREDIENTS

12 ounces firm tofu, cubed
1 tablespoon vegetable oil
2 tablespoons ginger root, grated
1 tablespoon garlic, chopped
2 tablespoons water
1 medium onion, minced
1 tablespoon garam masala or curry powder
1 teaspoon salt
1 teaspoon turmeric
1 teaspoon coriander
Pinch of cayenne pepper
¼ cup vegetable stock (see recipe on page 81) or water
14-ounce can diced tomatoes, with juice
1½ cups frozen peas
1 teaspoon sugar
Basmati or other rice, cooked to serve 4

PREPARATION

1 In a saucepan, sauté the tofu cubes in oil over high heat until they are golden on two sides. Remove from the pan and set aside.

2 Add the ginger and garlic to the hot pan, and fry over high heat with the water for 1 minute.

3 Add the onion, and steam-fry until it is soft, about 5 minutes (add more water if necessary).

4 Add the seasonings and the stock, and stir well.

5 Add the tomatoes, peas, tofu, and sugar, and simmer for 10 minutes.

6 Serve over the rice.

Korma with Tofu and Peas

• • •

This Indian dish, so simple to prepare, tastes special nonetheless—perfect for special occasions.

• • •

Serves 6

INGREDIENTS

16 ounces firm tofu, sliced in half
Vegetable oil for deep-frying and sautéing
2 large tomatoes, chopped
3 tablespoons cashew pieces
2 large onions, grated
1-inch piece ginger root, grated
4 garlic cloves, minced
2 cinnamon sticks
2 bay leaves
1 teaspoon chili powder
1$\frac{1}{3}$ cups water
1$\frac{1}{3}$ cups yogurt
2 teaspoons cumin
1 teaspoon coriander
2 teaspoons garam masala
$\frac{2}{3}$ cup frozen peas
1 teaspoon sugar
Salt to taste
Basmati or other rice, cooked to serve 6

PREPARATION

1 Cut one half of the tofu into small cubes, and, in a large frying pan, deep-fry until golden. Drain and set aside.

2 In a food processor or blender, add the tomatoes and cashew pieces, and blend thoroughly.

3 In a saucepan, sauté the onions in 1 tablespoon of oil until lightly browned.

4 Lower the heat, stir in the ginger, cinnamon sticks, bay leaves, and garlic, and cook for 3 to 4 minutes.

5 Stir in the chili powder, then add the water, yogurt, and tomato-cashew mixture. Bring to a boil.

6 Add the cumin, coriander, and garam masala. Simmer for a few minutes.

7 Add the deep-fried tofu cubes and the peas, and cook for 3 minutes longer.

8 Crumble the remaining tofu into the saucepan, along with the sugar and salt. Cook for 5 minutes, and then serve over the rice.

Tofu in Ginger-Coconut Sauce

• • •

Even the most finicky of eaters will not be able to get enough of this pungent Vietnamese dish.

• • •

Serves 4

INGREDIENTS

12 ounces firm tofu, drained and cubed
3 tablespoons peanut oil
8 scallions, thinly sliced
Salt to taste
1 bunch fresh cilantro leaves
$\frac{1}{2}$ cup ginger root, finely diced
Grated rind of 1 lemon
1 jalapeño pepper, seeded and diced
15-ounce can unsweetened coconut milk, plus water to make 2 cups
3 pieces galanga (optional)
1 teaspoon soy sauce
Pepper to taste
Basmati or other rice, cooked to serve 4

PREPARATION

1 In a frying pan, sauté the scallions in 2 tablespoons of oil until lightly browned.

2 Season with salt, then add half the cilantro. Stir for 1 minute, and remove from the heat. Set aside.

3 In a wok, heat the remaining oil, and add the ginger, grated lemon rind, and jalapeño. Stir-fry for 30 seconds.

4 Add the coconut milk mixture and galanga, and bring to a boil.

5 Lower the heat, add the tofu, and simmer for 10 minutes, or until the sauce has thickened.

6 Add the soy sauce, season with plenty of pepper, and then add the sautéed scallions and remaining cilantro.

7 Serve over the rice.

Cajun Pizza with Tofu and Roasted Red Peppers (see above)

Cajun Pizza with Tofu and Roasted Red Peppers

• • •

This isn't your run-of-the-mill cheese pizza. This pie is easy to make, and has a peppery, Cajun kick you won't be able to resist.

• • •

Yields 8 slices

INGREDIENTS

12 ounces extra-firm tofu
1 tablespoon vegetable oil
1 teaspoon cayenne pepper, or to taste
1 teaspoon crushed red pepper
1 teaspoon black pepper
1 teaspoon cumin
1 14-inch, prepared pizza crust
1½ cups pizza sauce
14 ounces roasted red peppers, drained
3 cups mozzarella cheese, shredded

PREPARATION

1 In a large mixing bowl, crumble the tofu. Add the oil and spices, and mix well. Marinate in the refrigerator for at least 30 minutes.

2 Place the pizza crust on a baking sheet, and generously cover with the sauce. Top with the tofu, peppers, and cheese.

3 Bake at 450°F for 8 to 12 minutes, or until the cheese is melted and the toppings are well heated.

Tofu-Stuffed Shells

• • •

Shell-ebrate with this lightning-quick, low-fat, deeply satisfying meal.

• • •

Yields 10 shells

INGREDIENTS

24 ounces firm tofu, mashed
2 quarts water
¼ cup fresh parsley sprigs, chopped
2 tablespoons onion powder
1½ teaspoons salt
½ teaspoon garlic powder
½ teaspoon dried basil
3½ cups of your favorite tomato sauce
4 ounces jumbo macaroni shells, cooked
Parmesan cheese (optional)

PREPARATION

1 In a large bowl, mix the tofu, parsley, onion powder, salt, garlic, and basil.

2 Spread 2 cups of the tomato sauce evenly onto the bottom of a 9 by 9-inch pan.

3 Spoon the tofu mixture into the cooked shells, about ⅓ cup per shell, and arrange the shells in the pan.

4 Pour the remaining sauce over the tops of the shells.

5 Top with Parmesan cheese, if desired, and bake at 350°F for 25 minutes, or until the tomato sauce is bubbly.

Fabulous No-Cheese Pizza

• • •

The tofu adds texture and protein to this vivacious, veggie-crammed pizza.

• • •

Yields 8 slices

INGREDIENTS

12 ounces firm tofu, crumbled
2 tablespoons olive oil
1 onion, chopped
2 garlic cloves, minced
1 16-ounce can tomatoes
2 tablespoons tomato paste
2 teaspoons dried oregano
1 teaspoon dried basil
Salt, to taste
Pepper to taste
1 14- to 16-inch prepared pizza crust
1½ cups mushrooms, finely chopped
1 small green bell pepper, thinly sliced
¼ cup olives, sliced (optional)
¼ cup artichoke hearts, sliced (optional)

PREPARATION

1 In a frying pan, sauté the onion and garlic in oil until tender.

2 Add the tomatoes, paste, herbs, and tofu.

3 Bring to a boil, then simmer for 30 minutes, or until thick. Add salt and pepper to taste.

4 Spread the sauce over the pizza crust, then evenly distribute the vegetables.

5 Bake at 450°F for 30 minutes.

Tofu-Veggie Calzone

• • •

Nothing will satisfy your hunger better than this "outside-in" filled pizza.

• • •

Serves 4

INGREDIENTS

8 ounces firm tofu, cubed
2 tablespoons olive oil
1 onion, chopped
1½ garlic cloves, chopped
1 carrot, chopped
2 celery sticks, chopped
1 small bell pepper, chopped
1 cup mushrooms, chopped
4 tablespoons tomato paste
1⅓ cups water
1 teaspoon dried basil
1 teaspoon dried oregano
2 cups whole wheat flour
Salt to taste
½ cup margarine or butter
Flour, for rolling out dough
Tomato sauce, for dipping

PREPARATION

1 In a saucepan, sauté the onion and garlic in the oil until the onion is translucent.

2 Add the carrot, celery, and pepper, and sauté for 5 minutes.

3 Add the mushrooms to the pan when the vegetables are nearly tender.

4 Stir in the tomato paste, ⅓ cup of the water, basil, and oregano, and bring to a boil.

5 Add the tofu, lower the heat, and simmer for 5 minutes.

6 In a large bowl, mix the flour and salt, then mix in the margarine or butter.

7 Add enough of the remaining water to make dough. Mix well.

8 Divide the dough into four pieces, and, on a floured surface, roll them into thin circles.

9 Spoon a quarter of the filling onto half of each circle. Fold the dough over to cover, and pinch it to seal.

10 Bake at 375°F for 25 to 35 minutes, or until the crust is browned.

11 Serve with your favorite tomato sauce on the side.

Pasta with Cream Sauce

• • •

This slimmed-down version of fettuccine alfredo retains all the creaminess and taste of the original, and none of its fat.

• • •

Serves 4 to 6

INGREDIENTS

24 ounces firm tofu
½ cup plain, low-fat yogurt
1 tablespoon sesame tahini
1 heaping tablespoon miso
1 tablespoon fresh lemon juice
Pinch of fresh nutmeg, grated
¾ pound pasta, any shape, cooked
1 cup Parmesan cheese, grated
Pepper to taste

PREPARATION

1 In a blender or food processor, blend the tofu, yogurt, tahini, miso, lemon juice, and nutmeg until completely smooth.

2 Spoon the cooked pasta into a serving bowl, and toss with the tofu cream sauce and the Parmesan. Add pepper to taste.

Spinach Risotto (see opposite page)

Penne with Oil, Garlic, and Zucchini

• • •

This simple dish is a garlic lover's dream come true.

• • •

Serves 4

INGREDIENTS

4 ounces firm tofu, crumbled
1 pound zucchini, cut into 2-inch julienne strips
⅓ cup olive oil
2 to 3 teaspoons garlic, finely minced
¾ pound penne, cooked al dente
½ to 1 cup Parmesan cheese, grated
3 tablespoons fresh parsley sprigs, chopped
Basil to taste
Sage to taste
Thyme to taste
Marjoram to taste
Salt to taste
Pepper to taste

PREPARATION

1 In a steamer insert, steam the zucchini for 5 minutes. Set aside.

2 Meanwhile, in a frying pan, heat the olive oil and garlic over very low heat, until the garlic turns golden. Remove from the heat. Add the tofu, and set aside.

3 Spoon the cooked pasta into a serving dish, and toss with the oil, garlic, and tofu mixture.

4 Mix in the zucchini, cheese, and spices, and serve immediately.

Spinach Risotto

• • •

You can whip this meal together in minutes—you probably already have all the ingredients you need in your kitchen.

• • •

Serves 6 to 8

INGREDIENTS

8 ounces firm tofu
10-ounce package frozen spinach
3 tablespoons vegetable oil
2 tablespoons spinach juice from thawing
1½ teaspoons salt
1 medium onion, finely chopped
2 garlic cloves, minced
3 to 4 cups rice, cooked
¼ teaspoon black pepper
¼ teaspoon nutmeg

PREPARATION

1 Thaw the frozen spinach and save the liquid.

2 In a blender or food processor, blend the tofu, 2 tablespoons of the oil, 2 tablespoons of the spinach juice, and salt until smooth and creamy.

3 In a saucepan, sauté the onion and garlic in the remaining oil, until the onion is translucent.

4 Remove from the heat, and add the rice, black pepper, nutmeg, spinach, and tofu mixture. Mix well.

5 Pour the resulting mixture into an oiled, 1-quart baking dish, and bake at 325°F for 30 minutes.

Basic Barbecue Tofu-Style

• • •

Tofu is the perfect meat alternative for shish kebobs. What follows is a basic recipe followed by five distinctive marinades. Experiment with different seasonal vegetables.

• • •

Serves 6

INGREDIENTS

16 ounces firm tofu, cut into 1-inch cubes
¼ cup olive oil
2 tablespoons red wine vinegar
1 teaspoon dried thyme
2 zucchini, cut into 1-inch rounds
2 red onions, cut into wedges
16 cherry tomatoes
2 green bell peppers, cut into large squares
8 metal skewers
Juice of 1 lemon
Salt to taste
Pepper to taste

PREPARATION

1 In a large mixing bowl, combine the oil, vinegar, and thyme.

2 Toss in the tofu and vegetables, and marinate in the refrigerator for at least 1 hour.

3 Thread the tofu and vegetables on the skewers, alternating the items.

4 Cook the skewers on a heated grill, occasionally basting with the remaining marinade, until the vegetables are slightly charred and crispy.

5 Sprinkle with lemon juice, salt, and pepper.

Basic Barbeque Tofu-Style (see above)

Bring a bit of summer indoors—
broil the skewers in the oven
for 3 minutes on each side.

If you are using wooden skewers,
soak them in water before
grilling, to prevent burning.

Soy-Ginger Marinade

INGREDIENTS

¼ cup soy sauce
1½ teaspoons ginger root, grated
1 tablespoon rice vinegar
1 tablespoon honey
1 cup water
1 tablespoon mirin

Barbecue Marinade

INGREDIENTS

1 onion, finely chopped
1 large garlic clove, minced
¼ cup apple butter
1 teaspoon Chinese chili paste
¼ cup fresh lemon juice
3 tablespoons corn oil
1 tablespoon vegetarian Worcestershire sauce
½ cup tomato sauce
2 teaspoons mustard powder
1 tablespoon sugar or natural sweetener
½ teaspoon salt

Note: For best results, place all the ingredients in a food processor, and process until well blended. Transfer the sauce to a saucepan, and simmer for 30 minutes before marinating.

Ginger-Tomato Marinade

INGREDIENTS

½ cup soy sauce
1 tablespoon garlic, crushed
1 tablespoon ginger root, finely grated
2 teaspoons dark sesame oil
2 teaspoons honey or rice malt
2 tablespoons tomato paste
1 tablespoon rice vinegar
1 tablespoon ground coriander
Freshly ground black pepper, to taste
½ cup water

Note: Bring all of the marinade ingredients to a high heat slowly, and pour over the skewers in a bowl. Marinate for 1 hour.

Mustard Marinade

INGREDIENTS

3 tablespoons prepared mustard
4 tablespoons sake or white wine
2 tablespoons vinegar
4 tablespoons vegetable oil
2 tablespoons maple syrup
1 teaspoon dried rosemary
1 teaspoon dried oregano
2 garlic cloves, minced
2 teaspoons ginger root, minced
3 to 4 tablespoons soy sauce

Sweet and Hot Marinade

INGREDIENTS

¼ cup pineapple juice
1 to 2 teaspoons dried rosemary
2 teaspoons dried sage leaves, finely chopped
1 tablespoon olive oil
2 tablespoons soy sauce
2 tablespoons lemon juice
1 teaspoon dried thyme leaves, finely chopped
2 teaspoons prepared mustard
Pinch pepper
Hot pepper sauce to taste

Cinnamon–Tomato Bow Ties

• • •

If you're tired of the same old pasta night after night, this dish will certainly resuscitate your taste buds.

• • •

Serves 6

INGREDIENTS

8 ounces firm tofu, crumbled
8 ounces bow tie pasta
Several quarts of water
3½ cups pear tomatoes, peeled and crushed
½ medium yellow onion, chopped
3 garlic cloves, minced
½ teaspoon ground cinnamon
½ teaspoon mild chili powder
½ teaspoon cumin
⅛ teaspoon mustard powder
⅛ teaspoon ground cloves
8 ounces ricotta cheese
½ cup plain, nonfat yogurt
3 tablespoons fresh basil leaves, minced
¼ teaspoon olive oil
¼ cup Parmesan cheese, finely grated

PREPARATION

1 In a large pot, boil the bow ties in several quarts of water until al dente. Drain, and set aside.

2 In a blender or food processor, purée the tomatoes, onion, and garlic until smooth.

3 Pour the mixture into a medium saucepan, and add the cinnamon, chili powder, cumin, mustard and cloves. Cook over medium-low heat for 10 minutes, stirring frequently.

4 In a large mixing bowl, combine the crumbled tofu, ricotta cheese, yogurt, and basil. Blend well.

5 In an oiled 9 by 9-inch pan, spread half the sauce evenly over the bottom.

6 Layer with half the noodles, and spread evenly with the tofu-cheese mixture.

7 Top with the remaining noodles and sauce. Sprinkle with Parmesan cheese, cover with aluminum foil, and bake for 20 minutes.

8 Uncover and bake for 5 minutes longer. Serve hot.

Capellini with Tofu-Basil Sauce

• • •

The herbed sauce creates a light and refreshing pasta dish—perfect for a summertime meal served with a bottle of your favorite white wine.

• • •

Serves 6

INGREDIENTS

16 ounces firm tofu, cubed
5 tablespoons olive oil
2 medium garlic cloves, minced
¼ cup pine nuts
½ teaspoon salt
¼ teaspoon black pepper
1 pound capellini pasta, cooked
½ cup fresh basil leaves, chopped
Romano cheese, grated (optional)

PREPARATION

1 In a large saucepan, heat 3 tablespoons of oil over medium-low heat. Sauté the garlic until softened, but not browned.

2 Add the pine nuts, increase the heat to medium, and cook, stirring frequently, until the nuts are lightly browned.

3 Season with salt and pepper, and add the tofu, tossing frequently for 3 minutes.

4 Remove the mixture from the heat, and season with additional salt and pepper, if desired.

5 In a serving bowl, mix the cooked pasta and the tofu mixture.

6 Add the remaining 2 tablespoons of oil, basil, and Romano cheese, if desired, and mix again. Serve immediately.

Baked Italian Eggplant

• • •

This casserole-type dish is a big holiday hit for vegetarians. Try it at your next family reunion, and see if anyone misses the meat.

• • •

Serves 5

INGREDIENTS

16 ounces soft tofu
1 medium onion, chopped
2 tablespoons oil
4 garlic cloves, minced
1 eggplant, diced in ¼-inch cubes
8 ounces tomato sauce
¼ cup water
2 teaspoons vegetable bouillon
¼ teaspoon Italian seasoning
¼ teaspoon garlic powder
3 eggs, lightly beaten
1 cup mozzarella cheese, grated
Parmesan cheese, grated

PREPARATION

1 In a saucepan, sauté the onion and garlic in oil until the onion is golden.

2 Add the diced eggplant, tomato sauce, water, bouillon, Italian seasoning, and garlic powder. Bring to a boil, reduce heat, and simmer, covered, for 10 minutes.

3 Meanwhile, in a large bowl, mash the tofu well with a fork. Add the eggs and mozzarella cheese, and mix well.

4 When the eggplant has simmered for 10 minutes, stir in the tofu mixture. Sprinkle with the Parmesan cheese

5 Pour the eggplant mixture into a 9 by 13-inch baking dish, and bake at 350°F for 35 minutes.

Tofu Casserole with Mashed Sweet Potato Crust

• • •

A family favorite, especially with lots of gravy. For best results, let the crust brown nicely before serving.

• • •

Serves 4 to 6

INGREDIENTS

CRUST

5 medium sweet potatoes, peeled and quartered
Water for boiling
1 garlic clove
1 celery stalk
1 bunch fresh parsley sprigs
8 peppercorns
1 medium onion
1 bay leaf
1 tablespoon light miso
1 tablespoon olive oil
Reserved potato water, from boiling potatoes
Paprika, for garnish

181

FILLING

- 16 ounces firm tofu, frozen, thawed, and crumbled
- 1 tablespoon olive oil
- ¾ cup red onion, diced
- 1 garlic clove, minced
- ½ pound mushrooms, sliced
- 4 tablespoons barbecue sauce
- 1 tablespoon instant gravy mix
- 1 teaspoon powdered vegetable broth
- 1 teaspoon dried thyme
- 1 teaspoon paprika
- 1 tablespoon soy sauce
- 1 cup frozen or fresh corn
- 1 cup spinach, chopped

GRAVY

- 2 tablespoons olive oil
- 2 tablespoons whole wheat pastry flour
- 1 tablespoon nutritional yeast flakes
- 2½ cups reserved potato water, from boiling potatoes
- 1 tablespoon instant gravy mix

PREPARATION

1 In a large pot, cover the quartered potatoes with water. Add the garlic, celery, parsley, peppercorns, onion, and bay leaf. Bring to a boil, cover, and simmer over medium-low heat for 15 to 20 minutes, or until the vegetables are very tender.

2 Transfer the potatoes from the water to a large bowl, reserving the potato water.

3 Add the miso, oil, and up to 1 cup of the potato stock to the potatoes, in ¼- to ⅓-cup increments, mashing as you add the stock. Add only enough water to moisten the potatoes adequately. Set aside.

4 Meanwhile, in a frying pan, prepare the filling by sautéing the onion and garlic in 1 tablespoon of oil. After 1 minute, add the mushrooms, and sauté for 2 minutes.

5 Add the tofu crumbles and sauté briefly.

6 Stir in the barbecue sauce, gravy mix, broth powder, thyme, paprika, and soy sauce. Mix well and cook, stirring frequently, for 10 minutes.

7 Add the corn and spinach to the filling, and mix well.

8 Pour the filling into a casserole dish. Pat down with the back of a large spoon.

9 Spread the potato crust evenly over the filling, smoothing the top with a spoon or spatula. Dust evenly with paprika.

10 Bake at 350°F for 30 to 40 minutes, or until the crust is golden.

11 While the casserole bakes, prepare the gravy. In a frying pan, heat the oil, and then add the flour and yeast, and whisk over medium heat to form a paste.

12 Slowly stir in 2½ cups of the reserved potato water, whisking as you stir to allow the gravy to thicken.

13 Stir in the instant gravy mix, and continue whisking until the gravy is thick and smooth. Add more potato water, if needed.

14 Serve with the potato crust on the bottom and the filling on top. Spoon the gravy over the top.

Tofu Pot Pie

...

Here's a delicious pot pie that brings back memories of the chicken ones mom used to make.

...

Serves 4 to 6

INGREDIENTS

- 16 ounces extra-firm tofu, cubed
- 4 teaspoons light sesame oil
- 1 cup onion, diced
- 1 carrot, diced
- 1 cup broccoli florets
- 1 cup fresh corn kernels
- 1 cup fresh or frozen green peas
- 1 cup cauliflower florets
- 1 teaspoon soy sauce
- 1½ cups water
- Pinch of powdered ginger
- 2 pie crusts (see recipe below)

WHOLE WHEAT PIE CRUST

3 cups whole wheat pastry flour
½ cup corn oil
Pinch of salt
½ cup water

PREPARATION

1 In a frying pan, sauté the tofu cubes in 2 teaspoons of the sesame oil until browned on both sides. Set aside.

2 In a saucepan, sauté the onions in the remaining sesame oil for 3 minutes.

3 Add the remaining vegetables, and cook, stirring, until tender.

4 Add the tofu cubes and the soy sauce. Add the water, and stir.

5 Bring the mixture to a boil over medium heat, and cook, stirring, until a thin glaze forms over the entire mixture. Stir in the powdered ginger, and set aside.

6 Press one pie crust into an oiled pie pan. Spoon the filling into the crust, and lay the second crust over the top.

7 Crimp the edges of both crusts between your fingers and thumb. Pierce the top crust in several places to allow steam to escape.

8 Bake at 350°F for 45 minutes, or until the crust is golden and the filling is bubbling.

THE CRUST

1 In a large mixing bowl, combine the flour, oil, and salt, and mix well.

2 Add the water, and continue to blend until the mixture becomes doughy.

3 Gather the dough between your hands, split it into two equal mounds, and knead each mound three to five times to shape into two balls.

4 Roll each ball out on a floured surface until it is the thickness of a pie crust.

Zucchini Frittata with Tofu

• • •

You may want to double this recipe, because your family will gobble up these crispy patties and beg for more.

• • •

Serves 4 to 6

INGREDIENTS

16 ounces firm tofu
3 tablespoons olive oil
1 large onion, thinly sliced
4 medium zucchini, thinly sliced
¼ cup fresh parsley sprigs, chopped
3 fresh garlic cloves, minced
1½ teaspoons salt
¾ cup flour
2 teaspoons baking powder
1 tablespoon soy sauce
8 ounces ready-made spaghetti sauce

PREPARATION

1 In a frying pan, sauté the onion, zucchini, parsley, and garlic until crisp-tender. Remove from the heat, and set aside.

2 In a large bowl, mash ½ cup of the tofu.

3 In a blender, blend the rest of the tofu until smooth.

4 Add the blended tofu to the mashed tofu, and add in the salt, flour, baking powder, and soy sauce. Mix well.

5 Stir in the sautéed vegetables. Scoop out half cupfuls of the mixture, and place them on an oiled baking sheet, flattened into circles. You should have seven to eight 5-inch patties.

6 Bake at 350°F for 15 minutes. Flip the patties, and bake for 15 minutes more, or until golden brown.

7 Serve with your favorite noodles and spaghetti sauce.

Recipe Tip

For a flavorful Frittata variation, replace the zucchini with 1 sliced leek, 8 ounces of sliced button mushrooms, and 3½ cups of chopped spinach.

Zucchini Frittata with Tofu (see page 183)

Curried Casserole with Tofu

* * *

Bored of the same old same old?
Don't worry, use curry!

* * *

Serves 4 to 6

INGREDIENTS

24 ounces firm tofu, cubed
¼ cup butter
3 tablespoons all-purpose flour
2 tablespoons curry powder
3 cups vegetable stock (see recipe on page 81)
Salt to taste
Pepper to taste
1 red bell pepper, diced
1 onion, chopped
¼ cup green beans, blanched
2 zucchini, sliced and blanched
1 head cauliflower, cut into florets and blanched
½ cup bread crumbs

PREPARATION

1 In a saucepan, melt the butter over medium heat, and add the flour and 1 tablespoon of the curry powder. Stir rapidly, and slowly add the stock until the mix begins to thicken.

2 Season with salt and pepper, and reduce heat to low.

3 In a frying pan, sauté the red pepper and onion until tender. Add the remaining curry, green beans, zucchini, and cauliflower.

4 Slowly add the sauce, then fold in the tofu.

5 Transfer the mixture to a casserole dish. Top with the bread crumbs, and bake at 350°F for 25 minutes.

Tofu and Artichoke Gratin

* * *

Flavorful and elegant, this is the perfect recipe for artichokes.

* * *

Serves 6

INGREDIENTS

16 ounces firm tofu, cubed
¼ cup corn oil
½ cup scallions, minced
¼ cup all-purpose flour
2 tablespoons fresh parsley sprigs, minced
2 garlic cloves, minced
½ cup vegetable stock (see recipe on page 81)
2 16-ounce cans artichoke hearts, drained and chopped
2 tablespoons lemon juice
2 tablespoons vegetarian Worcestershire sauce or soy sauce
¼ teaspoon hot pepper sauce
½ teaspoon salt
⅛ teaspoon pepper
¼ cup Romano cheese, grated
½ cup bread crumbs

PREPARATION

1 In a saucepan, sauté the scallions in oil over medium heat, stirring, for 1 minute.

2 Stir in the flour, and cook over medium-low heat, stirring, for 2 minutes.

3 Add the parsley and garlic, and cook, stirring, for 1 minute.

4 Add the stock, and bring to a boil. Then cook the mixture, stirring, for 3 minutes.

5 Stir in the artichoke hearts, tofu, lemon juice, Worcestershire sauce or soy sauce, hot pepper sauce, salt, and pepper. Cook over low heat for 5 minutes, then spoon into a large baking dish.

6 Sprinkle with the cheese and bread crumbs and bake at 375°F for 20 minutes, or until hot and lightly browned on top.

Tofu-Walnut Loaf

• • •

Serve this luscious loaf to your
favorite people, and top with
your favorite sauce.

• • •

Serves 6

INGREDIENTS

12 ounces firm tofu, mashed
1 tablespoon olive oil
2 cups mushrooms, finely chopped
½ cup celery, finely chopped
½ cup onion, finely chopped
1 teaspoon garlic, minced
½ cup brown rice, cooked
¼ cup wheat germ, toasted
½ cup whole wheat bread crumbs
2 large eggs, lightly beaten
½ cup walnuts, finely chopped
2 tablespoons Parmesan cheese, grated
1 tablespoon soy sauce
½ teaspoon ground sage
½ teaspoon pepper
6-ounce can tomato paste
¼ cup water

PREPARATION

1 In a saucepan, sauté the mushrooms,
celery, onion, and garlic in oil until tender.

2 Remove the pan from the heat. Stir in the
remaining ingredients, and mix thoroughly.

3 Gently press the mixture into a loaf pan,
and bake at 375°F for about 45 minutes.

Recipe Tip

The Tofu-Walnut Loaf tastes great
with sautéed diced zucchini in
place of the mushrooms.

Peanut Noodles with Asian-Style Vegetables and Tofu

• • •

Pretty and delicious, this pasta has
plenty of vegetables, and a terrific
Asian-style sauce.

• • •

Serves 4 to 6

INGREDIENTS

10 ounces extra-firm tofu, cubed
1 cup broccoli
8 scallions
1 medium zucchini
1 yellow squash
2 tablespoons peanut oil
2 tablespoons ginger root, minced
1 large carrot, peeled, cut into thin strips
1 celery stalk, thinly sliced
1 red bell pepper, cut into thin strips
2 tablespoons dry sherry
Salt to taste
Pepper to taste
12 ounces linguine, cooked
Spicy Peanut Sauce (see recipe on page 207)
1 cup lightly salted roasted peanuts

PREPARATION

1 Cut the tops of the broccoli into florets.
Then peel the stems, and cut them into
thin strips. Set aside.

2 Cut the white parts of the scallions into
thin strips. Then chop the green parts. Set
aside.

3 Cut the zucchini lengthwise in half, then
cut it crosswise into ⅓-inch-thick slices.
Set aside.

4 Cut the yellow squash lengthwise in half,
then crosswise into ⅓-inch-thick slices.
Set aside.

➡

Peanut Noodles with Asian-Style Vegetables and Tofu
(see opposite page)

5 In a large frying pan, heat the peanut oil over medium-high heat. Add the ginger, and stir for 30 seconds. Add the broccoli, carrot, and celery, and sauté for 5 minutes.

6 Add the white parts of the scallions, along with the zucchini, yellow squash, bell pepper, and sherry, and sauté until the vegetables are crisp-tender.

7 Add the tofu, and stir gently for 2 minutes, or until heated through. Season to taste with salt and pepper.

8 Place the cooked linguine in a large mixing bowl. Add the Spicy Peanut Sauce, and toss to coat.

9 Transfer the linguine to a serving platter, and top with the vegetable mixture. Sprinkle with peanuts and the chopped green parts of the scallions.

Macaroni and Cheese with Tofu

• • •

Ah...the perfect comfort food—and it may comfort you to know that the tofu helps lower the fat count without sacrificing the taste.

• • •

Serves 4

INGREDIENTS

12 ounces firm tofu, pressed and crumbled
2 eggs
¼ cup heavy cream
2 cups sharp Cheddar cheese
Salt to taste
Pepper to taste
¼ teaspoon onion powder, or to taste
¼ teaspoon garlic powder, or to taste
¼ teaspoon nutmeg, or to taste
¼ teaspoon mustard powder, or to taste
¼ teaspoon cayenne pepper (optional)
3 cups macaroni, cooked

PREPARATION

1 In a large bowl, combine the eggs, cream, and cheese. Mix well.

2 Stir the tofu into the cheese mixture.

3 Season to taste with the rest of the ingredients. Add the cooked macaroni, and mix well.

4 Pour the mixture into a casserole dish, and bake at 375°F for 40 to 45 minutes, or until golden brown and crunchy on top.

Recipe Tip

For a taste of veggies, sauté onions, garlic, and mushrooms, and stir into the macaroni mixture before baking.

Ziti Terrine with Tofu and Vegetables

• • •

This meal tastes great as is, though we've found that a tomato sauce complements this dish nicely.

• • •

Serves 2 to 4

INGREDIENTS

8 ounces firm tofu, cut into ¼-inch cubes
3 fennel bulbs
1 bunch broccoli
5 tablespoons olive oil
1 large onion, minced
½ cup tomato paste
1 cup water, plus extra for cooking
½ teaspoon salt
1 cup dried bread crumbs
1 cup grated Romano cheese
¼ teaspoon black pepper
1 pound ziti, cooked al dente

PREPARATION

1 Remove the outer layer of the fennel bulbs. Quarter the bulbs lengthwise, then cut into thin slices. Cut the center stalk into ¼-inch pieces. Set aside.

2 Cut the broccoli florets off the stems. Peel the stems, then slice them thinly.

3 In a steamer insert, lightly steam the broccoli florets and stem slices. Set aside.

4 In a large saucepan, sauté the onion in 3 tablespoons of the olive oil for about 2 minutes.

5 Add the tomato paste, and cook for 2 minutes. Mix in 1 cup of water.

6 Add the fennel and enough water to cover the fennel by two-thirds. Add the salt.

7 Cover, reduce heat, and simmer for 15 minutes, or until the fennel is tender.

8 Uncover, increase the heat to high, and stir until the liquid is reduced by half.

9 Transfer the liquid to a large pot or mixing bowl. Add the steamed broccoli, but save 1 cup of the florets for garnish.

10 In a large frying pan, heat the last 2 tablespoons of oil over medium heat. Add the tofu and ⅓ cup of the bread crumbs and the tofu, and stir for 2 minutes, or until the crumbs turn golden brown.

11 Remove from the heat, and continue stirring for 2 minutes. Then add to the vegetables in the bowl.

12 Mix in the Romano cheese, pepper, and ziti.

13 Coat an oiled baking dish with the remaining bread crumbs. Transfer the vegetable-ziti mixture to the pan, using the back of the spoon to pack it down well.

14 Bake at 325°F for about 45 minutes.

15 When the dish is done, invert it onto a platter to serve, and garnish with the reserved broccoli florets.

Rigatoni with Fried Tofu, Roasted Peppers, and Olives

• • •

Elegant in its simplicity, this garlicky pasta dish is a wonderful place to begin the great tofu experiment.

• • •

Serves 4

INGREDIENTS

16 ounces extra-firm tofu, cubed
1 tablespoon canola oil
1 tablespoon soy sauce
1 pound rigatoni
3 tablespoons olive oil

Rigatoni with Fried Tofu, Roasted Peppers, and Olives
(see page 189)

6 garlic cloves, minced

7-ounce jar of roasted red peppers, drained and diced

10 black olives, pitted and halved

½ cup fresh parsley sprigs, chopped

¼ cup fresh basil leaves, chopped

½ teaspoon salt

Pepper to taste

¼ cup grated Parmesan cheese

PREPARATION

1 In a large frying pan, fry the tofu in the canola oil until golden brown. Stir and flip occasionally. Transfer to a large bowl, and drizzle with the soy sauce. Toss well and set aside.

2 In a large pot, bring several quarts of water to a boil. Cook the rigatoni in the boiling water until al dente. Drain, reserving ½ cup of the water.

3 Meanwhile, in the large frying pan, sauté the garlic in the olive oil for 30 seconds.

4 Add the peppers, and cook 2 minutes longer.

5 Stir in the olives, parsley, basil, salt, pepper, and tofu. Toss well.

6 Stir the reserved pasta water into the sauce. Cook for 1 minute.

7 Place the rigatoni in a serving bowl, and pour on the sauce. Mix well, sprinkle on the Parmesan, toss, and serve.

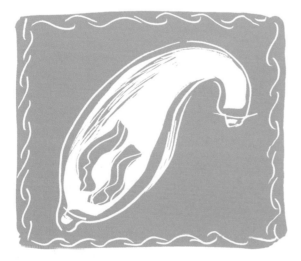

Tricolored Rotini and Asparagus with Tofu-Dill Sauce

• • •

This is another superb asparagus dish—the tart and tangy sauce and the asparagus pieces add real pep to your pasta.

• • •

Serves 4 to 6

INGREDIENTS

8 ounces soft tofu, patted dry and coarsely diced

1 tablespoon olive oil

2 garlic cloves, finely minced

¼ cup lemon juice

1 tablespoon Dijon mustard

2 tablespoons fresh dill sprigs, chopped

¼ teaspoon salt

⅛ teaspoon pepper

⅓ cup corn oil

1 pound tricolored rotini

½ pound fresh asparagus, cut in diagonal 1-inch pieces

PREPARATION

1 In a small frying pan, sauté the garlic over medium-low heat for 3 minutes.

2 Pour the contents of the frying pan into a food processor or blender. Add the tofu, lemon juice, mustard, dill, salt, and pepper, and blend until smooth.

3 With the processor or blender running, add the corn oil in a stream, and blend the sauce until emulsified.

4 Meanwhile, cook the rotini in a large pot of boiling water until tender. During the last 3 to 4 minutes of cooking time, add the asparagus to the cooking pasta. Drain, and toss with the sauce.

Fusilli with Yellow Squash, Tofu, and Capers

• • •

There's nothing silly about this seriously savory meal.

• • •

Serves 4 to 6

INGREDIENTS

4 ounces firm tofu, cut into ¼-inch cubes
3 tablespoons olive oil
2 large garlic cloves, minced
¼ cup scallions, minced
4 medium yellow squash, cut into ¼-inch cubes
½ teaspoon salt
¼ teaspoon hot red pepper flakes
1 tablespoon capers
1 pound fusilli pasta, cooked
½ cup fresh parsley leaves, chopped
¼ cup fresh mint leaves, chopped
Pepper to taste

PREPARATION

1 In a large saucepan, sauté the garlic in the oil until browned.

2 Add the scallions, and cook until tender but not browned.

3 Add the squash, salt, and red pepper flakes. Cover and cook over moderately low heat, stirring occasionally, for 5 minutes, or until the squash has softened.

4 Add the tofu and capers, reduce the heat to low, and simmer for 10 minutes.

5 Pour the contents of the saucepan into a serving bowl. Add the parsley, mint, and pepper to taste. Add the fusilli, and toss.

Moroccan Couscous with Tofu

• • •

Savor the exceptional conglomeration of veggies in this recipe we adapted from one we found on the back of a couscous box.

• • •

Serves 4 to 6

INGREDIENTS

12 ounces extra-firm tofu, frozen, thawed, and cubed
4 cups of vegetable stock (see recipe on page 81)
8 saffron threads, crushed
1 large tomato, cut into 1-inch cubes
1 small yellow onion, sliced
2 scallions, peeled and minced
1 garlic clove, minced
½ pound butternut squash, peeled and cubed
1 carrot, peeled and cut into 2-inch pieces
1 medium turnip, peeled and quartered
½ teaspoon salt
¼ teaspoon black pepper
1 zucchini, cut into 2-inch pieces
5 ounces chickpeas, cooked
2 teaspoons olive oil
1 cup couscous
½ teaspoon ground ginger
½ teaspoon ground cumin
¼ cup raisins
2 tablespoons soy sauce
1 tablespoon fresh parsley sprigs, chopped
1 tablespoon fresh cilantro leaves, chopped

PREPARATION

1 In a large pot, combine the vegetable broth, saffron, tomato, onion, scallions, garlic, squash, carrot, turnip, salt and pepper. Bring to a boil, reduce to a simmer, and cook for 15 minutes.

2 Add the zucchini and chickpeas, and cook for 10 minutes.

3 In a saucepan, sauté the couscous, ginger, and cumin in 1 tablespoon of the olive oil for 3 to 4 minutes. Remove from the heat.

4 In a separate, smaller pot, bring 1¼ cups of the broth from the vegetable mixture to a boil. Add the broth to the couscous along with the raisins.

5 Turn off the heat, cover the sauce pan, and let the couscous stand for 5 minutes.

6 In a frying pan, sauté the tofu in the rest of the oil and soy sauce for 5 minutes, or until the tofu is browned.

7 Fluff the couscous with a fork, and transfer to a serving platter.

8 With a slotted spoon, remove the vegetables from the broth and arrange them on and around the couscous.

9 Add the tofu to the platter, sprinkle with ½ cup of the remaining vegetable broth, and garnish with parsley and cilantro.

Moroccan Couscous with Tofu
(see opposite page)

Ziti with Watercress, Tofu, and Pine Nuts

• • •

This recipe adds a pungent punch to your pasta with the inclusion of fresh watercress.

• • •

Serves 4

INGREDIENTS

8 ounces firm tofu, cubed
¼ cup pine nuts
2 tablespoons olive oil
1 garlic clove, minced
¼ teaspoon hot red pepper flakes
2 cups watercress, chopped
1 cup vegetable stock (see recipe on page 81)
1 pound ziti, cooked until tender
½ cup Romano cheese, grated
Salt to taste
Pepper to taste

PREPARATION

1 In a frying pan, toast the pine nuts over medium-low heat, shaking the pan frequently, until lightly browned. Remove from the heat, and set aside.

2 Heat the oil in the frying pan, and add the garlic, tofu, and red pepper flakes. Sauté until the tofu is golden. Remove the contents with a slotted spoon, and set aside.

3 Add the watercress to the frying pan, and cook over medium heat for 1 minute.

4 Add the vegetable stock, and simmer for 5 minutes.

5 In a serving bowl, add the pasta, watercress mixture, tofu, cheese, salt, and pepper. Toss well, and top with the pine nuts before serving.

Mushroom-Almond Tofu

• • •

Easy enough for everyday, this meal is also special enough for company.

• • •

Serves 4 to 6

INGREDIENTS

16 ounces firm tofu, frozen, thawed, and cubed
2 tablespoons hot water
3 tablespoons soy sauce
2 tablespoons almond butter
¼ teaspoon garlic powder
¼ teaspoon black pepper
1 tablespoon vegetable oil
12 ounces flat noodles, cooked
1 tablespoon vegetable oil
½ pound mushrooms, sliced
½ cup almonds, sliced
¼ cup fresh parsley sprigs, chopped
3 cups water
3 tablespoon arrowroot or cornstarch

PREPARATION

1 In a food processor or blender, mix the hot water, 2 tablespoons of the soy sauce, almond butter, garlic powder, and black pepper.

2 Place the tofu in a large mixing bowl, and pour the blended ingredients over the tofu pieces. Make sure each tofu piece absorbs some of the mixture.

3 Lay the tofu pieces on an oiled baking sheet, and bake at 350°F for 15 minutes.

4 Turn the pieces over, and bake for 1 minute longer.

5 Meanwhile, in a frying pan, sauté the mushrooms, almonds, and parsley in 1 tablespoon of the oil until the mushrooms are tender.

6 In a small mixing bowl, whisk the water, arrowroot or cornstarch, and the remaining soy sauce.

7 Pour the whisked ingredients into the frying pan with the mushrooms, and stir over low heat until the sauce is hot and thick.

8 Arrange the tofu over the cooked noodles on a platter. Pour the sauce over the tofu and noodles, and serve.

Pasta and Olives with Kale-Tofu Sauce

...

For a crunchy topping, broil this meal in a baking dish for 5 to 10 minutes before serving.

...

Serves 4

INGREDIENTS

16 ounces soft tofu
Water for boiling
2 tablespoons olive oil
2 medium onions, diced
2 cups kale, chopped
3 tablespoons light miso
½ teaspoon ground bay leaf
2 cups black olives, pitted and sliced
1 pound noodles, cooked

PREPARATION

1 In a saucepan, boil the tofu in enough water to cover it. Cook for 2 to 3 minutes. Remove the tofu from the water, and set aside.

2 In a frying pan, sauté the onions and kale in oil until the kale is wilted.

3 In a blender, blend the tofu, onion, and kale until pasty.

4 Add the miso and bay leaf, and blend some more.

5 Stir in the olives, and set aside.

6 Combine the tofu mixture with the noodles, and serve.

Tofu Pilaf with Peaches and Almonds

...

This steamed rice dish is totally peachy, and just a little bit nutty!

...

Serves 4

INGREDIENTS

16 ounces firm tofu, cubed
2 tablespoons almonds, slivered
2 tablespoons corn oil
1 fresh peach, peeled, pitted, and diced
1 scallion, chopped
1 teaspoon ginger root, minced
1 cup basmati rice
2 cups water
1 teaspoon grated lemon rind
1 teaspoon fresh mint leaves, minced
1 tablespoon fresh parsley sprigs, minced
Salt to taste
Pepper to taste

➡

PREPARATION

1 In an oiled baking pan, spread the nuts and cook at 350°F for 5 minutes, stirring once. Set aside.

2 In a saucepan, sauté the tofu and peach in 1 tablespoon of the oil over medium heat for 2 minutes. Stir gently. Remove from the pan, and set aside.

3 In the same pan, add the remaining 1 tablespoon of oil and the scallion, and sauté, stirring, for 2 minutes.

4 Add the ginger, and cook 1 minute longer.

5 Add the rice, stirring to coat with the oil, and cook for 1 minute.

6 Stir in 2 cups of water and the grated lemon rind. Bring the liquid to a boil over high heat. Lower the heat, cover, and simmer for 30 minutes, or until the liquid is absorbed, and the rice is tender.

7 Stir in the toasted almonds, tofu-peach mixture, mint, and parsley. Season to taste with salt and pepper, and serve.

Tofu Florentine

• • •

Calling all spinach lovers! With a delectable, creamy sauce and enough spinach to make even Popeye proud, this recipe is for you!

• • •

Serves 4 to 6

INGREDIENTS

16 ounces firm tofu
3 tablespoons corn oil
1 medium onion, minced
3 cups packed fresh, trimmed spinach, cooked and drained
¼ teaspoon salt
⅛ teaspoon black pepper
Pinch dried nutmeg
½ cup low-fat milk
3 cups pasta shells, cooked
1 cup mozzarella cheese, shredded

PREPARATION

1 In a large frying pan, sauté the onion in the oil until translucent.

2 Chop the cooked spinach, stir it into the onions, and set aside in a large mixing bowl.

3 In a food processor or blender, combine the tofu, salt, pepper, nutmeg, and milk, and blend until smooth.

4 Combine the tofu mixture with the spinach, mixing well. Toss with the cooked pasta shells.

5 Pour the mixture into an oiled baking dish. Top with the cheese, and bake at 350°F for 40 minutes.

Shepherd's Pie with Tofu

• • •

Here is the British working-class special, still as tasty and hearty as ever—even without the meat.

• • •

Serves 4 to 6

INGREDIENTS

8 ounces firm tofu, frozen, thawed, and grated
4 medium potatoes, peeled and cubed
Water for boiling
¼ cup low-fat milk
½ teaspoon salt
3 tablespoons safflower oil
2 large carrots, diced
1⅓ cups fresh broccoli florets and stalks, finely chopped
1 cup frozen peas, thawed
3 scallions, chopped
2 tablespoons fresh parsley sprigs, chopped
2 tablespoons soy sauce
2 tablespoons dry red wine

PREPARATION

1 In a medium-sized pot, boil the potato cubes until tender. Transfer to a large mixing bowl, and mash well, adding the milk, salt, and 1 teaspoon of the oil. Set aside.

2 In a large frying pan, sauté the carrots and broccoli in the rest of the oil. When the vegetables are crisp-tender, add the remaining ingredients, and sauté for 3 minutes more. Stir frequently.

3 Pour the mixture into a casserole dish, and top with the mashed potatoes, spreading them evenly.

4 Bake at 375°F for 30 minutes, or until the top of the potatoes begins to turn golden and crusty. Let stand for 5 minutes before serving.

Recipe Tip

For more soy protein in your Shephard Pie, use the Tofu-Enhanced Mashed Potatoes (see recipe on page 142).

Dressings,
AND
Sauces, Spreads

Spread, pour, dunk, douse, immerse, and plunge
to your heart's delight. From mild to wild,
these dressings, sauces, and spreads
will tantalize your tastebuds.

• • •

Citrus Tofu Dressing

• • •

When you're looking for something with a mild but slightly fruity flavor to top your greens, try this simple recipe.

• • •

Yields 1 cup

INGREDIENTS

4 ounces silken tofu
½ small onion, finely diced
2 tablespoons tahini
2 teaspoons balsamic vinegar
1 teaspoon soy sauce
Juice of 1 orange

PREPARATION

1 In a blender, purée all the ingredients until smooth.

2 For a thinner dressing, add a small amount of water until the desired consistency is reached.

Creamy Dill Dressing

• • •

Use this versatile dressing on everything from roasted new potatoes to fresh spinach.

• • •

Yields 1¼ cups

INGREDIENTS

8 ounces silken tofu, drained
1 small garlic clove, minced
1 cup tightly packed fresh dill sprigs
¼ cup lemon juice
3 tablespoons olive oil
1 tablespoon Dijon mustard
1 teaspoon salt

PREPARATION

1 In a blender, mix the tofu and garlic until smooth.

2 Gradually add the remaining ingredients and continue blending.

3 Refrigerate for several hours prior to serving.

> **Recipe Tip**
>
> Refrigerating the Creamy Dill Dressing overnight deepens the flavor. It can be refrigerated for up to 5 days.

Creamy Italian Dressing

• • •

A favorite for children as well as adults, this dressing will liven up even the most ordinary garden salad.

• • •

Yields 1½ cups

INGREDIENTS

8 ounces firm tofu
½ cup water
4 tablespoons olive oil
3 tablespoons lemon juice
2 garlic cloves, minced
1 tablespoon onion, minced
1 teaspoon Italian herbs
1 tablespoon dried parsley
¼ teaspoon salt

PREPARATION

1 In a blender, mix all the ingredients until smooth.

2 Refrigerate before serving.

Blue Cheese Dressing

...

Do you have a taste for the refined?
This healthier version of a
classic is an ideal condiment.
It livens up both salads
and sandwiches.

...

Yields 1½ cups

INGREDIENTS

4 ounces firm tofu
4 ounces blue cheese, crumbled
1 teaspoon onion, minced
1 teaspoon mustard powder
½ teaspoon salt
⅛ teaspoon black pepper
2 tablespoons white wine vinegar
¼ cup vegetable oil

PROCEDURE

1 In a blender, mix the tofu, onion, mustard, salt, and vinegar until smooth.

2 Slowly add the vegetable oil, and continue to blend.

3 Stop the blender, and stir in the blue cheese.

Recipe Tip

Blue cheeses are very strong
in flavor and aroma.
Commonly available varieties
include Gorgonzola,
Roquefort, and Stilton.

Russian Dressing

...

This slightly sweet, slightly tart dressing
is wonderful drizzled over fresh lettuce
with sunflower seeds and mandarin
orange slices.

...

Yields 1½ cups

INGREDIENTS

8 ounces soft tofu
⅓ cup tomato ketchup
2 tablespoons vinegar
2 tablespoons vegetable oil
1 tablespoon prepared mustard
1 teaspoon onion powder
½ teaspoon salt

PREPARATION

1 In a blender, mix all the ingredients until smooth.

2 Refrigerate prior to serving.

Cool and Creamy Avocado Dressing

...

This dressing is simply divine on a hot
summer afternoon, drizzled over sliced
fresh tomatoes from the garden, or
spooned over a Mexican-inspired
tostada salad.

...

Yields 1¼ cups

INGREDIENTS

2 ounces silken tofu, mashed
1 ripe avocado, peeled, pitted, and mashed
¼ cup white wine vinegar
2 tablespoons olive oil
1 tablespoon fresh lime juice
Dash of salt

PREPARATION

1 In a blender, combine all the ingredients, and blend until creamy.

2 Refrigerate prior to serving.

Recipe Tip

Add chopped chilies, fresh or canned, to the Avocado Dressing for some added heat.

Caesar Dressing

• • •

Mmm...fresh green lettuce, large crunchy croutons with a hint of garlic and cheese, and this zesty dressing...a healthy indulgence on a hot day.

• • •

Yields 2 cups

INGREDIENTS

12 ounces firm tofu
1 tablespoon extra-virgin olive oil
2 teaspoons Dijon mustard
2 teaspoons capers, drained and rinsed
2 teaspoons vegetarian Worcestershire sauce
2 teaspoons soy sauce
1 small garlic clove, pressed
3 tablespoons fresh lemon juice
4 tablespoons Parmesan cheese
½ teaspoon sugar
⅛ teaspoon black pepper
¼ teaspoon salt
2 tablespoons water

PREPARATION

1 In a blender, combine all the ingredients, and blend until smooth and creamy.

2 Refrigerate before serving.

Spicy Lemon Dressing

• • •

Looking for layers of flavors that will surprise and delight you? This exotic recipe is wonderful on salads and steamed vegetables.

• • •

Yields 2 cups

INGREDIENTS

8 ounces soft tofu, drained
Juice of 1 lemon
1 teaspoon curry powder
½ teaspoon cayenne pepper
½ teaspoon ground ginger
3 garlic cloves, minced
1 teaspoon salt
½ cup olive oil

PREPARATION

1 In a blender, combine all the ingredients except the olive oil, and mix until smooth.

2 Empty the resulting paste into a small bowl, and stir in the oil.

3 Refrigerate before serving.

Creamy Ginger Dressing

• • •

When you've got an Asian-inspired meal planned, serve this lively ginger dressing over a small side salad with grated carrots.

• • •

Yields 2 cups

INGREDIENTS

8 ounces silken tofu
¼ cup tahini
1 scallion, finely chopped
¼ cup white wine vinegar
2 teaspoons honey
½ teaspoon fresh ginger root, grated
½ teaspoon salt

PREPARATION

1 In a blender, combine all the ingredients, and blend until smooth.

2 If you want a more fluid dressing, simply add a couple tablespoons of water.

Garlic Dressing

• • •

For you garlic lovers out there, this ultra-simple recipe is right up your alley.

• • •

Yields 1½ cups

INGREDIENTS

8 ounces soft tofu, drained
4 tablespoons lemon juice
4 garlic cloves, minced
½ cup olive oil
2 tablespoons tahini
Dash of salt

PREPARATION

1 In a blender, combine all the ingredients except the olive oil, and mix until smooth.

2 Empty the resulting paste into a small bowl, and stir in the oil.

3 Refrigerate before serving.

Raspberry and Walnut Dressing

• • •

So, you don't want to settle for your run-of-the-mill salad topper? Try this elegant combination of fruity flavors and crunchy nuts on your next spinach salad.

• • •

Yields 4 cups

INGREDIENTS

28 ounces firm tofu, drained and crumbled
½ cup skim milk
1 tablespoon olive oil
3 tablespoon raspberry vinegar
1 garlic clove, minced
2 scallions, finely chopped
2 to 3 tablespoons dried cherries
2 tablespoons walnuts, chopped
1 tablespoon honey
2 teaspoons dried parsley

PREPARATION

1 In a blender, purée the tofu until smooth.

2 Add the milk, olive oil, vinegar, garlic, and scallions. Pulse, then blend.

3 Add the cherries, walnuts, honey, and parsley. Pulse, then blend.

4 Refrigerate the dressing for at least 1 hour before serving.

Honey Dijon Sauce

• • •

Entertaining on a budget? Looking for something easy to make that tastes great? Here's an ultra-simple accompaniment to a platter of sliced fresh vegetables.

• • •

Yields 1¾ cups

INGREDIENTS

12 ounces soft tofu
5 tablespoons Dijon mustard
4 tablespoons honey

PREPARATION

1 In a medium-sized mixing bowl, stir together the ingredients until smooth.

2 Keep refrigerated.

Tofu Horseradish Sauce

• • •

When combined with tofu and some other simple ingredients, horseradish makes a deliciously pungent sandwich-topper or dip.

• • •

Yields 1 cup

INGREDIENTS

4 ounces soft tofu, drained and mashed
3 tablespoons white horseradish
1 tablespoon vegetable oil
1 tablespoon vinegar
1 teaspoon sugar
½ teaspoon salt

PREPARATION

1 In a blender, combine all the ingredients, and blend until smooth.

Hot and Sweet Dragon Sauce

• • •

This sauce features a lip-smacking sweetness with a sneak-attack bite that'll make your tongue burn with delight. The perfect accompaniment for Asian appetizers.

• • •

Yields 1½ cups

INGREDIENTS

2 ounces soft tofu, drained and mashed
1 cup soy sauce
½ cup brown sugar
2 fresh red cayenne peppers, sliced
3 garlic cloves, crushed
Juice of 1 lime

PREPARATION

1 In a small saucepan, combine all the ingredients, and simmer on low heat for 5 to 10 minutes.

2 Remove the sauce from the heat, and allow it to cool before serving.

Hollandaise Sauce

• • •

Just imagine bright green, steaming asparagus spears with this delicate sauce poured on top—a match made in heaven.

• • •

Yields 1½ cups

INGREDIENTS

8 ounces soft tofu, drained
½ teaspoon salt
½ cup vegetable oil
1 teaspoon sugar
Juice of 1 lemon
½ teaspoon white pepper

PREPARATION

1 In a blender, combine all the ingredients, and blend until smooth.

2 This can be served chilled or warm. If you are heating the sauce over the stove, be sure not to let it boil.

Recipe Tip

For some kick in your Hollandaise Sauce, add ¼ teaspoon of cayenne pepper.

Thousand Island Dressing

• • •

Favored by many for its rich texture and tangy flavor, this dressing packs a mild kick, thanks to the addition of chili sauce.

• • •

Yields 2 cups

INGREDIENTS

12 ounces silken tofu
¼ cup water
2 tablespoons white wine vinegar
1 tablespoon lemon juice
2 teaspoons sugar
6 tablespoons chili sauce
2 tablespoons chopped pickles
¼ cup green bell pepper, chopped
2 tablespoons scallions, chopped

PREPARATION

1 In a blender, combine the tofu, water, vinegar, lemon juice, sugar, and chili sauce, and blend until smooth.

2 Pour the mixture into a small bowl. Stir in the pickles, pepper, and scallions.

3 Refrigerate prior to serving.

Low-Calorie Dijon Vinaigrette

• • •

Just because you're watching your waist doesn't mean you need to sacrifice taste. Feel free to use this dressing to your heart's content.

• • •

Yields ⅔ cup

INGREDIENTS

3 ounces soft tofu
2 garlic cloves, minced
¼ teaspoon salt
½ teaspoon dried basil
⅛ teaspoon black pepper
¼ cup Dijon mustard
3 tablespoons red wine vinegar
1 tablespoon white vinegar
1 tablespoon onion, grated
Hot pepper sauce, to taste

PREPARATION

1 In a blender, mix the tofu and garlic until very creamy.

2 Pour the mixture into a bowl, and add the remaining ingredients. Mix well.

3 Transfer the dressing to a covered jar, and chill before serving.

4 Shake and serve.

Parsley Dressing

• • •

This gorgeous green dressing is as much a feast for the eyes as it is for the mouth. The flavor of parsley is put front and center, highlighted by accents of lemon and onion.

• • •

Yields 2 cups

INGREDIENTS

16 ounces soft tofu
1 cup onions, minced
½ cup fresh parsley sprigs, finely chopped
3 tablespoons lemon juice
½ teaspoon white pepper
½ teaspoon sugar
1 teaspoon salt
¼ cup water
3 tablespoons olive oil

PREPARATION

1 In a blender, combine all the ingredients, and blend until smooth.

Poppy Seed Fruit Salad Dressing

• • •

Toss this sweet-and-sour poppy seed dressing over a big bowl full of fresh melon, bananas, orange segments, and grapes.

• • •

Yields 2 cups

INGREDIENTS

4 ounces silken tofu
½ cup apple cider vinegar
⅓ cup honey
¼ cup vegetable oil
2 tablespoons onion, finely diced
2 tablespoons poppy seeds
1½ teaspoons mustard powder
1 teaspoon salt

PREPARATION

1 In a blender, combine all the ingredients, and blend until smooth.

2 Refrigerate prior to serving.

Warm and Crunchy Nut Sauce

• • •

Once you taste this savory sauce, we think you'll be hooked. Served warm over steamed vegetables or noodles, this distinctive, nutty sauce is a real crowd pleaser.

• • •

Yields 1 cup

INGREDIENTS

3 ounces firm tofu, cubed
¼ cup onion, chopped
1 teaspoon olive oil
1 garlic clove, minced
½ teaspoon ginger root, minced
¼ green bell pepper, finely chopped
1 tablespoon chunky peanut butter
½ cup water
½ teaspoon celery salt
2 tablespoons cashew pieces

PREPARATION

1 In a saucepan, sauté the onion and garlic in oil. Once the onion is tender, add the ginger and pepper. Cook 1 minute more.

2 Stir in the peanut butter, then the water and celery salt. Stir until smooth.

3 Let this mixture simmer for about 5 minutes, adding more water, if necessary.

4 Add the tofu and cashews and heat through.

Mushroom Sauce

• • •

Use your favorite mushrooms—shiitake, portabello, or your basic button variety— in this simple pasta sauce.

• • •

Yields 2½ cups

INGREDIENTS

12 ounces firm tofu, crumbled
1½ cups mushrooms, sliced
2 garlic cloves, minced
1 teaspoon dried basil
1 teaspoon dried oregano
2 tablespoons olive oil
1 15-ounce can tomato sauce

PREPARATION

1 In a medium saucepan, sauté the tofu, mushrooms, and spices in oil until the mushrooms are slightly wilted.

2 Add the tomato sauce and continue to cook, stirring well, until heated through.

Oregano and Olive Sauce

• • •

Bursting with the rich Italian flavors of oregano and olives, this chunky sauce is divine when spread over a slice of homemade bread or tossed with your favorite pasta.

• • •

Yields 3 cups

INGREDIENTS

12 ounces firm tofu, cubed
2 tablespoons olive oil
2 tablespoons dried oregano
1 cup pitted green or black olives
3 large garlic cloves, minced
1 cup tomato sauce

PREPARATION

1 In a large frying pan or wok, fry the tofu cubes in oil over medium heat. Fry each side of the cubes until they are golden brown.

2 Add the oregano, sprinkling it evenly over the tofu.

3 Add the garlic and olives, stirring evenly.

4 Once the garlic begins to brown, add the tomato sauce, and stir. Serve hot.

Tofu Spaghetti Sauce

• • •

This looks, smells, and tastes like traditional Bolognese sauce, but it's missing the meat and the fat. Over pasta, layered in lasagna, or served by itself with garlic bread, this sauce will become a staple in your kitchen.

• • •

Yields 5 cups

INGREDIENTS

12 ounces soft tofu, drained and mashed, frozen and thawed
1 medium onion, chopped
4 garlic cloves, minced
3 tablespoons olive oil
6 cups tomato sauce
3 fresh tomatoes, chopped
1 bay leaf
2 teaspoons Italian seasoning
¼ teaspoon black pepper
1 cup button mushrooms, sliced

PREPARATION

1 In a large saucepan, sauté the onion and garlic in the oil until light golden brown. Watch carefully—you don't want them to burn.

2 Add the spices, tomato sauce, fresh tomatoes, mushrooms, and tofu.

3 Bring the sauce to a boil, reduce the heat, and simmer, covered, for 30 minutes.

4 If you want a really smooth sauce, transfer the mixture to a blender after cooking, and purée to the desired consistency.

5 Serve warm over cooked spaghetti or other pasta.

Recipe Tip

For a heartier spaghetti sauce, add ½ cup sliced carrots and ½ cup sliced zucchini at the beginning of the cooking process.

PREPARATION

1 In a blender, combine all the ingredients, and mix until creamy.

2 Transfer the sauce to a saucepan, and cook over medium heat, stirring frequently. Serve hot.

Alfredo Pasta Sauce

• • •

Fear not! We've taken the guilt out of this traditionally fat-laden sauce by substituting tofu for the usual heavy cream. Spoon it over fettuccine. Use it for a white pizza sauce. Try dipping hot garlic bread sticks into it for a tasty appetizer.

• • •

Yields 1½ cups

INGREDIENTS

12 ounces soft tofu, drained
1 teaspoon garlic, minced
¼ cup Parmesan cheese, grated
¼ cup Romano cheese, grated
1 tablespoon olive oil
1½ teaspoons dried basil
1 tablespoon dried parsley
¼ teaspoon black pepper
1 teaspoon onion powder

Spicy Peanut Sauce

• • •

If you've never experienced the pleasure of this sweet and spicy sauce, here's your chance. Slather it on sautéed tofu, toss it with Asian noodles...you'll find you simply can't have enough!

• • •

Yields 3 cups

INGREDIENTS

2 ounces soft tofu, drained and mashed
2 tablespoons brown sugar
1 tablespoon soy sauce
1 cup crunchy peanut butter
4 garlic cloves, minced
2 fresh red chili peppers, sliced
1 teaspoon lemon juice
½ teaspoon salt
2 cups water

PREPARATION

1 In a blender, mix the tofu, sugar, soy sauce, garlic, peppers, lemon juice, and salt until smooth.

2 Transfer the mixture to a large mixing bowl, and alternately add the water and peanut butter. Stir thoroughly.

3 In a saucepan, warm over medium heat and serve.

Recipe Tip

The Tofu Thai Curry Paste can be refrigerated for up to a week in a sealed container.

Tofu Thai Curry Paste

• • •

Use this unusual blend to create vegetable and tofu stews. The fresh lemongrass combined with other spices captures the essence of traditional Thai cooking.

• • •

Yields ½ cup

INGREDIENTS

2 ounces silken tofu
¼ cup scallions, finely chopped
¼ cup fresh basil leaves, chopped
4 garlic cloves, minced
2 tablespoons ginger root, grated
1 tablespoon grated lemon rind
1 tablespoon fresh lemongrass, minced
1 tablespoon brown sugar
1 or 2 fresh red or green chili peppers, minced
3 tablespoons fresh lemon juice
1 tablespoon ground coriander
1 teaspoon turmeric
½ teaspoon salt

PREPARATION

1 In a blender, combine all the ingredients, and purée until smooth.

2 In a saucepan, warm over medium heat and serve.

Mock Béarnaise Sauce

• • •

The flavor of tarragon in this sauce enhances just about anything. Serve it with steamed artichokes for an elegant side dish or appetizer.

• • •

Yields 1½ cups

INGREDIENTS

4 ounces silken tofu, blended
4 scallions, minced
⅔ cup dry white wine
2 tablespoons vinegar
2 teaspoons thyme leaves, minced
½ teaspoon dried sage
1 tablespoon tarragon leaves, minced
½ teaspoon black pepper
¼ teaspoon saffron threads
½ teaspoon grated lemon rind
½ teaspoon grated orange rind
¼ cup lemon juice
¼ cup orange juice
2 teaspoons nutritional yeast (optional)
½ cup milk
Salt to taste

PREPARATION

1 In a saucepan, bring the scallions, wine, and vinegar to a boil.

2 Cook to reduce by half, then add the thyme, sage, tarragon, pepper, saffron, grated fruit rinds, and juices.

3 Cook to reduce by half again. Remove from the heat, and stir in the yeast, tofu, and milk. Salt to taste, and serve warm.

Tofu Tartar Sauce

• • •

Traditionally served with fried seafood, this sauce also makes a good dip for fried okra or french fries.

• • •

Yields 2½ cups

INGREDIENTS

8 ounces soft tofu, drained
½ cup lemon juice
½ cup vegetable oil
2 tablespoons sugar
1 teaspoon prepared mustard
1 teaspoon salt
1 small onion, fincly chopped
½ cup sweet pickle relish
½ teaspoon black pepper

PREPARATION

1 In a blender, mix the tofu, lemon juice, oil, sugar, mustard, salt, and pepper until creamy.

2 Transfer the mixture to a small bowl, and stir in the onion and relish.

3 Chill prior to serving.

Recipe Tip

For a spicier Tartar sauce, add 3 cloves of chopped garlic and 2 finely diced shallots. For some extra zing, add 2 tablespoons of capers.

Tofu Sour Cream

• • •

A favorite topper for baked potatoes, chili, and more, use this low-calorie, no cholesterol dressing in recipes that call for sour cream.

• • •

Yields 1¼ cups

INGREDIENTS

8 ounces soft tofu
¼ cup vegetable oil
2 tablespoons lemon juice
1½ teaspoons honey or sugar
½ teaspoon salt

PREPARATION

1 In a blender, combine all the ingredients, and blend until creamy.

2 Store in the refrigerator until ready to use.

Tofu "Cheese" Sauce

• • •

Enjoy the indulgence of creamy cheese-like sauce on everything from baked potatoes and nachos to steamed broccoli and cauliflower, without the guilt of the real thing.

• • •

Yields 1½ cups

INGREDIENTS

8 ounces firm tofu, crumbled
⅓ cup lemon juice
⅓ cup nutritional yeast
⅓ cup tahini
3 tablespoons tamari
3 tablespoons water
1 teaspoon dried basil
1 garlic clove, minced
¼ teaspoon black pepper

PREPARATION

1 In a blender, combine all the ingredients, and blend until creamy.

2 In a saucepan, warm the mixture thoroughly over medium heat.

3 Serve warm.

Recipe Tip

The Tofu Béchamel Sauce can be kept for up to a week in the refrigerator.

VARIATION: For a New Orleans Béchamel Sauce, add a few drops of hot pepper sauce.

Tofu Béchamel Sauce

• • •

This ultra-rich cream sauce is extremely versatile. Use it to cream vegetables, to create a base for other sauces, or as a sauce over pasta. When baked, the sauce firms up, making it suitable for use in soufflés and quiches.

• • •

Yields 2 cups

INGREDIENTS

12 ounces soft tofu
1 tablespoon miso
2 teaspoons soy sauce
½ cup plain yogurt
¼ cup water
¾ teaspoon ginger root, grated
2 tablespoons tahini
2 tablespoons dry sherry
1 tablespoon lemon juice
Nutmeg, grated, to taste

PREPARATION

1 In a blender, combine all the ingredients, and mix until smooth and creamy.

2 Transfer the mixture to a saucepan, and heat slowly over medium heat, stirring thoroughly.

3 Serve warm.

Tofu Raita with Mint and Cilantro

• • •

Traditionally served with spicy Indian curry dishes to ease the heat factor, raita is also a wonderful cooling condiment to a fiery curried soup.

• • •

Yields 1 cup

INGREDIENTS

6 ounces silken tofu
Juice of 1 lime
1 tablespoon miso
¼ cup mint leaves, chopped
¼ cup cilantro leaves, chopped
½ cucumber, peeled and finely diced
Dash of salt

PREPARATION

1 In a blender, mix the tofu, lime juice, miso, herbs, and salt until smooth.

2 Pour the mixture into a bowl, and stir in the cucumber.

3 Refrigerate for at least 2 hours before serving.

2 Pour this mixture over whatever you plan to grill, and marinate it in the refrigerator overnight.

Tofu Ricotta

• • •

Transform your favorite Italian recipes with this low-fat alternative to traditional ricotta cheese.

• • •

Yields 2 cups

INGREDIENTS

12 ounces firm tofu, drained and crumbled
2 tablespoons olive oil
2 medium onions, chopped
4 garlic cloves, minced
2 tablespoons soy sauce
½ cup water
½ teaspoon dried basil
½ teaspoon dried oregano
1 tablespoon fresh parsley sprigs, chopped

PREPARATION

1 In a medium-sized saucepan, sauté the onion and garlic in oil.

2 Once the onions are golden and transparent, add the tofu, soy sauce, water, and herbs. Stir until blended.

3 Cover the mixture and simmer on low heat for 15 minutes. Store in refrigerator until ready to use.

> ### Recipe Tip
> For a half-creamy/half-chunky Tofu Ricotta, blend half of the tofu in a blender, and mash the other half.

Jamaican Jerk Sauce

• • •

Marinate any grillable food in this flavorful sauce before tossing it on the barbecue. Adjust the heat level by adding more or fewer chili peppers.

• • •

Yields 1 cup

INGREDIENTS

4 ounces silken tofu
4 to 6 scallion greens, finely chopped
¼ cup apple juice
3 garlic cloves, minced
2 tablespoons soy sauce
2 tablespoons fresh hot chili pepper, minced
2 tablespoons vinegar
1 tablespoon brown sugar
1 tablespoon vegetable oil
1 tablespoon ginger root, grated
1½ teaspoons allspice
½ teaspoon cinnamon
¼ teaspoon nutmeg
½ teaspoon black pepper
½ teaspoon dried thyme

PREPARATION

1 In a blender, combine all the ingredients, and mix until smooth and creamy.

Raspberry-Mint Barbecue Sauce

• • •

Brush this colorful sauce over squares of tofu, vegetable kebabs, even sliced pineapple, for a tasty treat from the grill.

• • •

Yields 1¼ cups

INGREDIENTS

4 ounces silken tofu
½ cup raspberry jam
¼ cup raspberry vinegar
2 tablespoons vegetable oil
2 tablespoons fresh mint leaves, minced

PREPARATION

1 In a blender, purée the tofu until smooth and creamy.

2 Add the vinegar, oil, and mint. Pulse.

3 Add the raspberry jam, blending on high until thoroughly mixed.

4 Refrigerate until ready to use.

Tofu Mayonnaise

• • •

Try this delicious mock mayonnaise wherever you'd use the real stuff. The only thing you'll miss is the fat.

• • •

Yields ⅔ cup

INGREDIENTS

4 ounces silken tofu
2 tablespoons fresh lemon juice
2 tablespoons vinegar
1 teaspoon olive oil
½ teaspoon minced garlic
Salt to taste
Pepper to taste

PREPARATION

1 In a blender, combine the tofu, lemon juice, oil, vinegar, and garlic, and mix until smooth.

2 Season to taste with salt and pepper.

3 Store in a lidded container and refrigerate until ready to use.

Recipe Tip

You can experiment endlessly with this mayonnaise recipe. Try adding cut onions, minced pickles, hot mustard, or even curry, to create the perfect spread.

Tangy Lemon Mayonnaise

• • •

Spread this tart topping onto a veggie burger, or sneak a dollop into a fresh pita sandwich for some eye-opening flavor.

• • •

Yields 1½ cups

INGREDIENTS

8 ounces soft tofu, drained
Juice of 1 lemon
½ teaspoon grated lemon rind
½ teaspoon salt
½ teaspoon prepared mustard
1 teaspoon honey
¼ cup vegetable oil

PREPARATION

1 In a blender, combine all the ingredients, and mix until creamy.

2 Refrigerate before serving.

Creamy Peach Chutney

• • •

This fruity chutney packs some zing with fresh lime, ginger, and hot peppers. Serve it as a side to an Indian entrée, or simply spread some on a sandwich.

• • •

Yields 1½ cups

INGREDIENTS

2 ounces silken tofu
1 cup water
2 firm fresh peaches, peeled, pitted, and diced
1 lime, with peel, finely diced
1 tablespoon sugar
¼ teaspoon salt
¼ cup vinegar
½ serrano chili pepper, minced
2 teaspoons ginger root, grated
1 red bell pepper, finely diced

PREPARATION

1 In a small saucepan, bring the water to a boil.

2 Add the lime, and simmer on low heat for about 10 minutes. Drain and set aside.

3 In a large frying pan, heat the sugar and vinegar until a syrup forms.

4 Add the chili and ginger, then the red bell pepper, peaches, and limes.

5 Stir well, and continue to heat for another 5 minutes.

6 Transfer to a bowl, and refrigerate for at least 2 hours.

Tofu Hummus

• • •

This creamy spread is extremely versatile. Slather it on a sandwich with fresh veggies, or dip into it with warm slices of pita bread.

• • •

Yields 2 cups

INGREDIENTS

8 ounces soft or silken tofu
¼ cup tahini
¼ cup lemon juice
1 cup chickpeas, cooked
1 teaspoon salt
2 garlic cloves, minced

PREPARATION

1 In a blender, mix all the ingredients until smooth.

2 Chill prior to serving.

Recipe Tip

You can add roasted garlic, sun-dried tomatoes, fresh dill, or chili peppers to your hummus recipe.

Creamy Apple-Cilantro Chutney

• • •

This sweet and oh-so-fresh chutney is a perfect accompaniment to any hot and spicy dish. Its cool flavors will calm and delight your taste buds.

• • •

Yields 1½ cups

INGREDIENTS

2 ounces silken tofu
2 apples, cored, peeled, and diced
½ cup fresh lemon juice
¼ cup fresh cilantro leaves, chopped
2 tablespoons water
½ teaspoon salt

PREPARATION

1 In a blender, combine all the ingredients except the apples, and blend untul smooth.

2 In a large mixing bowl, stir the apples into the tofu mixture until well-blended.

Tofu Tahini Spread

• • •

The delicate flavor of this spread is best enjoyed when served on fresh-baked bread or your favorite crackers.

• • •

Yields 2 cups

INGREDIENTS

12 ounces firm tofu
2 tablespoons tahini
1 tablespoon miso
2 tablespoons soy sauce
2 scallions, finely chopped
1 carrot, finely chopped
Dash of ground black pepper

PREPARATION

1 In a blender, combine the tofu, tahini, miso, pepper, and soy sauce, and blend until smooth.

2 Transfer the mixture to a bowl, and stir in the scallions and carrots.

3 Chill prior to serving.

Tangy Tahini Spread with Capers

• • •

This spread is just as good on a crusty hunk of bread as it is served with a plate of fresh vegetables. The flavors of lemon, mustard, and capers, along with the crunch of celery and peppers, will make this tahini variation a favorite.

• • •

Serves 9

INGREDIENTS

12 ounces firm tofu
½ cup tahini
2 tablespoons soy sauce
2 tablespoons miso
Juice of 1 lemon
1 teaspoon Dijon mustard
2 tablespoons capers, drained
¼ cup celery, finely chopped
¼ cup red bell pepper, finely chopped
1 shallot, finely chopped
¼ teaspoon salt
⅛ teaspoon black pepper

PREPARATION

1 In a blender, combine all the ingredients, and mix until thoroughly blended.

2 Refrigerate for at least 2 hours prior to serving.

Olive and Cashew Spread

• • •

This spread, with its tangy, salty taste and smooth texture, makes an ideal sandwich filling.

• • •

Yields 2 cups

INGREDIENTS

8 ounces soft tofu
2 tablespoons vegetable oil
3 tablespoons lemon juice
¼ teaspoon salt
¼ cup roasted cashews, chopped
6 tablespoons green olives, pitted and sliced

PREPARATION

1 In a blender, combine the tofu, oil, lemon juice, and salt, and blend until creamy.

2 Transfer the mixture to a bowl, and stir in the olives and cashews.

3 Refrigerate before serving.

Fresh Chive Spread

• • •

The unique taste of fresh chives is spotlighted in this easy-to-make spread. Serve it with a plate of crackers, and watch this delicious spread disappear.

• • •

Yields 2½ cups

INGREDIENTS

12 ounces firm tofu, drained and crumbled
3 tablespoons rice vinegar
1 teaspoon onion powder
1 teaspoon salt
¼ cup olive oil
¼ cup fresh chives, finely chopped

PREPARATION

1 In a blender, mix the tofu, vinegar, onion powder, and salt until smooth.

2 With the blender still running, add the oil.

3 Pour the mixture into a bowl, and add the chives. Stir until mixed.

3 Chill prior to serving.

Recipe Tip

This chive spread will keep well for up to a week when refrigerated.

Spicy Jalapeño Spread

• • •

Who needs cheese when you can spread this fiery mixture over crackers? If you're a glutton for punishment, substitute ultra-hot habañero peppers for the jalapeños.

• • •

Yields 1 cup

INGREDIENTS

12 ounces soft tofu, drained and mashed
¼ teaspoon ground cumin
¼ cup red bell pepper, minced
¼ cup onion, minced
1 tablespoon dried parsley
1¼ tablespoons plain yogurt
¼ teaspoon dried dill
¼ teaspoon mustard powder
2 jalapeño chili peppers, finely chopped

PREPARATION

1 In a bowl, stir together the cumin, bell pepper, onion, parsley, and yogurt.

2 Add the dill, mustard, and jalapeños, and mix well.

3 Add the tofu, stirring thoroughly until the mixture is well-blended. Serve at room temperature.

Sun-Dried Tomato Spread

• • •

With a lovely red color and the rich flavor of sun-dried tomatoes and garlic, this spread is a tasty way to add variety to any sandwich.

• • •

Yields 1 cup

INGREDIENTS

4 ounces soft tofu, mashed
½ cup oil-packed sun-dried tomatoes, drained and coarsely chopped
2 tablespoons tomato paste
2 tablespoons lemon juice
1 tablespoon red wine vinegar
1 garlic clove, minced
1 teaspoon dried basil
1 teaspoon honey
Black pepper to taste
Salt to taste

PREPARATION

1 In a blender, combine all the ingredients and blend until smooth.

2 Serve at room temperature.

> **Recipe Tip**
>
> Covered and refrigerated, the Sun-Dried Tomato Spread will keep for up to three days. Bring to room temperature before serving.

Pumpkin Spread

• • •

A comforting dessert or a light afternoon snack, this sweet and slightly spicy spread is sinfully delicious on a warm piece of nutty toast.

• • •

Yields 1 cup

INGREDIENTS

8 ounces firm tofu
1 cup canned pumpkin
2 tablespoons miso
1 tablespoon maple syrup
½ teaspoon ground nutmeg
½ teaspoon ground allspice
¼ teaspoon ground cloves
1 teaspoon curry powder
Pinch of salt

PREPARATION

1 In a blender, combine all the ingredients, and blend until creamy.

2 Serve chilled or warm.

Desserts

You've been good. You haven't snacked all day, and
now it's time to indulge. But fear not! These
sumptuous, scrumptious desserts should
make you feel a little less guilty
about that second serving.

• • •

Kiwi-Strawberry Smoothie

• • •

A flavorful ending to a meal, or a great healthy snack, this recipe packs an unexpected hint of nutmeg for a subtle taste surprise.

• • •

Serves 4 (8-ounce glassfuls)

INGREDIENTS

16 ounces silken tofu
2 cups fresh or frozen strawberries
2 medium kiwi fruits, peeled and cubed
2 bananas, sliced
¼ teaspoon ground nutmeg

PREPARATION

1 Rinse and hull the fresh berries, or partially thaw the frozen berries.

2 In a blender, combine the tofu, kiwi, strawberries, bananas, and nutmeg, and blend until smooth.

3 Pour into 8-ounce glasses and garnish with a fresh slice of kiwi.

PREPARATION

1 In a blender, combine all of the ingredients, and purée until smooth.

2 Serve in chilled 8-ounce glasses with a pineapple or banana slice garnish.

Recipe Tip

Once ripe, bananas can be stored in the refrigerator for three or four days. The skin will darken, but the edible fruit will remain unchanged.

Chocolate "Milk" Shake

• • •

This non-dairy take on the old-fashioned chocolate milk shake will send your taste buds spinning.

• • •

Serves 2 (8-ounce glassfuls)

INGREDIENTS

6 ounces silken tofu
1 ripe banana
½ cup water
2 tablespoons chocolate syrup
2 tablespoons maple syrup

PREPARATION

1 In a blender, combine the banana, tofu, water, chocolate syrup, and maple syrup, and purée until smooth.

2 Serve in chilled 8-ounce glasses with straws.

Banana-Berry Shake

• • •

Looking for an easy cool-down? Nothing takes away the heat of a hot afternoon like this refreshing fruity beverage.

• • •

Serves 2 (8-ounce glassfuls)

INGREDIENTS

6 ounces silken tofu
1 cup pineapple juice
1 ripe banana
½ cup fresh or frozen strawberries
½ teaspoon vanilla extract
¼ cup sugar

Vanilla Pudding

• • •

Surprised to discover that this nostalgic
favorite is dairy-free? It's just as
good as the original; in fact,
we think it's even better.

• • •

Serves 4

INGREDIENTS

18 ounces soft tofu
¼ cup vegetable oil
1 cup sugar or ⅞ cup honey
1 tablespoon vanilla extract
Pinch of salt

PREPARATION

1 In a blender, combine all of the ingredients, and mix until smooth.

2 Pour into individual pudding cups.

3 Chill in the refrigerator until set, and serve.

**Baked Raisin and Nut Pudding
(see this page)**

Baked Raisin and Nut Pudding

• • •

The subtle flavors of this dessert
make it the perfect accompaniment
to after-dinner coffee.

• • •

Serves 8 to 10

INGREDIENTS

12 ounces soft tofu
½ cup butter
1 cup light molasses
1 cup honey
½ teaspoon baking soda
½ cup flour
½ cup raisins
½ cup chopped walnuts or pecans
Whipped cream (optional)

PREPARATION

1 In a blender, combine all of the ingredients except the flour, and mix until smooth.

2 Add the flour and mix once again.

3 Fold in the raisins and nuts until well-blended.

4 Pour into a greased 2-quart casserole dish, and bake at 350°F for 45 minutes.

5 Serve with a dollop of whipped cream.

Chocolate Pudding

• • •

Can you recall the simple childhood joy
of savoring a spoonful of creamy
chocolate pudding? Enjoy that
feeling again, now
without the guilt.

• • •

Serves 4

INGREDIENTS

18 ounces soft tofu
1 ¼ cups sugar
⅓ cup cocoa
¼ cup vegetable oil
1 ½ teaspoons vanilla extract
¼ teaspoon salt

PREPARATION

1 In a blender, combine the ingredients, and mix until smooth.

2 Pour into individual serving dishes.

3 Chill in the refrigerator until set, and serve.

Recipe Tip

For a frozen dessert, simply
place the chocolate pudding
in the freezer. Let thaw for
15 minutes before serving.

Banana Pudding

• • •

Enjoy the simple flavor of this rich
dessert by itself, or incorporate it as
an indulgent filling in a favorite
layered cake recipe.

• • •

Serves 3

INGREDIENTS

12 ounces silken tofu
2 ripe bananas
1 teaspoon lemon juice
¼ cup vegetable oil
½ cup sugar
¼ teaspoon salt
2 teaspoons vanilla extract
2 tablespoons milk

PREPARATION

1 In a blender, combine all of the ingredients, and mix until creamy.

2 Pour the mixture into individual serving dishes.

3 Chill in the refrigerator until set, and serve.

Swirled Berry Ice

• • •

This new slant on the traditional fruit sorbet has the look and taste of a gourmet treat. Shhh! No one needs to know it took only minutes to make!

• • •

Serves 4

INGREDIENTS

12 ounces soft tofu
1 pound fresh or frozen strawberries, raspberries, or blueberries
½ cup frozen apple juice concentrate
¼ cup yogurt
1 tablespoon honey

PREPARATION

1 Rinse and hull the fresh berries, or partially thaw frozen berries.

2 In a blender, combine the tofu and berries, and purée until smooth.

3 Add the apple juice concentrate, yogurt, and honey. Process for 1 to 2 minutes.

4 Serve immediately in small bowls with berry garnish; or, transfer to a storage container, cover, and chill.

Berry Sinful Strawberry Cream

• • •

Showcase the season's freshest berries with this mouth-watering indulgence.

• • •

Serves 4

INGREDIENTS

16 ounces firm tofu
1 pound fresh strawberries
2 teaspoons lemon juice
½ cup sugar
¼ teaspoon vanilla extract

PREPARATION

1 Set aside several strawberries.

2 In a blender, combine the remaining berries with the other ingredients, and mix until smooth.

3 Pour the mixture into individual serving dishes.

4 Chill in the refrigerator until set, and serve.

5 Garnish with the reserved strawberries.

Recipe Tip

Substitute blueberries or raspberries for the strawberries.

Swirled Berry Ice (see this page)

Apple Tofu Strata

• • •

Picture an apple pie without the crust...tart fruit mixed with the richness of brown sugar and cream. Absolute Heaven!

• • •

Serves 6 to 8

INGREDIENTS

4 ounces soft tofu, mashed
4 cups apples, very finely diced
¼ cup brown sugar
¼ teaspoon butter
½ cup whipping cream
2 cups crushed graham crackers

PREPARATION

1 In a large bowl, mix the apples and sugar, being sure that the apple pieces are evenly coated.

2 Spread the apple mixture evenly onto a lightly-buttered baking sheet, and bake at 350°F for 5 minutes.

3 Set aside to cool.

4 In a medium-sized baking dish, arrange the apple mixture, tofu, whipping cream, and graham crackers in layers: imagine you're making a dessert lasagna, building layer upon layer.

5 Refrigerate overnight.

6 Scoop out individual servings onto small plates or bowls.

Recipe Tip

Try serving the Apple Tofu Strata warm for an entirely different experience.

Ginger Peach Whip

• • •

The wonderfully sweet flavor of fresh peaches comes to life with the spicy accent of ginger.

• • •

Serves 6

INGREDIENTS

12 ounces soft tofu
4 ripe medium peaches
⅓ cup honey
½ tablespoon ground ginger

PREPARATION

1 In a saucepan, poach three of the peaches in boiling water for about 1 minute. Immediately transfer to a bowl of ice water to cool. Using a small knife, pull the skins off.

2 Cut the peaches into smaller pieces, and place in a blender. Add the tofu and honey, and blend until smooth.

3 Divide the mixture into six dessert bowls, and chill in the refrigerator for several hours.

4 Garnish each of the servings with a slice from the remaining peach and the ground ginger. You might also choose to garnish with fresh mint leaves or a small ginger cookie and a light dusting of nutmeg.

Basic Tofu Flan

• • •

If you've never experienced the pleasure of this traditional Spanish dessert—and even if you have—this is an absolute must-try recipe. Even though we've substituted tofu for eggs, we swear you won't know the difference.

• • •

Serves 6

INGREDIENTS

12 ounces soft tofu
6 ounces cream cheese
¼ cup milk
2 teaspoons vanilla extract
¼ cup honey
6 teaspoons brown sugar

PREPARATION

1 In a blender, combine all the ingredients except the brown sugar, and mix until completely smooth.

2 Pour the mixture into six custard dishes or small oven-safe bowls, and bake at 350°F for 15 minutes or until firm.

4 Remove from the oven and dust each custard with 1 teaspoon of brown sugar.

5 Return to the oven, and continue baking for 5 more minutes, or until the tops have browned.

6 Allow to cool to room temperature before refrigerating for at least 1 hour.

Recipe Tip

If you prefer, flan may be served warm; however, the consistency improves with chilling.

Touch-of-Orange Tofu Flan

• • •

So you like the basic flan recipe, but you're looking for a little "oomph?" This recipe showcases the delicate citrus flavor of oranges. It's the perfect accompaniment to a steaming cup of espresso.

• • •

Serves 8 to 10

INGREDIENTS

12 ounces soft tofu, crumbled
⅔ cup frozen orange juice concentrate, thawed
3 tablespoons vegetable oil
1 teaspoon vanilla extract
½ teaspoon salt
1 cup sugar
½ cup unbleached white flour
1 teaspoon baking powder
¼ teaspoon baking soda
2 tablespoons grated orange rind

PREPARATION

1 In a blender, combine the tofu, juice concentrate, 2 tablespoons of the oil, vanilla, and salt, and mix until creamy.

2 In a mixing bowl, stir together the sugar, flour, baking powder, and baking soda.

3 Slowly add this mixture to the contents of the blender, and mix until smooth.

4 Pour the mixture into a well-oiled and floured 9½ by 13-inch pan, and bake at 400°F for about 30 minutes.

5 Slice with a sharp, wet knife to serve. Garnish with grated orange rind.

Almost-as-Good-as-Your-Grandma's Rice Pudding

• • •

We bet you won't be able to taste the difference between this guilt-free recipe and the more traditional dessert. Go ahead! You'll be pleasantly surprised.

• • •

Serves 6 to 8

INGREDIENTS

16 ounces soft tofu
3 eggs
1 cup honey
2 teaspoons lemon juice
1 teaspoon grated lemon rind
½ teaspoon salt
½ teaspoon cinnamon
1 tablespoon vanilla extract
1 cup unsweetened, dried, shredded coconut
1 cup cooked rice
¾ cup raisins

PREPARATION

1 In a blender, combine all the ingredients except the coconut, rice, and raisins. Mix until smooth.

2 Pour the mixture into a large bowl.

3 Add the cooked rice, coconut, and raisins, and mix until well-blended.

4 Empty the contents into an oiled 2-quart casserole dish, and bake at 350°F for 1 hour.

5 Serve warm or chilled. Garnish with a light dusting of cinnamon.

Bread Pudding with a Lemon Twist

• • •

Be on the lookout, lemon lovers! This comforting dessert dish is for you.

• • •

Serves 4

INGREDIENTS

12 ounces soft tofu
4 eggs
1 cup honey
½ cup water or milk
2 tablespoons lemon juice
1 teaspoon grated lemon rind
¼ teaspoon salt
1 teaspoon butter
2 cups dried bread cubes
Dash of cinnamon
Dash of nutmeg

PREPARATION

1 In a blender, combine all of the ingredients except the bread. Mix until smooth.

2 Empty the mixture into a large mixing bowl.

3 Add the dried bread cubes, stirring gently with a large spoon.

4 Pour into a buttered 2-quart casserole dish and bake at 350°F for 30 to 45 minutes.

5 Serve warm or chilled. Garnish with a dusting of cinnamon and nutmeg.

PB & J Cookies

• • •

Who would have thought your kids would go crazy over a tofu recipe! Just out of the oven or tucked into a lunchbox, these treats are destined to become a family favorite.

• • •

Yields 24 Cookies

INGREDIENTS

2 ounces soft tofu
1½ cups ground almonds
1½ cups peanut butter
2 cups vegetable oil
½ cup maple syrup
3 ripe bananas
3 cups pastry flour
1½ teaspoons baking powder
Dash of salt
1½ cups strawberry or grape jelly

PREPARATION

1 In a blender, grind the almonds to a fine powder.

2 Add the tofu, peanut butter, oil, maple syrup, and bananas. Mix until creamy.

3 Empty the contents into a large mixing bowl, adding the flour, baking powder, and salt. Stir until fully blended. The dough will be thick.

4 Lightly oil several baking sheets.

5 Roll the batter into 1-inch balls, and place them onto the baking sheets. Press gently on each ball with your thumb to create an indentation.

6 Spoon approximately 1 teaspoon of jelly into the thumbprint of each cookie, and bake at 375°F for 20 to 25 minutes or until the cookies are lightly brown.

Sunny Coconut Cookies

• • •

The unexpected combination of sunflower seeds and coconut creates a marvelous union of flavors.

• • •

Yields 16 to 20 cookies

INGREDIENTS

6 ounces soft tofu
1 egg
¾ cup honey
½ cup vegetable oil
1 teaspoon vanilla extract
1½ cups pastry flour
¾ teaspoon baking powder
½ teaspoon salt
1 cup shredded coconut
½ cup sunflower seeds
¼ teaspoon nutmeg

PREPARATION

1 In a blender, purée the tofu, egg, honey, oil, and vanilla until smooth.

2 In a large mixing bowl, combine the flour, baking powder, salt, coconut, seeds, and nutmeg. Stir until well-blended.

3 Add the contents of the blender to the dry ingredients in the bowl, and stir until a thick batter is formed.

4 Drop the dough by spoonfuls onto oiled baking sheets, and bake at 400°F for 10 minutes, or until golden brown.

Walnut Chocolate Chip Cookies

• • •

This favorite crowd-pleaser is sure
to bring smiles...that is, if the
cook's willing to share!

• • •

Yields 16 to 20 cookies

INGREDIENTS

6 ounces soft tofu
1½ cups pastry flour
¾ teaspoon baking powder
½ teaspoon salt
6 ounces milk chocolate chips
½ cup chopped walnuts
1 egg
¾ cup sugar
½ cup vegetable oil
1 teaspoon vanilla extract

PREPARATION

1 In a large mixing bowl, combine the flour, baking powder, salt, chocolate, and nuts in a bowl.

2 In a blender, mix all of the remaining ingredients until smooth.

3 Add the blender contents to the mixing bowl, and stir until well-mixed.

4 Drop spoonfuls of the dough onto oiled baking sheets, and bake at 400°F for about 10 minutes.

Spice-of-Life Cookies

• • •

Oh, the decadence! One whiff of these
spicy cookies baking in the oven will
have your senses dancing.

• • •

Yields 20 to 24 cookies

INGREDIENTS

8 ounces soft tofu
1 teaspoon dried ginger
1 teaspoon cinnamon
½ teaspoon ground nutmeg
½ teaspoon salt
½ cup butter, softened
⅔ cup honey
1 egg
1 teaspoon vanilla extract
1½ cups flour
½ cup raisins
½ cup chopped walnuts
½ teaspoon baking soda

PREPARATION

1 In a blender, combine the tofu, spices, butter, honey, egg, and vanilla. Mix until very smooth.

2 In a large mixing bowl, stir together all the remaining ingredients.

3 Add the blender contents to the dry ingredients and stir well.

4 Drop spoonfuls of the dough onto oiled baking sheets, and bake at 400°F for 10 to 15 minutes.

Recipe Tip

Try substituting chopped dates,
or even dried cranberries or
cherries, for the raisins.

Basic Graham Cracker Pie Crust

• • •

Okay, okay...so there's no tofu in this one. But we wanted to give you an alternative to the store-bought variety we require in so many of the following pie recipes.

• • •

Yields 1 9-inch pie crust

INGREDIENTS

2 cups graham crackers, crumbled
6 tablespoons margarine

PREPARATION

1 Using a blender, chop the graham crackers until they are finely ground.

2 Add the margarine, and pulse the blender until the mixture has the appearance of coarse crumbs.

3 Empty the mixture into a 9-inch pie plate, pressing it firmly into the bottom and sides.

4 Fill and bake according to the recipe instructions.

Basic Tofu Cheesecake

• • •

You'll swoon with pleasure when you try this rich recipe. Top it with everything from fresh berries to crushed cookies. Ecstasy!

• • •

Yields 2 9-inch cheesecakes

INGREDIENTS
(ALL AT ROOM TEMPERATURE)

18 ounces soft tofu
1 cup sugar
12 ounces cream cheese
1 tablespoon vanilla extract
2 ready-made graham cracker pie crusts

PREPARATION

1 In a blender, purée the tofu until smooth.

2 Add the sugar, cream cheese, and vanilla, and blend until creamy.

3 Pour the mixture into the pie crusts, spreading evenly. Bake at 325°F for 50 minutes, or until the tops are very slightly browned.

4 Turn off the oven, leaving the cheesecakes inside. Let them sit for 1 hour.

5 Remove the pies and let them cool to room temperature, then refrigerate overnight.

6 Serve slightly chilled.

Recipe Tip

For a vegan cheesecake, use soy cream cheese (available in health food stores).

VARIATION: For a wonderful fall dessert, add ½ cup pure maple syrup to the recipe. Garnish with a drizzle of syrup and crushed pecans.

Tropical Cheesecake Escape (see opposite page)

Tropical Cheesecake Escape

• • •

Picture yourself enjoying a picnic on a sandy beach, a soft, warm, ocean breeze washing over you. Slowly, you take a bite of this exotic dessert... you will feel transported.

• • •

Serves 8

INGREDIENTS

12 ounces soft tofu, crumbled
2 8-ounce cans of crushed pineapple, drained
1/3 cup sugar
1/2 teaspoon grated orange rind
1 1/2 teaspoons vanilla extract
2 tablespoons all-purpose flour
1 tablespoon unsalted butter or margarine
1 large egg white
1 ready-made graham cracker pie crust

PREPARATION

1 In a blender, combine the tofu and pineapple, and mix until fairly smooth.

2 Add the remaining ingredients, and continue blending until creamy.

3 Pour the batter into the pie crust, spreading evenly. Bake at 325°F for 50 to 60 minutes, or until a toothpick inserted in the center comes out clean.

4 Remove from the oven, and cool for about 1 hour to room temperature.

5 Chill in the refrigerator for at least 3 hours.

6 Serve slightly chilled, and garnish with an orange or pineapple slice.

Recipe Tip

Add 1 cup of cubed mango in place of one of the cans of pineapple.

Pumpkin Cheesecake

• • •

The texture of pumpkin works wonderfully with creamy silken tofu. This cheesecake is the perfect addition to a holiday table, but we think it's so good you'll want to enjoy it year-round.

• • •

Yields 2 9-inch cheesecakes

INGREDIENTS
(ALL AT ROOM TEMPERATURE)

18 ounces silken tofu
1 cup canned pumpkin
12 ounces cream cheese
1 1/4 cups sugar
1/2 teaspoon ground nutmeg
1 teaspoon ground cinnamon
1/4 teaspoon ground cloves
1 tablespoon vanilla extract
2 ready-made graham cracker pie crusts

PREPARATION

1 In a blender, purée the tofu and pumpkin until smooth.

2 Add the cream cheese, sugar, spices, and vanilla. Mix until well blended.

3 Pour the mixture into the pie crusts, spreading evenly. Bake at 325°F for 50 minutes, or until the cheesecakes are firmly set.

4 Turn off the oven, leaving the cheesecakes inside. Let sit them for 1 hour.

5 Remove the cheesecakes and let them cool to room temperature, then refrigerate overnight.

6 Serve chilled.

Frozen Peanut Butter Pie

• • •

A treat for young and old, this easy-to-make frozen dessert is the ultimate in comfort food.

• • •

Yields 1 9-inch pie

INGREDIENTS

12 ounces soft tofu
¾ cup peanut butter
½ cup honey
4 tablespoons maple syrup
1 teaspoon vanilla extract
¼ cup vegetable oil
Dash of salt
1 ready-made graham cracker pie crust

PREPARATION

1 In a blender, combine all of the ingredients, and mix until smooth.

2 Pour the mixture into the pie crust. Decorate with chocolate shavings.

3 Freeze for several hours. Let thaw 10 minutes prior to serving.

Recipe Tip

For some crunch, use chunky peanut butter. You could even sprinkle some chocolate chips into the mix.

Tofu Pecan Pie

• • •

Usually considered one of the more guilty indulgences of the pie world, this version of the traditional pecan pie is light on fat without sacrificing any of the taste. Top with a dollop of whipped cream for an "oh-my" experience.

• • •

Yields 1 9-inch pie

INGREDIENTS

6 ounces silken tofu
1 cup brown sugar
¼ cup margarine
1 teaspoon vanilla
⅓ cup molasses
¼ teaspoon salt
1½ cups whole pecan pieces
1 ready-made graham cracker crust

PREPARATION

1 In a blender, combine all of the ingredients except the pecans, and mix until smooth.

2 Carefully fold the pecans into the mixture, and pour into the pie crust.

3 Lightly dust the top of the pie with some brown sugar, and bake at 350°F for approximately 45 minutes.

Lemon Coconut Pie

• • •

The subtle hint of lemon gives this pie a delicate yet distinctive flavor.

• • •

Yields 1 9-inch pie

INGREDIENTS

16 ounces soft tofu
Juice of 1 lemon
¼ teaspoon vanilla extract
½ cup brown sugar
Grated rind of 1 lemon
¼ cup shredded coconut
1 ready-made graham cracker pie crust
Lemon slices for garnish

PREPARATION

1 In a blender, purée the tofu until smooth. Add the lemon juice, vanilla, and brown sugar, and continue mixing.

2 Add the grated lemon rind and shredded coconut, and blend on high speed.

3 Pour the mixture into the pie crust and refrigerate, covered, overnight.

4 Serve chilled, garnished with lemon slices.

Easy-as-Pie Banana Cream Pie

• • •

Nothing could be easier! Throw the ingredients in a blender, chill, and "voila!"...a rich, sumptuous dessert your whole family will enjoy.

• • •

Serves 8 to 10

INGREDIENTS

16 ounces soft tofu, crumbled
3 ripe bananas
½ cup honey
½ cup margarine or butter, melted
1 tablespoon vanilla extract
1 tablespoon lemon juice
1 ready-made graham cracker pie crust
Banana slices for garnish

PREPARATION

1 In a blender, combine all the ingredients, and mix until smooth.

2 Pour the mixture into a pie crust, and refrigerate for at least 3 hours.

3 Serve chilled, garnished with fresh banana slices.

"Just Peachy" Peach Pie

• • •

This recipe puts the flavor of fresh peaches in the spotlight. A delightful end to a relaxed Sunday brunch.

• • •

Yields 1 9-inch pie

INGREDIENTS

12 ounces soft tofu
2½ cups peaches, thinly sliced
¼ cup honey
½ teaspoon ground cinnamon
⅛ teaspoon ground nutmeg
2 tablespoons flour
4 ounces cream cheese
2 eggs
1½ teaspoons vanilla extract
¼ teaspoon salt
1 ready-made graham cracker pie crust

PREPARATION

1 In a bowl, mix the peaches, honey, spices, and flour. The peaches should be well-coated.

2 Spoon the peach mixture into the pie crust, and set aside.

3 In a blender, combine the remaining ingredients, and mix until smooth.

4 Pour this mixture over the peaches. Do not stir.

5 Bake at 350°F for 50 to 60 minutes.

6 Serve warm or chilled, and garnish with a peach slice.

Sweet Potato Pie

• • •

This seemingly-sinful dessert is so packed with healthy ingredients that it's actually good for you. Don't worry—it'll be our little secret.

• • •

Yields 1 9-inch pie

INGREDIENTS

12 ounces soft tofu
2 cups cooked sweet potatoes, pureed
2 eggs
1 cup orange juice
½ cup butter
½ cup honey
½ teaspoon salt
½ teaspoon vanilla
¼ cup molasses
¼ teaspoon ground nutmeg

PREPARATION

1 In a blender, combine all of the ingredients, and mix until smooth.

2 Pour the mixture into a pie crust, and bake at 350°F for 35 to 40 minutes, or until slightly firm.

3 Chill for at least 3 hours.

Recipe Tip

Add the grated rind of half a lemon or orange for a surprising kick.

Not-So-Old-Fashioned Pumpkin Pie

• • •

The addition of a sweet and crunchy topping to this classic will make this your new standard recipe.

• • •

Yields 1 9-inch pie

INGREDIENTS

PIE

12 ounces soft tofu
2 cups canned pumpkin
1 cup brown sugar
1 teaspoon ground cinnamon
½ teaspoon ground ginger
¼ teaspoon ground nutmeg
¼ teaspoon ground gloves
1 ready-made graham cracker pie crust

TOPPING

¼ cup brown sugar
2 tablespoons all-purpose flour
2 tablespoons cold butter or margarine
¾ cup chopped walnuts

PREPARATION

1 In a blender, mix the tofu, pumpkin, brown sugar, and spices until smooth.

2 Pour the mixture into the pie crust, and bake at 425°F for 15 minutes.

3 Remove from the oven, and lower the temperature to 350°F.

4 In a small mixing bowl, combine the brown sugar and flour, slowly cutting the butter or margarine until crumbly. Stir in the walnuts.

5 Sprinkle the topping over the pie, and return it to the oven for 40 minutes.

Chocolate Almond Pie

• • •

Looking to get rave reviews at your next dinner party? For those with refined tastes, this elegant dessert fits the bill.

• • •

Yields 1 9-inch pie

INGREDIENTS

12 ounces soft tofu
¾ cup sliced almonds
1 cup brown sugar
1 cup unsweetened cocoa powder
1 teaspoon almond extract
1 teaspoon unflavored vegetarian gelatin
1 ready-made graham cracker pie crust

PREPARATION

1 Spread the sliced almonds on a baking sheet, and bake at 350°F for 5 to 10 minutes. You only want them to brown slightly, so watch to make sure they don't burn. Set aside to cool.

2 In a blender, purée the tofu until smooth. Add the brown sugar, and continue blending.

3 Add the cocoa, almond extract, and gelatin, continuing to mix until creamy.

4 Pour the mixture into the pie crust, sprinkling the almond slices on top for garnish.

5 Refrigerate overnight. Serve chilled.

Recipe Tip

For even more almond flavor, add a splash of amaretto liqueur during the blending process.

Chocolate Almond Pie (see above)

Tofu Key Lime Pie

• • •

This creamy-tart dessert is a favorite
throughout the country.

• • •

Yields 1 9-inch pie

INGREDIENTS

12 ounces soft tofu, mashed
1 cup ricotta cheese
1 14-ounce can sweetened condensed milk
½ cup freshly squeezed Key lime juice (about
   8 limes)
1 tablespoon unflavored vegetarian gelatin
1 ready-made graham cracker pie crust

PREPARATION

1 In a blender, combine the tofu, ricotta, and
condensed milk, and mix until smooth.

2 In a saucepan, combine the lime juice and
gelatin.

3 Cook the mixture over low heat for several
minutes, stirring constantly, until the
gelatin has dissolved.

4 Add to the tofu mixture, and mix well.

5 Pour the filling into the pie crust, and
refrigerate for at least 3 hours.

6 Garnish each slice with a thin slice of lime.

Recipe Tip

Key limes are not available
in all supermarkets, so use
regular limes if you're
in a pinch.

Poppy Seed Cake with Lemon Icing

• • •

As if this cake isn't exquisite on its own,
we've added a creamy icing that takes
this favorite dessert to a new level.

• • •

Serves 6 to 8

INGREDIENTS

BATTER

8 ounces soft tofu, drained and mashed
⅔ cup sugar
½ cup vegetable oil
1 tablespoon baking powder
¼ teaspoon baking soda
1 egg, beaten
1 teaspoon vanilla extract
½ cup plain bread crumbs
1 cup orange juice
2½ cups flour
1/4 cup poppy seeds

ICING

12 ounces firm tofu, drained and mashed
½ cup maple syrup
4 tablespoons freshly squeezed lemon juice
Grated rind of 1 lemon
2 teaspoons vanilla extract
Pinch of salt

PREPARATION

1 In a blender, combine the tofu, sugar, oil,
baking powder, baking soda, egg, vanilla,
and bread crumbs, and blend until thoroughly mixed.

2 Pour the mixture into a large mixing bowl,
and slowly add the orange juice, flour, and
poppy seeds. Stir well.

3 Pour the batter into a buttered and lightly
floured 9 by 13-inch pan, and bake at
350°F for 45 minutes.

4 Set aside to cool.

5 In a blender, combine all of the icing
ingredients, and mix until creamy. If you

prefer a smoother icing, add 1 to 2 tablespoons of vegetable oil.

6 Transfer the icing to a bowl, and refrigerate for about 2 hours, or until thickened.

7 Spread the icing onto the cake with a knife or spatula, being sure to thoroughly cover the top and sides. Enjoy!

Apple Walnut Cake

• • •

This delicious cake tastes especially good when topped with a scoop of your favorite vanilla ice cream or frozen yogurt.

• • •

Serves 8 to 10

INGREDIENTS

8 ounces soft tofu, drained and mashed
2 cups flour, sifted
2 teaspoons baking powder
½ teaspoon baking soda
2 teaspoons ground cinnamon
1 teaspoon ground nutmeg
1¼ cups brown sugar
½ cup vegetable oil
2 eggs, beaten
2 cups apples, shredded
1 cup walnuts, chopped

PREPARATION

1 In a large bowl, mix the flour, baking powder, and baking soda. Set aside.

2 In another bowl, mix the spices, sugar, oil, eggs, and tofu until well-blended.

3 Add this tofu mixture, along with the apples and walnuts, to the flour mixture. Stir all of the ingredients together.

4 Pour the batter into a buttered and floured 9 by 13-inch baking pan, and bake at 350°F for 40 minutes.

5 Let the cake cool before serving.

Recipe Tip

Add ½ cup raisins or dried dates for even more texture to the Apple Walnut Cake.

Citrus-Glazed Yogurt Cake

• • •

This deliciously tangy recipe is the ideal dessert when you're craving the flavor of fresh citrus fruit.

• • •

Serves 8 to 10

INGREDIENTS

BATTER

2 ounces soft tofu, drained and mashed
1¼ cups plain yogurt
2¼ cups sugar
3 eggs, beaten
¼ cup melted butter or margarine
3 cups flour, sifted
1 teaspoon baking soda

CITRUS GLAZE

½ cup sugar
2 teaspoons grated orange rind
1 teaspoon grated lemon rind
3 cups orange juice

PREPARATION

1 In a blender, combine the yogurt, tofu, and sugar, and mix for a few seconds.

2 Add the eggs, butter, flour, and baking soda, and continue mixing until smooth.

3 Pour the mixture into a buttered 9 by 13-inch pan, and bake at 375°F for 30 minutes. Set aside to cool.

4 In a small saucepan, combine the glaze ingredients, and bring to a boil. After 5 minutes, remove from the heat and let cool.

5 With a spoon, pour the glaze over the surface of the cake.

6 Refrigerate overnight, and serve with fresh orange or lemon slices for garnish.

Carrot Cake

• • •

You probably consider this cake to be healthy already, what with all those carrots. But the addition of tofu makes it even more so, and, we think, even more delicious.

• • •

Yields 2 8-inch cakes

INGREDIENTS

8 ounces soft tofu
½ cup vegetable oil
1 cup honey
2 cups flour
2 teaspoons baking soda
2 teaspoons vanilla extract
2 teaspoons cinnamon
½ teaspoon salt
¼ cup carrots, grated
1 cup walnuts, chopped (optional)

PREPARATION

1 In a blender, combine all of the ingredients except the carrots and walnuts, and mix until smooth.

2 Empty the mixture into a large mixing bowl, and slowly fold in the remaining ingredients.

3 Pour into two oiled and floured 8-inch cake pans, and bake at 325°F for 45 minutes.

4 Remove from the oven, and allow to cool. Serve as is or with the Tofu Cream Cheese Frosting (see recipe below).

Tofu Cream Cheese Frosting

• • •

Everyone's favorite frosting, perfect for topping carrot cake or simple oatmeal cookies, is now packing some protein with the addition of tofu. You'll never have a reason, or desire, to buy packaged frosting again!

• • •

Yields 2 cups

INGREDIENTS

4 ounces soft tofu, drained and mashed
⅓ cup butter or margarine
2 cups powdered sugar
⅓ cup cream cheese
1 teaspoon vanilla extract

PREPARATION

1 In a large mixing bowl, combine all of the ingredients, and beat with an electric mixer until creamy.

2 Refrigerate for 1 hour prior to use.

Cranberry Pumpkin Cake

• • •

Nothing says autumn like the tart flavor
of cranberries and the rich sweetness
of pumpkin. Serve this cake during
the year's cold months, and bring
a warm smile to any
lucky recipient.

• • •

Serves 12

INGREDIENTS

18 ounces extra-firm tofu
1 8-ounce can of pumpkin
⅓ cup honey
¼ cup water
1 teaspoon vanilla extract
1 egg
¾ cup milk
3 cups flour
1½ cups brown sugar
1 teaspoon baking powder
1 teaspoon baking soda
1 teaspoon cinnamon
½ teaspoon ground nutmeg
¼ teaspoon ground cloves
1 teaspoon ground ginger
1 cup dried cranberries
½ teaspoon salt
1 teaspoon powdered sugar

PREPARATION

1 In a blender, purée the tofu until smooth.
Add the pumpkin, honey, water, and
vanilla, and pulse until smooth.

2 Add the egg and milk to the mixture, and
continue to blend until creamy.

3 In a large mixing bowl, stir together all the
dry ingredients, except the cranberries.

4 Add the blended mixture to the dry
mixture, and stir well.

Cranberry Pumpkin Cake (see above)

5 Fold in the cranberries.

6 Pour into an oiled baking pan, and bake at 350°F for 50 minutes.

7 Allow to cool, and dust with a light layer of powdered sugar.

Recipe Tip

Add ½ cup of crushed walnuts or pecans when folding the cranberries into the Cranberry Pumpkin Cake batter.

Chocolate Raspberry Decadence

• • •

Luscious. Sumptuous. Sinful. Need we say more?

• • •

Yields 1 9-inch cake

INGREDIENTS

CAKE

12 ounces firm tofu
⅔ cups sugar
2 tablespoons maple syrup
¼ cup warm water
¼ cup vegetable oil
1 tablespoon vanilla extract
1 tablespoon apple cider vinegar
1¾ cups flour
¾ cup unsweetened cocoa powder
1 teaspoon baking powder
1 teaspoon baking soda
⅛ teaspoon salt
1 cup fresh raspberries

RASPBERRY TOPPING

1 cup fresh raspberries, plus extra for garnish
2 tablespoons chocolate syrup

PREPARATION

1 In a blender, purée the tofu until smooth.

2 In a large mixing bowl, combine the tofu with the sugar, maple syrup, water, oil, vanilla, and vinegar. Stir vigorously until creamy.

3 In a separate bowl, mix the flour, cocoa, baking powder, baking soda, and salt.

4 Slowly add the dry mixture to the large bowl. Mix just until blended.

5 Pour the batter into a lightly oiled baking pan, and bake at 350°F for 30 to 35 minutes, or until the cake feels springy to the touch.

6 Remove from the oven, and cool.

7 In a blender, purée the fresh raspberries. Strain the berries through a wire strainer or cheesecloth to remove the seeds.

8 Combine the raspberry purée and chocolate syrup in a small mixing bowl, stirring until very smooth.

9 Pour the topping over each individual serving, and garnish generously with fresh raspberries.

Double Chocolate Fantasy

• • •

Here's a temptation that will send any chocoholic into a feeding frenzy. With the addition of chocolate chips in the batter, be prepared for an exquisite dessert experience.

• • •

Serves 10

INGREDIENTS

24 ounces soft tofu
¾ cup honey
½ cup cocoa powder
3 teaspoons vanilla extract
½ cup semi-sweet chocolate chips
1 ready-made graham cracker pie crust or 10 pudding cups

PREPARATION

1 In a blender, whip the tofu until smooth.

2 Heat the honey for 90 seconds in a microwave, or several minutes on the stove.

3 In a large mixing bowl, pour the honey over the cocoa powder, and stir until well-blended.

4 Add the vanilla.

5 Pour the tofu into the bowl and stir for several minutes until creamy.

6 Fold in the chocolate chips, distributing them evenly.

7 Pour the mixture into a pie crust or pudding cups, and refrigerate for approximately 1 to 2 hours.

8 Garnish with more chocolate chips or a flourish of fresh banana slices.

Shortcake Squares

• • •

Here's a simple but elegant sweet that will add class to your morning coffee or afternoon tea.

• • •

Yields 10 to 12 shortcake squares

INGREDIENTS

4 ounces soft tofu
2 cups flour
⅓ cup sugar
⅓ cup vegetable oil
¾ cup water
2 teaspoons baking powder
½ teaspoon salt

PREPARATION

1 In a bowl, combine the flour and sugar, and slowly add the oil. Set aside.

2 In a blender, combine the tofu, water, and salt, and mix until smooth.

3 Empty the mixture into the mixing bowl with the dry ingredients, and stir well.

4 Roll out the dough onto a lightly floured board until it is ¼ inch thick.

5 Slice the dough into squares, approximately 2 to 3 inches wide.

6 Place the squares on an oiled cookie sheet, brushing each dough square with a generous coating of oil.

7 Bake at 400°F for 15 minutes.

8 Serve at room temperature.

> ### Recipe Tip
>
> Serve the Shortcake Squares with a dollop of fresh berries or jam.

Strudel

• • •

This comforting cake reminds us of the
fresh-baked strudel we used to buy
at the neighborhood bakery
when we were kids.

• • •

Serves 8

INGREDIENTS

12 ounces soft tofu, mashed
2 tablespoons yogurt
⅓ cup raisins
1 teaspoon vanilla extract
½ cup sugar
2 tablespoons margarine
8 sheets of frozen filo pastry dough, thawed
1 tablespoon powdered sugar

PREPARATION

1 In a large mixing bowl, combine the tofu,
yogurt, raisins, vanilla, and sugar, and stir
until blended.

2 Melt the margarine, and brush some onto
each sheet of pastry dough.

3 Spread one-eighth of the tofu filling onto
each sheet and roll up, turning the ends
over.

4 Place all eight sheets onto an oiled baking
sheet, and bake at 425°F for 20 to 30
minutes, or until lightly browned.

5 Sprinkle with powdered sugar, and serve.

Recipe Tip

Add diced apples or peaches
to the tofu mixture for a
delicious fruity strudel.

Black Forest Cake

• • •

If your idea of a blissful dessert
incorporates the delicious combination
of chocolate and cherries, do we
have a treat for you! It's a more
involved recipe, but well
worth the trouble.

• • •

Serves 12

INGREDIENTS

BATTER

1 cup water
1 cup honey
½ cup applesauce
1 teaspoon vanilla extract
1 teaspoon vinegar
2 cups flour
¾ cup unsweetened cocoa
1 tablespoon baking powder
1 teaspoon baking soda

SYRUP

½ cup water
¼ cup honey
2 lemon or orange slices
⅓ cup cherry liqueur or rum

ICING

10 ounces firm tofu
1 cup cashews
½ cup water
2 teaspoons vanilla extract
½ cup honey
3 ounces semi-sweet chocolate, melted
1 16-ounce can pitted cherries, drained

PREPARATION

1 In a large mixing bowl, combine the water,
honey, applesauce, vanilla, and vinegar.
Whisk until smooth.

2 In another bowl, combine the flour, cocoa,
baking powder, and baking soda.

3 Slowly add the dry ingredients to the wet
ingredients, whisking thoroughly.

4 Pour the resulting batter into an oiled and lightly floured 9-inch cake pan, and bake at 350°F for 35 minutes, or until springy.

5 Cool completely, then carefully remove the cake from the pan. With a sharp knife, cut the cake in three horizontal layers. Set aside.

6 For the syrup, combine the water, honey, and lemon or orange slices in a small saucepan, and bring to a light boil. Boil for 3 minutes, and remove from the heat.

7 Once the syrup has cooled, add the liqueur. Set aside.

8 For the icing, combine the cashews, water, and vanilla in a blender, and mix until smooth.

9 Add the tofu and honey, and blend again.

10 Set aside 2 cups of this icing to be used on the top and sides of the cake.

11 Add the melted chocolate and 2 or 3 tablespoons of the prepared syrup to the remaining blender contents. Blend again until smooth.

12 Chill both icings.

13 To assemble the cake, position the bottom cake layer on a serving platter.

14 Brush some of the syrup onto the bottom layer, and spread half of the chocolate icing on top.

15 Place the center layer on top of the first. Brush with more syrup, and spread the remaining chocolate icing on top.

16 Spread most of the canned cherries on top of the chocolate icing.

17 Place the top cake layer on top. Brush with syrup.

18 Coat the entire top and sides with the vanilla icing you set aside.

19 Place a small circle of the remaining cherries in the center of the cake, and garnish with chocolate shavings.

20 Chill for several hours before serving.

Tofu Ice Cream

• • •

Tasty enough to be served by itself, this simple ice cream recipe also makes the perfect topping for your favorite cake or pie.

• • •

Yields 3 cups

INGREDIENTS

8 ounces soft tofu
2 teaspoons vanilla extract
2 tablespoons vegetable oil
6 tablespoons sugar
¾ cup milk

PREPARATION

1 In a blender, mix all of the ingredients until smooth.

2 Pour the mixture into a suitable container and place in the freezer. Stir frequently while it is freezing to prevent crystallization. For best results, use an ice cream maker.

3 Transfer the ice cream to the refrigerator for 10 to 15 minutes prior to serving.

Recipe Tip

Add ½ cup fresh fruit or nuts to the ice cream before freezing. For a yummy chocolate dessert, add ½ cup cocoa powder.

5 Combine the water and remaining sugar in a small saucepan, and bring to a boil.

6 Cook, uncovered, over medium heat for 15 minutes.

7 Carefully dip the tofu into this sugar syrup and place them on a plate to cool.

8 Place the coated tofu in a serving dish, and pour the milk mixture over them.

9 Chill thoroughly before serving.

Tofu Roshmalay

• • •

This recipe combines fragrant Indian spices with tofu to create a distinctively delicious and nutritious treat.

• • •

Serves 6 to 8

INGREDIENTS

16 ounces firm tofu, drained and cubed
Freshly ground seeds from 6 cardamom pods
½ cup sliced almonds
⅛ teaspoon freshly ground nutmeg
1¼ cups sugar
2 cups milk
2 tablespoons margarine
2 teaspoons rose water
½ teaspoon vanilla extract
8 tablespoons water

PREPARATION

1 In a small mixing bowl, combine the ground cardamom seeds with the almonds, nutmeg, and half the sugar.

2 In a small saucepan, add these dry ingredients to the milk and margarine and gradually bring to a boil.

3 Turn the heat down low and simmer, uncovered, for approximately 10 minutes.

4 Remove from the heat, and add the vanilla and rosewater. Let cool.

Terrific Tofu Tiramisu

• • •

Traditionally, this Italian dessert tops the chart in fat content. But with our tofu version, you can dine virtually guilt-free while still savoring the wonderfully rich flavors.

• • •

Serves 8 to 10

INGREDIENTS

8 ounces soft tofu, mashed
¾ cup prepared espresso coffee
½ cup sweet Marsala wine
½ cup mascarpone (Italian cream cheese)
½ cup sugar
1 teaspoon grated orange rind
12 ladyfingers
1 teaspoon bittersweet cocoa powder

PREPARATION

1 In a small mixing bowl, whisk together the espresso and wine. Set aside.

2 In a blender, combine the tofu, mascarpone, sugar, and 2 tablespoons of the espresso-wine mixture. Mix until smooth.

3 Stir in the grated orange rind.

4 One at a time, dip the ladyfingers into the espresso-wine mixture, just enough to be moistened.

5 Place half of the ladyfingers in a single layer on the bottom of a medium-sized serving dish.

6 Cover with half of the tofu mixture. Then repeat with another layer of ladyfingers and tofu.

7 Cover the dish with plastic wrap, and chill in the refrigerator for up to 8 hours.

8 Sprinkle with a dusting of cocoa powder prior to serving.

Recipe Tip

The Terrific Tofu Tiramisu is best when prepared the day it is to be served.

Berries and Cream Pastries (see above)

Berries and Cream Pastries

• • •

So you've got a dinner party tonight, and you're in need of a last-minute dessert that will be pleasing to the eye and mouth? These gorgeous little pastries take very little time, and will have your guests singing your praises.

• • •

Serves 6

INGREDIENTS

6 ounces soft tofu
6 frozen pastry shells
¼ cup vegetable oil
¼ cup powdered sugar
1 teaspoon vanilla extract
½ teaspoon lemon juice
⅛ teaspoon salt
2 pints fresh berries (strawberries, black-berries, raspberries, etc.), washed and trimmed
½ cup sugar

PREPARATION

1 Bake the pastry shells according to package instructions.

2 While those are in the oven, prepare the cream filling by combining the tofu, oil, confectioner's sugar, vanilla, lemon juice, and salt in a blender. Mix until smooth.

3 In a large mixing bowl, stir the berries into the sugar.

4 Fill each cooled pastry shell with the prepared cream filling, and top with a spoonful of the berry mixture.

Baked Pears

• • •

Most of us aren't used to eating pears warm; but this wonderful baked dish will convert you with just one tasty bite.

• • •

Serves 8

INGREDIENTS

4 ounces silken tofu

3 large ripe pears, peeled, cored, and sliced in half

½ cup milk

3 eggs

¼ cup flour

⅓ cup sugar

¼ teaspoon baking powder

Dash of salt

1 teaspoon grated lemon rind

1 tablespoon cinnamon

PREPARATION

1 Cut the pears into ⅛-inch-thick slices, and arrange in overlapping rows on the inside of a baking pan. Arrange another layer on top.

2 In a blender, combine the milk, tofu, and eggs, and mix until smooth.

3 Add the flour, sugar, baking powder, and salt. Continue blending.

4 Stir in the grated lemon rind.

5 Pour this mixture evenly over the pears, and bake at 350°F for 30 minutes, or until lightly browned.

6 Serve warm, garnished with a dusting of cinnamon.

Stuffed Peaches

• • •

This dish of fresh peaches topped with citrus-almond cream is simplicity perfected.

• • •

Serves 6

INGREDIENTS

4 ounces extra-firm tofu, mashed

½ cup ricotta cheese

2 tablespoons orange juice

2 tablespoons honey

¼ teaspoon almond extract

2 tablespoons slivered almonds

1 teaspoon grated orange rind

3 fresh ripe peaches, peeled, halved, and pitted

PREPARATION

1 In a blender, combine the tofu, ricotta, orange juice, honey, and almond extract. Mix until smooth.

2 Stir in the almonds and grated orange rind.

3 Pour into a dish and refrigerate, covered, for at least 1 hour.

4 Scoop the mixture onto the peach halves right before serving. Garnish with almond slivers.

> ### Recipe Tip
>
> To peel a peach, simply immerse it in boiling water for 1 minute. Drop the peach in cold water, then use a knife to remove the peel in downward pulls.

Crème-Filled Fruit Crêpes

• • •

Impress your guests with these elegant, delicate-tasting crêpes. Garnished with fresh fruit or a dollop of whipped cream, they'll make quite a statement on your next brunch table.

• • •

Yields 12 crêpes

INGREDIENTS

CRÊPE BATTER

- 1 cup skim milk
- 2 eggs
- ½ cup all-purpose flour
- ¼ cup wheat germ
- ½ teaspoon vegetable oil

CRÈME FILLING

- 8 ounces silken tofu, mashed
- 1 cup ricotta cheese
- ¼ cup sugar or honey
- 1 tablespoon orange juice
- 1 teaspoon grated orange rind
- 1 cup fresh berries, peaches, or other fruit
- Dash of cinnamon

PREPARATION

1 In a large mixing bowl, vigorously stir together the milk, eggs, flour, wheat germ, and oil.

2 Cover and refrigerate for 1 to 2 hours. The batter will thicken as it stands.

3 Lightly oil a crêpe pan or large frying pan. Heat the pan over medium heat until hot.

4 Remove the pan from the heat, and pour approximately ¼ cup of the batter into the middle of the pan. Quickly turn the pan with your wrist so the batter covers the entire bottom of the pan with a thin film.

5 Return the pan to the heat, and cook until the crêpe is lightly browned. Flip once. Cool on a paper towel.

6 Repeat the process with the remaining batter.

7 In a blender, combine the filling ingredients and mix until smooth.

8 To assemble a crêpe, place the "less-cooked" side up. Spread about 2 tablespoons of the filling over the center; fold the sides of the crêpe over to cover the filling, overlapping the edges at the center.

9 Serve warm.

> ### Recipe Tip
>
> After making the crêpes, you may place them between sheets of waxed paper and refrigerate for up to two days. For longer storage, wrap the stacked crêpes in aluminum foil and place in the freezer for up to two months. The filling must be made the same day you plan to serve the crêpes.

Basic Tofu Brownies

• • •

Everyone's favorite gooey chocolate treat makes a healthy and delicious comeback with the simple addition of tofu.

• • •

Serves 6 to 8

INGREDIENTS

4 ounces soft tofu, drained and mashed
⅔ cups flour
1 teaspoon baking powder
2 eggs, beaten
½ cup sugar
½ cup butter or margarine, melted
½ cup unsweetened cocoa powder
1 teaspoon vanilla extract

PREPARATION

1 In a small mixing bowl, stir together the flour and baking powder.

2 In another larger bowl, mix the tofu, eggs, sugar, butter, cocoa, and vanilla until creamy. Add the flour mixture, and continue to stir.

3 Pour the batter into a buttered and lightly floured 8 by 8-inch baking pan, and bake at 350°F for 30 minutes.

Recipe Tip

Add ½ cup walnuts or chocolate chunks to the brownie batter before baking.

Tofu Fudge

• • •

Fudge made out of tofu? Really! Not only can it be done, but we'll prove that it's just as good as the original.

• • •

Serves 4 to 6

INGREDIENTS

4 ounces soft tofu, drained and mashed
2 tablespoons butter or margarine, melted
½ cup cocoa powder
¼ teaspoon salt
⅔ cup sugar
1 teaspoon vanilla extract
1 teaspoon baking powder
½ cup flour
⅔ cup walnuts, chopped

PREPARATION

1 In a blender, combine the tofu, butter, cocoa, salt, sugar, and vanilla in a blender, Mix until smooth.

2 In a large mixing bowl, combine the tofu mixture with the baking powder, flour, and walnuts. Stir well.

3 Pour the batter into a buttered 8 by 10-inch baking pan, and bake at 350°F oven for 30 minutes.

4 Cool, and cut into small squares.

Banana Parfaits

• • •

The added flavor of ginger gives just enough kick to this fruity and exotic dessert.

• • •

Serves 4

INGREDIENTS

12 ounces soft tofu, mashed
10 vanilla wafer cookies
¼ cup ricotta cheese
⅓ cup sugar
1 ripe banana, plus extra for garnish
1 tablespoon freshly squeezed lemon juice
1 tablespoon crystallized ginger, minced
Whipped cream (optional)

PREPARATION

1 Put the cookies into a plastic bag, and carefully crush them into coarse crumbs.

2 In a blender, mix the remaining ingredients until smooth.

3 Spoon ¼ cup of the tofu mixture into the bottom of four clear glasses. Add a thin layer of cookie crumbs. Repeat until the glasses are full.

4 Refrigerate for up to 3 hours prior to serving. Garnish with a dollop of whipped cream and fresh banana slices, if desired.

Tofu Pashka

• • •

This tangy Russian recipe is served during holiday festivities. Incorporate it into your own family's culinary celebrations, then sit back and enjoy the applause.

• • •

Serves 4

INGREDIENTS

12 ounces firm tofu, drained
¼ cup margarine
5 tablespoons yogurt
4 tablespoons sugar
½ cup ground almonds
⅓ cup finely chopped orange and lemon peel
½ cup raisins
1 teaspoon vanilla extract
Honey, to taste
Dash of cinnamon

PREPARATION

1 In a large mixing bowl, combine the tofu and margarine, and stir together until somewhat smooth.

2 Add the rest of the ingredients, except for the honey and cinnamon, and mix well.

3 Empty the mixture into four small serving dishes, press down firmly with a spoon, cover, and refrigerate.

4 Chill for several hours prior to serving. Garnish with a light drizzle of honey and a dash of cinnamon.

Metric Equivalents

Dry Weights
In grams (g)

U.S.	Metric
1 ounce	28 g
2 ounces	57 g
4 ounces (¼ pound)	114 g
⅓ pound	148 g
8 ounces (½ pound)	230 g
⅔ pound	297 g
¾ pound	336 g
16 ounces (1 pound)	454 g

Temperature Equivalents

°F	°C
200°F	90°C
250°F	120°C
275°F	135°C
300°-325°F	150°-160°C
325°-350°F	160°-180°C
350°-375°F	180°-190°C
375°-400°F	190°-200°C
400°-450°F	200°-230°C
450°-500°F	230°-260°C

Fluid Measurement
In milliliters (mL) or liters

U.S.	Metric
¼ teaspoon	1.25 mL
½ teaspoon	2.5 mL
1 teaspoon	5 mL
2 teaspoons	10 mL
1 tablespoon (3 teaspoons)	15 mL
2 tablespoons (1 ounce)	30 mL
¼ cup	60 mL
⅓ cup	80 mL
½ cup	120 mL
¾ cup	180 mL
1 cup	240 mL
4 cups (1 quart)	1 liter

Length

U.S.	Metric
1 inch	2.5 centimeters

Index

Acknowledgments

We'd like to thank the following people whose help was instrumental
in bringing this book to fruition:

Deborah Morgenthal, for her guidance and leadership.

Nicole Tuggle, who, with her vigilance and undying enthusiasm, plowed
through any obstacle in order to get this book to our publisher in time.

Theresa Gwynn, whose patience and good humor held up under the
pressure of dealing with us on a daily basis. Her design
truly brings this book to life.

Dana Irwin, for her wonderful illustrations.

Evan Bracken and Richard Hasselberg, for their beautiful photography.

Skip Wade, who, with his innate sense of style,
helped readers dine with their eyes.

A special thanks to Robert G. Wysong and David W. Rowland, Executive
Sous Chefs at Grove Park Inn Resort, Asheville, NC, for preparing the
gorgeous recipes photographed in this book.

Stephen and Jessica King, for the use of their kitchen.

Catharine Sutherland, for taking on the daunting task
of proofreading and indexing.

Megan Kirby, for her computer expertise.

Ted Cheney, for teaching us to write well.

Joe Rhatigan, our man Friday.

Rob Pulleyn, for believing in this project from the very beginning.

Finally, we want to thank our friends, family, co-workers, and yes, even
strangers, for encouraging us and giving us the honest feedback
we needed for our recipes. Without their time and consideration,
this book would not have been possible.